CW00925275

# Humanism
## in
# Renaissance Scotland

John Mair lecturing at Paris (c. 1505)
From *In Petri Hyspani Summulas Commentaria*

# Humanism
# in
# Renaissance Scotland

edited by
John MacQueen

Edinburgh University Press

© Edinburgh University Press 1990
22 George Square, Edinburgh

Set in Linotron Palatino by
Photoprint, Torquay, and
printed in Great Britain by
Page Bros (Norwich) Ltd

British Library Cataloguing
  in Publication Data
Humanism in Renaissance Scotland.
1. Scotland. Humanism, history
I. MacQueen, John 1929–
144.09411

ISBN 0 7486 0111 2
ISBN 0 7486 0186 4 pbk

The publisher acknowledges subsidy from
the Scottish Arts Council towards
the publication of this volume

# Contents

# Abbreviations

| | |
|---|---|
| *Adv.* | Advocates |
| *APS* | *Acts of the Parliament of Scotland*, 1124–1707, ed. T. Thomson & C. Innes, 12 vols. (Edinburgh, 1814–75) |
| *ASD* | *Annali di Storia del Diritto* |
| *AUR* | *Aberdeen University Review* |
| *BL* | British Library |
| *c.* | (around) |
| *cf.* | (compare) |
| *CIC* | *Corpus Iuris Civilis*, 3 vols., ed. T. Mommsen *et al.* (Berlin, 1904–6) |
| *Cont LH* | *A General Survey of Events, Sources, Persons and Movements in Continental Legal History*, various authors, Continental Legal History Series, vol. 1 (London, 1912) |
| *DJR* | G. Buchanan, *De Jure Regni apud Scottos Dialogus* (Edinburgh, 1579) |
| *DOST* | *Dictionary of the Older Scottish Tongue* |
| *DVS* | J. Skene, *De Verborum Significatione* (Edinburgh, 1597) |
| *ed., eds.* | editor, editors. |
| *e.g.* | (for example) |
| *et al.* | (and others) |
| *EUL* | Edinburgh University Library. |
| *f., ff.* | (following; f. = '+ single page'; ff. = '+ more than one page') |
| *fig.* | figure |
| *FMLS* | *Forum for Modern Language Studies* |
| *fn.* | footnote |
| *fol., fols.* | folio, folios |
| *Gen.* | general |
| *ibid.* | (in the same place) |
| *i.e.* | (that is) |
| *IR, Innes Rev.* | *Innes Review* |
| *JF* | T. Craig, *Jus Feudale*, trans. J.A. Clyde (Edinburgh, 1934) |
| *JHI* | *Journal of the History of Ideas* |
| *MS, MSS* | manuscript, manuscripts |

| | |
|---|---|
| *NE* | *Nicomachean Ethics* (Aristotle) |
| *NLS* | *National Library of Scotland* |
| *no.* | (number) |
| *n.s.* | new series |
| *p., pp.* | page, pages |
| *passim* | (throughout) |
| *Proc.Arist.Soc.* | *Proceedings of the Aristotelian Society* |
| *pt.* | part |
| *r* | *recto* |
| *repr.* | reprinted |
| *RM (Latin)* | J. Skene, *Regiam Majestatem Scotiae . . .* (Edinburgh, 1609) |
| *RMS* | *Registrum Magni Sigilli Regum Scotorum*, edd. J.M. Thomson and others (Edinburgh, 1882–1914) |
| *RSS* | *Registrum Secreti Sigilli Regum Scotorum*, edd. M. Livingstone and others (Edinburgh, 1908–) |
| *SHR* | *Scottish Historical Review* |
| *sig.* | signature (in printed books) |
| *SND* | *Scottish National Dictionary* |
| *SRO* | Scottish Record Office |
| *STC* | *Short Title Catalogue* |
| *trans.* | translated |
| *Univ.* | University |
| *UL* | University Library |
| *v* | *verso* |
| *viz.* | (namely) |
| *vol.* | volume |

# Notes on Contributors

ALEXANDER BROADIE is Reader in Philosophy, University of Glasgow, specialising in logic and philosophy in Pre-Reformation Scotland. His publications include *George Lokert: Late Scholastic Logician, Introduction to Medieval Logic* and *The Scottish Tradition of Philosophy*.

JOHN W. CAIRNS is Lecturer in Scots Law at the University of Edinburgh. He has mainly published on the legal history of Scotland in the 17th and 18th centuries and is currently researching a book on legal education in 18th-century Scotland.

JAMES K. CAMERON, Professor of Ecclesiastical History, University of St Andrews since 1970, has contributed extensively on Renaissance and Reformation subjects at national and international conferences and has published articles in a wide variety of periodicals and essay collections. He is a former President of the Ecclesiastical History Society and is a member of the Grotius Commission of the Royal Dutch Academy of Arts and Sciences.

JOHN DURKAN is honorary Senior Research Fellow of Glasgow University attached to the Department of Scottish History and former President of the Scottish Church History Society. He has contributed articles on aspects of late medieval and modern culture and religion to various periodicals and has lectured widely in Scotland and Canada. His publications include *William Turnbull, Bishop of Glasgow* and *Early Scottish Libraries* (with Anthony Ross). He is presently completing *Schools and Schoolmasters 1560–1603*, a work commissioned by the Scottish Record Society.

CLARE FARROW studied Art History at University of St Andrews and specialised in contemporary and renaissance art, completing a thesis on *Mary Queen of Scots and the Visual Arts* – an analysis of French and Scottish portraiture, jewellery, costume and the masque. She currently works in London as House Editor of *Art and Design* magazine.

T. DAVID FERGUS is Lecturer, School of Law, University of Glasgow, specialising in Roman Law and Legal History. He is co-author of *An Introduction to European Legal History*.

ALEXANDER KELLER is currently Senior Lecturer in the History of Science at University of Leicester, where he has taught since 1963, his principal interest being the beginnings of mechanisation in the Renaissance. He has contributed widely in various periodicals and collections and is author of *A Theatre of Machines*.

MARTIN KEMP, Professor of Fine Arts at University of St Andrews since 1981 is Honorary Professor of History, Royal Scottish Academy and was a Trustee of the National Galleries of Scotland and the Victoria and Albert Museum. He has published extensively on the Renaissance, including, *Leonardo da Vinci. The Marvellous Works of Nature and Man*. He is currently completing *The Science of Art. Optical Themes in Western Art from Brunelleschi to Seurat*.

HECTOR MACQUEEN is Lecturer in Scots Law at the University of Edinburgh. He has published on various aspects of the legal history of Scotland, in particular its medieval law, as well as on topics of modern law.

JOHN MACQUEEN is an Endowment Fellow of the University of Edinburgh. Earlier appointments were as Masson Professor of Medieval and Renaissance Literature (1963–71), Director of the School of Scottish Studies (1969–88) and Professor of Scottish Literature and Oral Tradition (1971–88).

RICHARD J. SCHOECK was educated in Canada and at Princeton and has taught widely throughout the USA and Canada. From 1975–87 he was Professor of English and Humanities at University of Colorado and is now Professor of Anglistik at University of Trier. He has published extensively, including *The Achievement of Thomas More* and *Intertextuality and Renaissance Texts*, and has edited and co-edited a wide variety of projects including two volumes of *Chaucer Criticism* and *Voices of Literature*.

# The Background of European Humanism: An Introduction
## R.J. SCHOECK

Renaissance humanism was international, and it was known and (in differing ways and degrees) it flowered in every European country during the fifteenth and sixteenth centuries. It is the purpose of the book that follows to study the ways in which European humanism took root in Scotland and to make clear the ways that Scotland contributed to the parent-growth. It is the purpose of this introduction to provide a sense of the background of European humanism.

The Renaissance – to take the more comprehensive term – was a complex period that extended from about 1350 (earlier in Italy) and lasted until about 1600 (somewhat later in some northern European countries). It is a period celebrated for its splendid achievements in art and music, thought, and letters, and it produced some of the most remarkable people of human history. But there were, one must emphasise at the outset, regional differences in chronology as well as social differences everywhere: the way of life and the modes of expression at Ferrara or Burgundy courts were nothing like those of the farms and villages of northern Italy or Flanders at precisely the same time. This period is marked by extraordinary heterogeneity of thought and expression, for Aristotelianism existed side by side with Platonism, neo-Stoicism and neo-Epicureanism, and throughout the period the system known as scholasticism continued in the universities. Not to be forgotten are the strong religious institutions, some old (like the Benedictines and the mendicant orders), some new (like the Brethren of the Common Life); but it is difficult to grasp a sense of that former intensity of devotion, often accompanied by a fervour for reading at least some of the classics, when one gazes upon the 'bare ruined choirs' of the Border country or seeks in vain for the ruins of the monastery in which Erasmus spent half a dozen years near Gouda.

So too the political thought presents a wide spectrum, from strong claims for absolute papal power in writers like Augustinus Trium-phatus to equally strong claims for the superior authority of emperors or councils of the Church in writers like Marsiglio of Padua. This introduction does not pretend to cover that full scope of Renaissance activity, and the literature discussing that prodigious activity is very considerable.[1]

One has only to consider such 'Renaissance' figures as Leonardo da Vinci, Valla, Ficino, Pico, Michelangelo, and then to place them alongside such contemporaries as Savonarola, Thomas More and John Colet, and Martin Luther, to see how contradictory some of the currents and achievements were during that period from 1350 to 1600. For this reason, the term 'Renaissance' is here used as a chronological designation only. What was most characteristic of this period was its high valuation of the classics and of classical studies; and in speaking of the heritage of classical antiquity, and especially its literature and philosophy, Kristeller has declared that 'classical studies occupied in the Renaissance a more central place in the civilisation of the period, and were more intimately linked with its other intellectual tendencies and achievements, than at any earlier or later time in the history of Western Europe.'[2] It is the humanist movement of the Renaissance period that was most intimately concerned with classical studies, and it was this movement that provided the 'figure in the carpet' that gave cultural expression during the Renaissance its unique qualities.

### Renaissance Humanism

The term 'humanism' is currently much misunderstood, and since the Romantic period it has come increasingly to mean different things: from belief in the mere humanity of Christ to the quality of being human, and thus to any system of thought or action concerned with merely human interests – as well, one must insist, with some of us still carrying the original concept developed during the Renaissance of a dedication to classical studies and to culture founded on classical ideals. Coined, apparently, in 1808, it is thus not a Renaissance word; but it was created on the foundation of the Renaissance term for a professor of humanism, the *umanista*.[3] And that term *umanista* (or *humanista*, or *humanist*) coined by analogy with *canonista* or *legista* evoked the well-understood concept of *studia humanitatis*, as celebrated particularly in Cicero and Quintilian, where it may at times have been something of a slogan but it did mean a code of values as well as a field of study. After the early fifteenth century, the *studia humanitatis* (i.e. humanism) was clearly understood as embracing a well-defined cycle of subjects and authors that always included grammar, rhetoric, and poetry, as well as history and moral philosophy and then, rather later, and in a widening circle, texts from jurisprudence and medicine.[4] While humanism *per se* was not a single philosophical system though it favoured Plato more than Aristotle, there was at the core of nearly all Renaissance humanistic studies and writings their favourite theme of the dignity of man – most famously celebrated by Pico della Mirandola in his *Oratio de hominis dignitate*, but to be found everywhere and nearly continuously: from the fifteenth century to Hamlet's 'O what a piece of work is man' and into the seventeenth century.[5] But humanism was not only a programme; it was a spirit, a new enthusiasm for the classics, and it led to the desire to comprehend the ancient world as a whole.

There were continuities with medieval culture and education, to be sure,[6] but the Renaissance version of the *studia humanitatis* gave a new emphasis to the reading and teaching of classical Latin and Greek authors – the Greek far more than had been done in Europe at least since Boethius, and the Latin now in a fresher light by virtue of the reorientation of the Latin language, literature and thought to the Greek sources and models. The early humanists all cried out for a return to the original texts ('ad fontes'[7]), and the contributions of the humanists of the late fifteenth and early sixteenth centuries to classical scholarship were very great: first in the effort to bring forth the *editiones principes* of the ancient authors (for whom there was often additionally a keen interest in uncovering either older manuscripts or the manuscripts of 'lost' texts, like the works of Quintilian, parts of Tacitus, and others). This early stage was followed by the effort over several generations of scholars to comment upon these freshly established texts and to offer textual emendations where necessary (and at times emendations were made where they were not needed, as twentieth-century scholarship has shown). This is now familiar ground, thanks to the scholarship of Sabbadini, Curtius, Garin, Kenney and others;[8] but it is ground that must be seen as part of the total landscape of Renaissance humanism.

Finally, one must observe that Renaissance humanism called for the writing of a great deal of original verse, drama, historical and critical prose, and even fiction, in what is called Neo-Latin, that is Latin written from about 1350 to post-Renaissance periods. If we now understand more fully the epithet given to George Buchanan by his contemporaries, *poetarum nostri saeculi facile princeps*,[9] we must also recognise that there were many others who were expressing in their own writing their understanding of classical forms and models; that Neo-Latin literature was a significant part of the totality of Renaissance literature in Latin and the vernaculars; and that for Renaissance humanists their work in Neo-Latin literary forms was also an area in which the fullness of their understanding of classical literature might be expressed, and their participation in tradition – in the process of receiving and transmitting a cultural heritage – might be fulfilled.[10]

### *The Diffusion of Humanism in Western Europe: 1. Italian*

That Italian culture enjoyed an eminent position during the Renaissance has not been questioned since the publication of Burckhardt's seminal book in 1860; and that Italian influences upon the civilisations

of the other European countries during the fifteenth and sixteenth
centuries were both wide and deep has been generally known
through the work of Roberto Weiss, Renaudet, Kristeller, and Denys
Hay.[11] Italian humanism clearly occupied, as Kristeller has summarised, a rather central position in the visual arts and music, in
literature, in political, scientific and economic theory, and in the
sciences and philosophy.[12] This view needs no discussion here, for
there is general agreement among scholars on the prime importance
of Italian humanism. One must beware, however, of ascribing an
exclusive role to Italian institutions and individuals in the genesis
of Renaissance humanism – for there are roots in Chartres, for
example, and in other cathedral and monastic schools – and one
must recognise that there were native roots in Britain, in the Low
Countries, and elsewhere so that local geniuses like Thomas More
and Erasmus could develop into major European humanists without
having made that trip to Italy that before 1500 was thought to be
essential in humanistic formation. Further, there were humanists of
the sixteenth century whose schooling and intellectual formation
was in France (as with Buchanan) or in the Low Countries during
the seventeenth century. One cannot generalise on individual figures
like More and Erasmus, or Buchanan: yet the bulk of the 'first-
generation' humanists – i.e. those who came of age by 1500 – had
visited Italy for at least a short period, and some had spent a good
number of years at Italian universities and academies. Then too,
Italian humanists came to Britain in ever-increasing numbers during
the fifteenth and sixteenth centuries. With these qualifications, then,
we may accept Italian humanism as the *fons et origo* of Renaissance
humanism.

In charting the diffusion of Italian humanism we shall want to
take account of the following: scholars and students who spent time
in Italy, Italians who lived outside Italy, and religious exiles,
especially after the Reformation. Two important channels for spread-
ing the influence of which we have been speaking were the
manuscripts copied by the humanists, and the correspondence with
Italians. Finally, humanists' books rolled off the presses of Aldus
Manutius and many others, and these found their way to every
library in Europe.

Most foreign students who went to Italy for study did so to obtain
degrees in law and medicine, in which the universities of Bologna
and Salerno especially enjoyed a long tradition. Thus such British
physicians as Thomas Linacre went to Italy to study medicine, as
did Copernicus, who also studied law. But many of the foreign
students also studied or cultivated the humanities while in Italy, and
they carried back home their appreciation of the *studia humanitatis*
and often precious manuscripts of the classics.[13] It is worth asking
whether the preservation of Roman civil law in Scotland may not

have owed much to the combination of legal and humanistic training received by Scottish students, who later became lawyers, jurists and public officials upon their return to Edinburgh, Aberdeen and St Andrews.

Many Italians of course lived outside Italy, as Weiss and Kristeller have documented: bankers and businessmen, legal officials, scholars – many of these were men of humanistic training and interests; and there were others who served as secretaries or tutors, as well as court poets or humanists. A number of Italian humanists taught at foreign universities, and their influence spread the cause of humanism.[14]

The correspondence of humanists like Erasmus is well-known, with its more than 3 000 letters to and from Erasmus;[15] and there were others with significant, even if not so extensive, letter collections. 'This is a rich source of information which has not yet been properly explored,' Kristeller rightly observes;[16] and the fitting of the correspondence into the larger European picture needs to be done.

The number of Italian humanist manuscripts preserved in Scottish libraries today is larger than generally realised, and this evidence needs much fuller exploration. Here, however, books acquired in later periods must be excluded from those acquired during the Renaissance period. Some personal libraries can be reconstructed, and some institutional library catalogues permit the establishment of *termini ad quem* for the use of books in this kind of study. One can point to the exemplars of Erasmus in the Library of New College, Edinburgh, for Erasmus is himself a key figure in the diffusion of European humanism, with much indebtedness in his writings to Valla and other Italian humanists.[17]

The spread of the Italian humanist script across Europe and into Britain has been studied only in part;[18] yet it points to the significance of humanist script as the hallmark of humanism itself, both for its greater beauty and because it replaced the more awkward Gothic scripts, which had the further disadvantage of being slower for the copyist and were often seen as emblematic of the age of scholasticism, that hated enemy of humanism. In the Low Countries and in the Rhineland the diffusion of the humanist script seems to have been owing to the teachers of the Brethren of the Common Life; but it cannot be said as yet whether there are similar patterns of diffusion in Britain.[19]

A number of the chapters of this book directly address the question of the diffusion of Italian humanism (either directly or through intermediary individuals and institutions); but one may conclude this section on the diffusion of Italian humanism with the exhortation, often pious but here called for, that much further study is needed.

*Diffusion: 2. French and Other Circles of Influence*

After 1500 the circles of influence increased in number, and they widened. Other Scots came to Paris to join those like the Stewarts who had studied there under Erasmus in the late 1490s.[20] Early in the sixteenth century there were Scots at Bordeaux, like Buchanan, who studied under the gentle, generous and learned Elie Vinet.[21] And there were Scots in growing numbers who came to Orléans to study civil law, for it was now the centre for the *mos gallicus*, the humanistic study of Roman law by going back to the original texts and reading those texts in their full linguistic and cultural context, as Budé had demonstrated in his celebrated treatise *De Asse* and in his *Annotations on the Pandects*.[22] Finally, there were currents of humanism at the courts, where Scots were often found in significant numbers.

The Low Countries became a remarkable focus of humanistic activity. In the fifteenth century there had been the Burgundian Court, surely the most splendid court in Europe at that time, from which the music of Ockegem, Josquin des Près and others went forth to charm the courts of Urbino and Ferrara in the last decades of the fifteenth century; and with the music went painting and the humanism of Erasmus and others. There is much to account for in the sixteenth century, but that is as yet an untold story.[23] We do know that after the founding of the University of Leiden in 1576 Scots came there for the study of law and medicine and of humanism as well under such celebrated scholars as J.J. Scaliger, Hugo Grotius, Daniel Heinsius and others. Much further study is needed of the Scots as students in the Low Countries and of their later role as teachers and disseminators of humanism.

*Conclusion*

During the Renaissance, classical studies in Scotland became, at their best, as high in their standards as anywhere else in Europe, and since the Renaissance there has always been a keen appreciation for classical learning, both in itself and as a means of inculcating civic and other virtues. The assertion that Spenser was a better moral teacher than Aquinas – even, a means of grace – is something of a humanist *topos*, and it has roots in Coluccio Salutati, the disciple of Petrarch. In Scotland, classical scholarship flourished in the universities, as is made clear later in this volume. Surely we can now recognise a little more clearly the extent to which that fine tradition of classical studies owes much to the Renaissance humanism of George Buchanan and others – with the presence of Erasmus always very much felt – for it is this heritage which gave birth to the tradition of classical learning.

At the end of the nineteenth century, a many-sided figure like

John Buchan, whose classical foundations were laid in Scottish schooling, felt it appropriate years later to write (in his autobiography) that one of the great virtues of the *studia humanitatis* was that it brought young men and women into intimate contact with the great minds of antiquity for a vital period of their intellectual and moral formation. That heritage of classical and Renaissance humanism was deep, and vital, and lasting.

## NOTES

1. For a comprehensive view of the changing interpretations of the Renaissance, see W.K. Ferguson, *The Renaissance in Historical Thought: Five Centuries of Interpretation* (Boston: Houghton Mifflin, 1948). A central work is Jacob Burckhardt's seminal study, *Die Cultur der Renaissance in Italien* (Basel, 1860), translated as *The Culture of the Renaissance in Italy* (London, 1944). Although Buckhardt's great book on the Renaissance has been described by Mircea Eliade as 'an exemplary instance of creative hermeneutics' and is still a book of lasting importance, it has limitations – the religious element of the Renaissance, for example, is largely ignored. See further the discussions by Hans Baron and others in the *Journal of the History of Ideas*, IV (1943), 1–74; E. Panofsky, 'Renaissance and Renascences,' *Kenyon Review* VI (1944), 201–36; and P.O. Kristeller, *Renaissance Thought II: Papers on Humanism and the Arts* (New York: Harper Torchbooks, 1965). On earlier renascences and revivals, see Treadgold, cited in n. 6 below.
2. Paul Oskar Kristeller, 'The Humanist Movement,' in *Renaissance Thought: The Classic, Scholastic, and Humanist Strains* (New York: Harper Torchbooks, 1961), pp.7–8. This book is an admirable survey of the distinct strains in Renaissance thought, of which the humanist is one.
3. The term *Humanismus* was coined in 1808 by F.J. Niethammer to emphasise classical studies as against the practical and scientific: see W. Rüegg, *Cicero und der Humanismus* (Zurich, 1946), 1 ff., and Kristeller, 'The Humanist Movement,' p. 9.
4. Thus Kristeller's influential and still largely accepted definition (ibid., 10), which emphasises that Renaissance humanism was 'rather a cultural and educational program which emphasised and developed an important but limited area of studies.'
5. See Charles Trinkaus, *In Our Image and Likeness: Humanity and Divinity in Italian Humanist Thought*, 2 vols. (Chicago: Univ. of Chicago Press, 1970). This Renaissance tradition should be studied against the earlier, for which see *Images of man in ancient and medieval thought: Studia Gerardo Verbeke*, ed. F. Bossier, et al. (Leuven: Leuven Univ. Press, 1976).
6. See Warren Treadgold, ed. *Renaissances Before the Renaissance – Cultural Revivals of Late Antiquity and the Middle Ages* (Stanford: Stanford University Press, 1984) for up-to-date examinations of previous revivals of classical cultural and for an implicit emphasis

on the continuity of the classical tradition. Walter Ullmann's *Medieval Foundations of Renaissance Humanism* (Ithaca, N.Y.: Cornell Univ. Press, 1977) is important as a medievalist's plea for the principle of continuity; but it is (as I have concluded elsewhere) an unsatisfactory book.

7. I have covered this point in 'The Humanistic Text,' in *Proceedings of the Patristics, Medieval and Renaissance Conference 1982*, ed. J. Schnaubelt (Villanova, Pa.: Augustinian Institute, 1984).

8. See further: E.R. Curtius, *Europäische Literatur und lateinische Mittelalter* (Bern, 1948); P.O. Kristeller, as above; R. Sabbadini, *Storia e critica di testi latini*[2] (Padua, 1971); E. Garin, *Der italienische Humanismus* (Bern, 1947), and E.J. Kenney, *The Classical Text: Aspects of Editing in the Age of the Printed Book* (Berkeley: University of California Press, 1974).

9. See the papers of Roger Green and others in *Acta Conventus Neo-Latini Sanctandreani*, ed. I.D. McFarlane (Binghamton, New York: Medieval & Renaissance Texts & Studies, 1986).

10. On Neo-Latin literature generally, see I. Jsewijn, *Companion to Neo-Latin Studies* (Amsterdam: North-Holland, 1977); and on the concept of imitation, see R.J. Schoeck, '"Lighting a Candle to the Place": On the Dimensions and Implications of *Imitatio* in the Renaissance,' *Italian Culture IV* (1983), 123–43.

11. For Italian humanism there are the studies of Roberto Weiss, 'Italian Humanism in Western Europe,' in *Italian Renaissance Studies*, ed. E.F. Jacob (London, 1960), 69–83; and Denys Hay, 'The Reception of the Renaissance in the North,' in *The Italian Renaissance in its Historical Background* (Cambridge, 1961), ch. 7 (pp. 179–203); and by P.O. Kristeller, 'The European Diffusion of Italian Humanism,' in *Renaissance Thought II* (New York: Harper Torchbooks, 1965), pp. 69–88.

   For England there are the earlier studies of W. Schirmer, but now standard is R. Weiss, *Humanism in England during the Fifteenth Century*, 2d ed. (Oxford: Blackwells, 1957). See now 'Humanism in England', by R. J. Schoeck, in *Renaissance Humanism*, ed. Albert Rabil, Jr. (Philadelphia: University of Pennsylvania Press, 1988) II, 5–38. The contributions in all three volumes of this impressive collection make an admirable summary of the state of scholarship on the full range of studies of Renaissance humanism.

   For France, see A. Renaudet, *Préréforme et Humanisme à Paris pendant les premières guerres d'Italie* (Paris, 1953); and F. Simone, *Il Rinascimento francese* (Turin, 1961).

12. See Kristeller, 'The European Diffusion,' pp. 69–70.

13. Cf. the documentation in Kristeller's immensely rich *Iter Italicum*.

14. Kristeller, 'The European Diffusion,' p. 75.

15. I am not aware of any studies of the Scottish elements in the correspondence of Erasmus – or indeed, as an overall view, in his other writings and career – but it may be noted that Erasmus had tutored Alexander Stewart, the natural son of James IV, together with James Stewart, earl of Moray, another natural son of James IV. (See epistles 1992 to W. Pirckheimer and 2018 of Erasmus to A. Valdes.) One finds that Erasmus wrote of the Scottish-English alliance in his *Institutio principis christiani* (see *ASD* IV–1, 208), where he deplored the invasion of 1513. Both in his *Adages* (II.v.1)

and in his letters (epistles 2283 to Hector Boece, and 2886 to James v) Erasmus praised James' policy of peace and the support of culture. In epistles 964 and 2283 to Henry viii Erasmus hoped that James v would follow the example of his father, James iv, and support humanistic studies.

16. Kristeller, 'The European Diffusion,' p. 76.

17. I have devoted a chapter to Valla and Italian humanism in my forthcoming biography of Erasmus (Volume I, Edinburgh University Press. 1990). Meanwhile, see E. Garin, *Italian Humanism* (Oxford: Blackwells, 1965); and P.O. Kristeller, *Eight Philosophers of the Italian Renaissance* (Stanford: Stanford Univ. Press, 1964).

18. For a general view, see B.L. Ullman, *The Origin and Development of Humanistic Script* (Rome, 1960); and, more briefly, Kristeller, 'The European Diffusion,' pp. 71–2.

19. I am indebted to Dr P.F.J. Obbema of Leiden for this point concerning the role of the Brethren of the Common Life in disseminating the new script north of the Alps.

20. See n. 15 above. On foreign students at Italian universities, see P. Kibre, *The Nations in the Mediaeval Universities* (Cambridge, Mass.: Harvard Univ. Press, 1948), esp. the bibl. pp. 189–208. An illuminating model for the study of foreign students in law at Bologna is provided by S. Stelling-Michaud, *l'Université de Bologne et la pénétration des droits romain et canonique en Suisse aux XIIIe et XIVe siècles* (Geneva, 1955).

21. I have commented on this role of Vinet in my paper 'On the Editing Of Classical Texts before Vinet: Early Printed Editions of Ausonius before 1580', in *Acta Conventus Neo-Latini Guelpherbytani* – Proceedings of the Congress of Neo-Latin Studies, Wolfenbüttel 1985 (Binghamton, New York: MRTS, 1988), 137–44.

22. An excellent introduction is provided by Myron P. Gilmore in *Humanists and Jurists: Six Studies in the Renaissance* (Cambridge, Mass.: Harvard Univ. Press, 1963). Donald R. Kelley, *Foundations of Modern Historical Scholarship* (New York: Columbia Univ. Press, 1970) investigates the implications of the *mos gallicus* in much greater detail and in a wider context. See further R.J. Schoeck, 'Humanism and Jurisprudence', in Rabil ed., *Renaissance Humanism*, III, 310–26.

23. One approach is provided by the catalogue of *Le livre scolaire chez Erasme* (Liège, 1969), with an introduction by L.E. Halkin, which demonstrates the pervasive and continuing influence of Erasmus upon 16th-century schoolbooks.

As the humanistic correspondence of others besides Erasmus – Lipsius notably, but others as well – receives scholarly editing, one can begin to study the correspondence of scholars as an indication of the international character of European humanism. There was, in fact, a *république des lettres* in the 16th and 17th centuries (see the Sir Thomas Browne Special Number of *English Language Notes*, 1982, for my introductory essay on this concept and reality), and scholars from Scotland played a strong role upon this European stage.

This introduction (written in 1986) includes references to scholarly literature only to 1986 (except for *Renaissance Humanism*, ed. A. Rabil, 1988).

## Aspects of Humanism in Sixteenth- and Seventeenth-
## Century Literature
### JOHN MACQUEEN

Scottish literary humanism is an elusive concept. The context is
Latin; the influence of classical Greek prose or poetry is slight. Some
characteristic continental features, such as manuscripts copied in the
humanist hand, are almost entirely lacking. Few traces survive of
the more extreme forms of the doctrine of the dignity of man. But
the foundation during the fifteenth and sixteenth centuries of the
four older Scottish universities opened the way for some humanistic
influence. Most of the poets and prose writers mentioned in this
chapter were graduates, the majority from St Andrews. A number
of their works may be described without qualification as humanistic
– in particular, Gavin Douglas's translation of the *Aeneid* (Bawcutt,
1976) the neo-Latin poetry of George Buchanan and his successors
(J.G. MacQueen, 1988, 213–25), the Christian Platonism of Florentius
Volusenus (J. and W. MacQueen, 1988, 240) and Drummond of
Hawthornden (J. MacQueen, 1982, 17–26). In addition, the books
and MSS which such men owned provide almost a plethora of
confirmatory evidence (Durkan and Ross, 1961; MacDonald, 1971).

Much is less obvious. In an article published many years ago (J.
MacQueen, 1967), I suggested that early traces were to be found in
the poetry of Robert Henryson (c.1420–90) and that Gavin Douglas's
*Palice of Honour* was a humanist manifesto, partly fantastic, partly
comical, but in intention serious throughout. James VI (1566–1625)
certainly saw himself as a humanist monarch when he produced his
defence of Scots poetry, *Ane Schort Treatise Conteining Some Revlis and
Cautelis to be obseruit and eschewit in Scottis Poesie* (1584) and founded
the Castalian Band of court poets (Craigie, 1955, 65–83; Jack, 1988,
126–7). The sonnet should probably be regarded as a humanist
literary form (Jack, 1988, 127). The reforming urge and basic secularism of Sir David Lindsay's *Ane Satyre of the Thrie Estaitis* represents
the movement under a more popular aspect (Brother Kenneth, 1962,
171–3; Carpenter, 1988, 204–7). The sense of long passages of time
to be found in pieces like Du Bellay's *Antiquités de Rome*, and often
regarded as characteristically humanistic (Gilmore, 1952, 201, 257),
recurs, for instance, in Drummond's sonnet 'Earth and all on it
changeable' (MacDonald, 1976, 108–9):

That space, where raging Waves doe now divide
From the great Continent our happie Isle,
Was some-time Land, and where tall Shippes doe glide,
Once with deare Arte the crooked Plough did tyle –

The study and imitation of classical Greek and Latin literature underlies all these various developments and one of the best indications of the existence and importance of humanistic studies in Scotland as elsewhere is the production of translations of the classics. Gavin Douglas's *Aeneid* is well-known, but another translator, whose interests were in prose rather than poetry, was John Bellenden (c.1495–1548), M.A. of St Andrews in 1512, Doctor of Theology of Paris at some uncertain date, from 1533 to 1538 archdeacon of Moray, precentor of Glasgow from 1538 to his death, and Rector of Glasgow University 1542–4. In 1533 he produced a version of the first five books of the Roman History of Livy (Craigie, 1901–3), an author particularly important for the Renaissance in Italy and elsewhere. The humanist Pope Nicholas v (1447–55) and his successors had 'subsidised attempts to find the lost decades of Livy in places as remote as Denmark and Crete' (Gilmore, 1952, 182); Boece rather improbably (below) held that the search had been extended to include Scotland.

Some fragments of this translation are to be found in British Library Add. MS. 36670, which in 1902 George Reid rescued from the binding of a book printed in 1537 (Craigie, 1903, 235–329). This MS is older than either of the better-known and more or less complete texts which have also survived, Advocates MS 18.3.12 (c.1540) in the National Library of Scotland, and the Boyndlie (1550–60), but its real importance lies in the fact that it is partly Bellenden's autograph, partly in the hand of his amanuensis, and that it contains an early stage of the text with auctorial revisions and scholia, no trace of which appears in the more complete versions. These give some idea of Bellenden's methods and purpose as translator, of the range of knowledge which he could bring to bear, and of the sources which he used for his commentary. The fragment, unfortunately, is restricted to portions of Books I and III.

The scholia are primarily illustrative, and so in a sense educational; they augment the translation where, as inevitably happens, it does not immediately succeed in making Livy's concepts clear to a sixteenth-century lay audience in Scotland. The translation itself also makes concessions; the method mainly adopted is the equation, wherever possible, of Livy's Rome with Bellenden's Scotland and Europe. By southern standards, Scottish society in the sixteenth century was unsophisticated, and for this reason Bellenden may have found parallels for his own local circumstances more in the earlier than the later stages of Roman history; Livy's fifth book ends with the triumph of Camillus after the capture of Rome by the Gauls in 390 B.C.

His modernisation and Scotticising of the text is sometimes carried out almost at an unconscious level. *Pontifex*, '(pagan) priest', for instance, Bellenden usually translates with the sense which it had in medieval Latin, 'bishop', a sense too which he sometimes extends. Livy's *pontificem deinde . . . Marcium Marci filium ex patribus legit* (I.20.5) he renders 'And eftir that he create ane grete Bischop namit Marcius the sone of Marcus, ane of the faderis of Rome' (Craigie, 1901, 48). In modern editions, the Latin contains no equivalent of 'grete', but Bellenden regarded Marcius as *pontifex maximus* ('greatest bishop', 'pope' in medieval Latin), and the translation of this and a slightly later sentence shows that he regarded the 'grete Bischop' as in some measure a pre-Christian Pope, who might have to deal with problems closely resembling those of his sixteenth-century counterpart, possibly including early analogues of Protestant heresies, of which it seems likely that Bellenden, an orthodox and successful churchman, strongly disapproved. 'This bischop suld be of sic preeminence and wisdom that he mycht support the peple by his consultatioun quhen ony doutsum mater occurrit, and to provide sic ways that nowther the religious maneris inducit be him suld be trublit be necligence, nor yit new superstitione brocht in abone the samyn' (I.20.6: *cetera quoque omnia publica priuataque sacra pontificis scitis subiecit, ut esset quo consultum plebes ueniret, ne quid diuini iuris neglegendo patrios ritus peregrinosque adsciscendo turbaretur*). The Latin contains no real equivalent of 'new superstitione', a phrase which for Bellenden almost certainly had overtones of Luther and Henry VIII of England.

*Nomen* in the sense 'gentile or family name' he regularly translates 'surname', a term which in Scots had particular associations with the great Border families – 'Middle March – Ellottis, Armenstranges, Niksonis, Crosares; West Marche – Scottis of Ewisdaill, Batesonis, Litillis, Thomesonis, Glenduniges, Irvingis, Bellis, Carraths, Grahames, Johnstones, Jardanes, Moffettis, Latimeris' (Kermack, 1967, 64). These surnames were also known as 'clans', a term which Bellenden on at least one occasion (Craigie, 1903, 198) applied to the early peoples of Italy. His use of 'surname' sometimes carries no great emphasis, as for instance when he is translating Livy's account of the way in which Romulus organised the joint population of Romans and Sabines: *Itaque cum populum in curias triginta diuideret, nomina earum* (i.e. the Sabine women captured by the Romans to be their wives) *curiis imposuit* (I.13.6) becomes 'Sone eftir Romulus dividit his pepill in sindry courtis, and namit ilk court with the surname of ane of thir Sabyne ladyis' (Craigie, 1901, 37).

Even here there are traces of the idea that the surname indicates not so much birth as a particular social and administrative group to which the individual belonged. More strikingly adapted to home circumstances is his version of the expedition of the Fabii, a distinguished Roman *gens*, who offered to maintain by their own family resources the war against the Veii, an Etruscan people who were dangerous rivals of the early Roman republic. The Senate would then be able to concentrate public resources on the struggle with other neighbouring peoples. In Livy's Latin the Fabii address the Senate with majestic brevity in rhyming prose: *Vos alia bella curate, Fabios hostes Veientibus date* (II.48.8). Bellenden avoids the rhyme and otherwise is more expansive: 'We desire that ye, the faderis foresaid, sustene the chargis of all vthir batallis, quhilkis ar movit agane youre commoun weill and ceite, and suffir ws, the surname and hous of Fabis, to were aganis the Veanis' (Craigie, 1901, 214). It will be noted that at this point the word *nomen* does not appear in Livy's text; Bellenden is translating *ad sensum* rather than *ad litteram* and, as it were, combining his text with a commentary, the purpose of which is to bring the situation home to a sixteenth-century Scots audience. Note how he introduces 'commoun weill' as well as 'surname' into his version, both concepts with which his contemporaries were wholly familiar. One should compare the importance attached to the figure of Iohne the Commoune Weill in Lindsay's *Ane Satyre of the Thrie Estaitis*, written a few years later.

Bellenden translates Livy into the world of the Border ballads, with the justification, as Macaulay long after realised when he composed *The Lays of Ancient Rome*, most of them based on incidents in the first five books of Livy, that a ballad-like element is very much part of the early stages of the history. It is certainly present in the narrative of the tragic but heroic events which follow the undertaking made by the Fabii. Here, for instance, is Bellenden's account of the departure of the Fabii from Rome to the territory of the Veii:

> On the day following the Fabis tuke thare armoure and wappynnis and convenit to the samyn place that was to thame assignit. Sone eftir thare cummyng, the consull, clothit in his cote armour and habit imperiall, departit fra his house and vesyit all his surname and lynnage, arrayit in gudelie maner afore him. Als son as he was enterit in myddis of thame, he gart display his baner. Suthlie thare was never ane armye sene afore thai dayis, beand of sa few nowmer that was of mare renovne & admiratioun to the pepill than was this foresaid cumpany of Fabis; for thai war iij$^c$ and vj knichtis in schyning armoure, all patricianis, all of ane hous, and euery ane of thame wourthy to haue bene governoure of ony nobill army abone the Romanis. Thir feirs and illustir campiouns, al of ane hous, went fordwart mynassing grete myscheif and sorow to Veane pepill.
>
> (Craigie, 1901, 215)

The end is equally dramatic:

> Now war the Fabis be fast rusching of the Ethruschis inclusit but ony out-passage, & the more the inemyis thristit in on thame, the more straitlie war thai drawin togiddir; and ay the more the Fabis semyt of few nowmer, the more the Ethruschis apperit of huge multitude. Than the Fabis, howbeit ilkane of thame was equalie debating with thare inemyis, left the chance thareof, and made thame all attanis perforce to mak ane outpassage throw thare inemyis. Finalie, be force of all thare bodyis and wapynnis at anys concurrand, thai made ane slop throw thare inemyis, at the samyn place quhare thai made this first onset. Als sone as thai war departit in this maner, thai fled vp throw ane strate montane, and be straitnes thareof made thame to new defence and batall. And becaus thai war montit abone thare inemyis, and sum parte deliuerit, as apperit, of the sorowfull chance in quhilkis thai war presentlie falling, thai began to draw new curage and are; syne straik doun thare inemyis ay as thai be force ascendit. Throw quhilk thir few knichtis had vincust and oure thrawin thare inemyis be straitnes of ground, war nocht the Veanis kest thame about the montane; and als sone as thai had won the hede thareof, thai discendit with grete violence on thare bakkis; throw quhilk the nobill Fabis, inclusit baith on bak & afore, fechtand with perseverant manhede to the deith, war all slane but ony exceptioun, and thare munitions made at Cremera tane. Treuth is iij[c] & vj Fabis all perist at this tyme, & nane of thare surname left on life except ane young childe, quhilk was left at hame, preseruit be favoure of goddis to be ane stok of thare hous, that the samyn mycht be ane beild to Romanis in tymes cummyn aganis inemyis baith in were & pece, quhen maist necessite occurrit.

> (Craigie, 1901, 218–219)

Bellenden must surely have had Flodden specifically in mind when he translated that particular passage:

> The stubborn spearmen still made good
> Their dark impenetrable wood,
> Each stepping where his comrade stood
> The instant that he fell.

The child who alone survives is clearly a ballad and folktale figure, destined to become ancestor of the *gens Fabia* so distinguished in the later Republic. Two other points are noteworthy. The Latin makes it clear that the Fabii made their initial escape from ambush by adopting an accepted early military formation, the *cuneus* or wedge; *eo nisi corporibus armisque rupere cuneo uiam* (II.50.9). Bellenden was either unaware of the technical significance of the word, or thought it impossible to render into Scots. His translation contains no equivalent. *Hostis*, 'enemy', occurs twice in the Latin; 'inemyis' eight times in the more emotive Scots, which seems aimed at the patriotic prejudices of its readers, for whom the word inevitably had overtones of their 'auld inemyis' of England. Roman and Scot are identified even, or indeed particularly, in disaster.

At times the Latin itself seems to promote the identification of Scotland with early Rome. The *quattuor iugerum agrum* (III.26.8) of the poor farmer and virtuous dictator Cincinnatus effortlessly becomes (Craigie, 1901, 281) 'foure oxin gang of land'; the *tugurium*, 'hut', in which he lives with his wife becomes 'the somer schele quhare he duelt' – a summer shieling, presumably, because he had a house in Rome where he passed the winter months, or so Bellenden seems to assume. *Seu fossam fodiens palae innixus, seu cum araret, operi certe, id quod constat, agresti intentus* (III.26.9) becomes 'owthir makand ane sewch or ellis haldand the pleuch. In quhatsumeuir sorte it happynnyt, treuth is, he was gevin to landwart besynes'. A comparison with the BL MS shows that Bellenden made several attempts at *fossam fodiens palae innixus* before he found the elegant and accurate 'makand ane sewch'. 'Landward', as is well known, is still a Scots legal and official term; 'landward parts' means 'the rural area in the neighbour-hood of a town, the rural part of a country district or parish'. The toga of Cincinnatus is simply his 'goun'; there is no hint that the garment implied any special status for the wearer; the forum is the 'merket', where for the duration of the emergency he 'commandit the ministracioun of lawis to ceis, and na buthis to be opynnit to his returnyng, that na private besines suld be done, bot alanerly sic thingis as concernis the ordinance of battale'. Rome is seen as if it were Edinburgh with its merkat cross where proclamations were made, its Luckenbooths or covered stalls, and its law-courts. The landscape in fact is a more salubrious version of that found in Dunbar's satirical 'To the Merchantis of Edinburgh'.

A similar effect is created when word spreads of the rape of Lucretia by Sextus Tarquinius (Craigie, 1901, 127): it 'causit the pepill to rusch out of all partis thareof to the merket. Incontinent ane officiare warnit thame all to compere afore Brutus, the tribune of the garde (for he was cled at this tyme with that office)'. Here the Scots legal term 'compere' translates *aduocauit*; *praeco*, 'herald', is 'ane officiare' – the toun officer, that is probably to say, 'an official attending on the provost, magistrates and councillors of a burgh in the council chamber and at public functions' (SND), and the *Celeres*, the royal bodyguard, become simply 'the garde', which suggests the Edinburgh City Guard of later notoriety.

To return to Cincinnatus, the *signifer*, 'standard-bearer, ensign', who leads out the dictator's army, becomes 'banerman', a term confined to Scots usage, and *signa constituunt*, 'they halted' (literally 'grounded their standards') becomes 'set doun thare tentis', again like a Scots rather than a Roman army.

Roman circus games gave Bellenden the unconscious opportunity

to distort the record in favour of burgh life. The circus he equated
with burgh playing places, and the games with the popular plays of
his time, performed in these enclosures. The only specimen to
survive is *Ane Satyre of the Thrie Estaitis*, written a few years after
Bellenden completed his translation. Bellenden believed that the
Roman 'plays' were originally performed on the streets, and that the
circus, like the playing place, was a later development. The Sabine
women, he believes, were raped while attending an early Roman
theatrical performance in the streets. The performance was preceded
by something resembling the banns or proclamation for the approaching Cupar performance of Lindsay's play. Romulus 'be his crafty
industry proclamyt ane solempne play, callit in thai dayis *consualia*,
quhilkis war dedicate in honour of Neptunus Chevelrier. Sone eftir,
he commandit generall edictis and proclamacioun to be maid in all
partis, to aduertis his nychtbouris thareof. The Romanis dressit furth
this play in the maist solempne maner thai culd or mycht, to mak it
the more sichty and glorius to the pepill. Mony vncouth and strange
pepill assemblit to this conuencioun, na les desirus to vesy this new
toun than to se this play, especialie the pepill quhilkis war nerrest
nychtbouris, as Cenynanis, Custumanis & Antempnatis; and beside
thir convenit ane huge nowmer of Sabinis with thare wyiffis, barnis
& servandis, quhilkis war all plesandlie lugit and intertenit within
the said tovne. Thir pepill, eftir thai had vesyit the situacioun, wallis
and policyis of this new toun, had grete admiracioun that the
Romanis war cummyn sa haistelie to grete pussance. At last, quhen
the houre of play was cummyn, and the pepill maist ernistlie gevand
thare ene to the contemplacioun thareof, raiss ane suddane effray
be slicht and craft industry. Incontinent, be sound of trumpett (as
was devisit) all the young men of the toun, armit in fere of were,
ran throw the stretis, revisand the virginis and madynnis that come
to this play' (Craigie, 1901, 28–29).

Especially notable and uniquely Scottish here is the use of the
word 'policy' in the sense 'The improvement, or development of a
town, estate or the like, amenity; the houses and other property
improvements involved in this' (SND), to provide a concise and
accurate translation of Livy's *frequentem tectis urbem* (I.9.9). Bellenden
fails to understand that the 'young men of the toun', whom he sends
running through the streets on no textual authority, were in fact
competitors in the games, who broke off from their contests to
ravish the girl spectators. It seems likely that he envisaged a street
performance, resembling the guild performances of mystery plays
which were a feature of Scots burghs as well as English towns in the
period from the fourteenth to the sixteenth centuries. The 'sound of
trumpett' which gave the signal for action may also have been introduced from such performances; the Latin – *signoque dato* – is much
less specific.

In this episode there is no reference to a playing place, a feature later introduced by the fifth king, Tarquinius Priscus:

> He was the first king that assignit grete boundis within Rome to be playing places, quhilk placis war namyt Circus. Thir playing placis war dividit with sic ordinance amang the faderis, horsmen, and vtheris nobillis of Rome, that euery ane of thame eftir thare estate had thare sete edifyit for contemplacioun of thir playis. Thir seittis war namyt *fori*, and war rasit on certane stakis xij fute of hicht fra the erde, that thir foresaidis nobillis mycht the more esely behald & vesy the playis quhen thai occurrit. Thir playis war sa ioyus and sa full of euery pleasour, that sindri valeyeant campiouns and horsmen, specially of Ethruria, come to vesy the samyn quhen thai occurrit. Thir sportis and ioyus merynes continewit yerelie amang the Romanis, and war callit sum tyme the Romane Playis and sum tymes the Grete Playis.

(Craigie, 1901, 83)

Bellenden misses the fact that the reference is to the foundation of a single notable arena, the Circus Maximus, which in its prime could seat more than a hundred thousand spectators and was one of the wonders of Rome. The visitors from Etruria came, not to see the plays, but to compete in the games, and the 'sindri valeyeant campiouns' were in fact boxers (*pugiles*). As a translation from the Latin, the paragraph thus contains more than one howler; it is important nevertheless because it projects on to antiquity features characteristic of Bellenden's own day. The translation may also be of some importance as indirectly supplying evidence for theatrical developments in Scotland.

After the defeat of the Latins, Tarquinius Priscus was also responsible for improvements in city hygiene by the construction of *cloacae*, 'sewers', from the lower parts of the city into the Tiber (Craigie, 1901, 88). Bellenden reveals the shortcomings of his times when he renders the passage in a way which misses the point: he seems unable to visualise the possibility of draining low-lying ground. 'He drew mony closettis, condittis, & synkis fra the hicht of the toun to the merkett and vthir law partis thareof to purge the sammyn of all corruptioun and filth; for on the plane and evin ground mycht na discensis be maid for purgacioun thareof.' The filth, in other words, is deposited, not as Livy has it in the Tiber, but in the lower parts of the town, including the market place, a scheme which uncomfortably calls to mind not only the Edinburgh of Dunbar, but also Dr Johnson's words to Boswell on his arrival in a later, but still insalubrious city, 'I smell you in the dark'. *Cloacae* is rendered by three terms, 'closettis, condittis and sinks'; the three are not synonyms, but represent different methods of waste-disposal available in Bellenden's time; the first is an early example

of the word used with the connotations of the later 'earth-' and
'water-closet' (DOST).

One weakness of the translation as preserved in the two main
MSS, is that many unfamiliar concepts are taken apparently for
granted, and indeed that the coinages, usually Latin, applied to
them, and often in Bellenden's text exemplified for the first time in
Scots or English, receive no kind of gloss or explanation. One
instance is the word 'dictator', applied first to the Alban, Mettius
Fufetius (Craigie, 1901, 52). Bellenden was not the first to use the
word, but obviously it was unfamiliar, and the fragmentary inter-
linear or marginal gloss to the BL MS reads thus (Craigie, 1903,
250, n.2): 'Dictator vas the gretest officer that vas amang the peple.
He had . . . jurisdictioun aboun the peple baith of lif and deth. He
changit all . . . at his plesour'. A little later (54) we find the word
'feciall', Latin *fetialis*; the BL MS glosses it (Craigie, 1903, 251, n.1),
'Feciall was ane preist quhilk had all the iurisdictioun abone the
peple to bynd and mak confederation in mast sover maner. Thir
preistis decernit gif batallis var . . . & als maid trevis . . . Ane of thir
feciallis (quhilkis var maist nobill) was chosin to be fader patrat &
was accustumit to pas with terribill censuris on the pepill quhair the
damage or vrangis first . . .'. Bellenden appears to be the first to use
the word in Scots or English. It is clear from the BL MS that his
original intention was to gloss his translation throughout; quite
possibly too that he was making a deliberate attempt to enrich the
resources of the vernacular. The other words which he glosses are
'emperour' (*imperator*, 'general'), 'the principal capitane havand
vitore on his enimis' – in view of the possible confusion with the
normal meaning of 'emperour' Bellenden is here very precise –
'candidatis', 'interregnis', 'proconsul', 'sextile' (of months. = 'August';
cf. 'September' from *septem*), 'talentis', 'census', 'classis', 'commentaris', 'turme', 'the rame', 'salynis' ('salt-pans'; cf. Saline, a place-
name in Fife).

As befits a humanist, his gloss on 'commentaris' (Craigie, 1903,
260, n.3) although much damaged, remains of interest. The immediate
reference is to Tullus Hostilius, the fourth king, reading the religious
handbook left by his predecessor Numa Pompilius. The gloss runs
'Commentaris ar callit certane bukis, in quhilk ar contenit allanerlie
the rubrikis or chaptouris of only greter mater, & sum tymes thai ar
callit the expositioun of . . . as the Commentaris of . . . or Lucan'.
A reference to Caesar's *Commentaries* on the Gallic Wars is perhaps
to be understood here: the reference to Lucan may indicate that his
historical and political epic, the *Pharsalia*, was regarded, like Caesar's
work, as a commentary, or alternatively Bellenden may be referring
to some humanist exposition of the poem.

All in all, the glosses reveal a considerable breadth of scholarly
knowledge. There are occasional references to classical sources other

than Livy. Valerius Maximus is cited five times, Pomponious Mela and Dionysius of Halicarnassus once each. It is perhaps worth noting that an anecdote in Valerius Maximus may be the ultimate source of *The Palice of Honour*, a poem by another Scots humanist and translator, Gavin Douglas (Bawcutt, 1967, Lxxxii, n.37).

It may seem strange, even eccentric, that Bellenden's *Livy* should figure largely in a relatively brief article on literary humanism in Renaissance Scotland. Yet there are good reasons. Livy as an author is particularly important to Scots humanism, which was essentially Latin and historical. The long struggle, intellectual as well as military, against English territorial ambitions had ensured that the Scots were already the historical nation. Again, the translation has received very little attention; in the recently published *History of Scottish Literature*, for example, only a dozen words are devoted to it (Lyall, 1988, 173). It occupies an important position, substantially later than the achievement of such men as James III's humanist Secretary, Archibald Whitelaw, who died in 1498, or even Gavin Douglas, who died in 1522 and whose version of the *Aeneid* was completed in 1513. It represents what at the time was possible for someone trained in a Scots university, who figured again in a Scottish academic context when in 1542 he became Rector of Glasgow University. It seems likely that he owed his Rectorship to his reputation as humanist and literary man (Batho and Husband, 1941, 433). His translations however were not primarily directed at the scholar or the general reader; like the earlier (1531) rendering of Boece's *History*, *Livy* was produced at the command of King James V, who, as a Renaissance ruler, thus acknowledged the importance of classical and historical studies for the conduct of public affairs.

Bellenden's career, with its emphasis on literary achievement, throws some light on the intellectual circumstances of the time, as does the contrast between his work and that of his older contemporary, John Major or Mair (1467–1550). Although Major figures elsewhere in this book, he has traditionally been regarded as the last of the Schoolmen, someone whose interests belonged, not to the Renaissance, but the Middle Ages. The inadequacy of this point of view has long been evident. Major was historian as well as theologian and logician, author of *Historia Majoris Britanniae tam Angliae quam Scotiae per Johannem Majorem natione quidem Scotum professione autem theologum* (1521), for whom the most eminent masters of his craft were the humanist idols Sallust and Livy. Interestingly, he was prepared to add Bede to the company. It will be noticed too that he wrote a history of Britain rather than of Scotland or England; almost certainly he would have been unsympathetic to some aspects of Bellenden's nationalism. He wrote entirely in Latin. His style however remained entirely that of an old-fashioned theologian, in defence of which he argued the passage of time; that sixteenth-century Scotland differed significantly from, rather than resembled pagan Rome, and that theology is a discipline peculiarly appropriate for the writer of history, who must make distinctions. 'And, indeed,' he adds, 'I have given my utmost endeavour to follow this course in all cases, and most of all where the question was ambiguous, to the end that from the reading of this history you may learn not only the thing that was done, but also how it ought to have been done, and that you may by this means and at the cost of a little reading come to know what the experience of centuries, if it were granted to you to live so long, could scarcely teach' (Constable, 1892, cxxxiv–cxxxv). To a degree he differs from such humanists as Bellenden because his ideas were more radical and advanced. From the point of view of the present article, however, this still leaves him something other than a full-blown humanist, and the contrast between him and Bellenden, one born in 1467, the other in 1495, gives proof of the advance of humanistic studies in Scotland in the early years of the sixteenth century.

The immediate contrast however is not so much between Major and Bellenden as between Major and Hector Boece (*c.*1465–*c.*1536). Bellenden however retains his relevance because, as has already been mentioned, he made a translation of Boece's *History* under the same royal patronage as his *Livy*, and presented it to the king in 1531. Several early MSS survive, together with an edition printed in Edinburgh by Thomas Davidson in 1541–2 (Chambers and Batho, 1938, viii–x; Aldis, 1970). Boece, like Major, was a product of the College of Montaigu in Paris, and later became first principal of Aberdeen University, where he brought to his post the interests and enthusiasms which in some measure he shared with another former member of the College of Montaigu, the greatest of sixteenth-century humanists, Erasmus. Boece modelled his Latin style principally on Livy, but he was also significantly affected by Tacitus, the range and power of whose writings had been brought to light, first by Enoch of Ascoli's discovery in 1455 of the 10th-century Jesi codex, and secondly by the printing at Rome in 1515 of Beroaldus' first complete edition (Hall, 1913, 274–5). Boece in other words stood near the beginning of Tacitean studies. His *History*, printed in Paris in 1527, six years after Major's, is limited to Scotland, and like the earlier, non-humanist *Scotichronicon* (*c.*1440–50), ends with the murder of James I in 1437. Something of the difference between Boece and Major may be gathered from a comparison of titles; Major's, already quoted, is medieval in its Latinity, and includes a pun on his own name. Boece's is more classical and grandiloquent, *Scottorum Historiae a prima gentis origine cum aliarum et rerum et gentium illustratione non vulgari.*

For the purposes of the present chapter, Books I–VII, covering the history of Scotland from Fergus I to Fergus II, are the most important.

The basic source, it seems fair to say, for this and much of the later material is *Scotichronicon*. Both Ferguses are there included – Fergus I establishing the monarchy in Scotland in 330 B.C., and the coronation ceremony of the genuinely historical Fergus II (Fergus son of Erc) taking place in 403, a century too early. Boece puts it in 422 and so reduces the error to some eighty years. In *Scotichronicon* III.2 forty-five kings are said to have reigned during the period separating the namesakes, but details are given only for a very few. Royal genealogies however are found in V.60, in X.2, and independently in a number of MSS, the most notable being the 12th-century Irish MS, Oxford Bodleian Rawlinson B.502, the 12th-century Trinity College, Dublin MS H.2.18 (the Book of Leinster), the 14th-century Poppleton MS (Paris, Bibliotheque Nationale, MS Latin 4126, and the 14th-century Trinity College, Dublin MS H.2.7 (O'Brien, 1962, i, 328f; Bannerman, 1974, 28–31; Anderson, 1980, 237–40); the names included in these have a more or less direct correspondence with those found in Boece, in whose work the two Ferguses are separated by a sequence of thirty-nine kings.

Boece however claims a different source, the notorious Veremund, details of whose work are given in a curiously roundabout way at a relatively late stage of the *History*. In VII.2 (Chambers and Batho, 1938, 269–70) he tells how Fergus II in his youth was allied with Alaric the Goth in the sack of Rome (410). As part of the spoils he received a 'kist of bukis', which he deposited in Iona. In the course of his visit to Scotland Aeneas Sylvius, later Pope Pius II (1458–64), made some attempt to visit the island to see if the collection included the lost decades of Livy, but gave up when James I was murdered in 1437 (Aeneas Sylvius in fact visited Scotland in 1435). Boece himself later recovered some fragmentary broken leaves through the agency of the king's Treasurer, Master John Campbell. No more than every tenth word could be read, but the style 'soundit mair to the eloquence of Salustius than of Liuius. Als war brocht to ws that samyn tyme the werkis of Veremundus, Archidene of Sanctandrois, contenand the history of this realme fra the first begynnyng of it to King Malcolme Canmoiris tyme, quhom we haif followit, with the maist wise Byschop Williame Elphinstoun, to the end of this oure quhatsumeuer werk'.

Veremund has been tentatively identified with Richard Vairement, a culdee of St Andrews in the 1250s, and 'the history of the realme' with the *Historia* which formed the eighteenth item in the lost *registrum* of the Augustinian priory attached to St Andrews cathedral (Skene, 1871, xxxviii–xxxix). The *registrum* disappeared shortly after 1660, but a list of its contents has survived (Anderson, 1980, 54–58). The evidence is at best tentative, and Boece at the least must have considerably expanded his source, which in the *registrum* occupied only forty-one folios.

The identification of Veremund is less important than the context in which Boece places him. The search for copies of classical MSS, especially those of 'lost' authors, as has been noted was a characteristic preoccupation of certain Italian humanists in the fifteenth century. Boece introduces one, not usually regarded as a collector, Aeneas Sylvius, whose visit to Scotland he sees as preluding the quest for MSS of Livy instituted by his predecessor in the papacy, Nicholas V (1447–55), a quest which in the case of Aeneas was directed towards the monastic library of Iona. When he himself resumed the search, he demonstrated his own status as humanist. There is a palpable note of disappointment at the condition of the recovered MSS, and a note of pedantic pleasure in the fact that although it was possible to read only every tenth word, yet the style was more like Sallust than Livy. There is no necessary suggestion that the MS of Veremund came from the same place, but mere association gives it something of the glamour of the classical discovery.

Long ago Thomas Innes noted (1879, 131) how Boece used Livy and other classical models to give flavour to the new anecdotes which he brought into his *History*. 'In effect,' he says, 'Boece was one of the first in these northern parts who, by assiduous reading, and imitation of the ancient Latin authors, began to restore the Latin tongue to its purity, instead of the barbarous style which, from the fall of the Roman empire, had overrun all till later ages'. In the course of his Section VI, he demonstrates the extent to which classical reading had influenced the very structure of the *History*. Innes refers (148) to 'the fabulous stories in his history, copied from the Roman or other histories, such as the Scottish women married to the Picts interceding between their husbands and parents, like the Sabine in Titus Livius; King Mainus, like Numa, establishing the sacred rites; the table of the laws made by Fergus I, Dornadilla, and others. And all politic deliberations he puts in his Scottish grandees' mouths, from the same Titus Livius and others'. The hostile tone here and elsewhere in the *Essay* is not difficult to explain. Innes was a Catholic priest, a Jacobite, who believed in the divine right of kings (Donaldson, 1988, 14); it was this, as well as his careful scholarship, which made him hostile to any parallel drawn between the history of Scotland and that of Rome under the kings and during the early republic, a parallel which Boece, Bellenden and (for Innes) the more obviously sinister figure of George Buchanan had emphasised. The fate of Queen Mary and her great-grandson, James VII and II, too much resembled that of Tarquin.

There is a genuine as well as a spurious aspect to Boece's antiquarianism. He attempts to follow Livy's example by making a pretext of investigating the origins of ancient monuments and calendar customs, which fascinate and often puzzle him. When Innes in the passage quoted refers to King Mainus establishing the sacred rites, he does Boece scant justice. Boece intended (Chambers and Batho, 1938, 57–58) not only to draw a parallel between Mainus and Numa Pompilius, but also to explain the existence and function of the megalithic stone circles found in Scotland together with the religious origins of certain superstitions which survived into his own day and later. The king ordained that on one stone of each circle sacrifices of corn, cattle or other fruits of the earth should be offered. These served the additional purpose of maintaining the priests ('kirkmen'). Each new moon a special sacrifice was to be offered to Diana, a custom which Boece describes as Egyptian and says continued in use for a very long time. Diana is thus signalled out because Boece has already made the point (Chambers and Batho, 1938, 32–33, 58–59) that the economy of the early Scots, as oppose to that of the more urban Picts, was based on hunting. The Egyptians are mentioned because it was from Egypt that the Scots began their migration to Spain, Ireland and Scotland. The kirkmen are the Druids mentioned by Tacitus. The two philosophers whom shipwreck brought to the court of King Iosyne (Chambers and Batho, 1938, 71–72) 'declarit thair religioun nocht to be commendit, becaus thai adorit the ymagis of brutell beistis, in form of levand goddis, as the Egipcianis vsit'; as a consequence people temporarily gave up their sacrifices to Isis and Apis. Diana as mentioned in the passage is perhaps to be identified with Isis. When Boece says that a ceremony was 'lang vsit', he probably implies that something like it was still followed in his own day.

The beginnings of archaeology are to be found in the collections made by Italian humanists and their patrons of objects and works of art found on ancient sites, whether by chance or deliberate excavation. Often these finds were a ready-made excuse for specu- lation. Boece shares this tendency. The *History* contains several notices of discoveries made in Scotland and the deductions made by him in consequence. See especially Chambers and Batho, 1938, 126– 7 (sepulchral customs) and 214 (coin hoards).

The supposed ancestral link between Scots and Egyptians allows Boece to see the Pictish sculptured stones found over much of north- eastern Scotland (Henderson, 1967, 104–60) as hieroglyphic memor- ials of the ancient kings. In I.8, for instance, he states that Fergus I 'gatt charteris and euidentis of the crovne of Scottlannd to him and his successouris in this sort; quhilkis charteris war gravin in merbill, with ymagis of bestis in forme of letteris, as wer vsit in thai dayis; syne gaif the samyn to maist religious preistis, to be obseruit in thair tempillis' (Chambers and Batho, 1938, 45). King Rutha erected monuments to keep alive the memory of valiant men, 'on the quhilkis wer engravit ymagerijs of dragonis, wolffis and vther bestis, because na inuencioun of letterez was in thai dayis, to put the dedis of nobill men in memory' (Chambers and Batho, 1938, 67). It is possible that he similarly regarded the 'tabullis' on which the laws of Dorvidilla and Fergus were preserved (Chambers and Batho, 1938, 59) as sculptured stones with hieroglyphic inscriptions. He also insists that connections with Egypt long remained open; thus he tells how King Ptolemy of Egypt dispatched 'certane oratouris' to investigate the geography of the world. King Rutha extended every hospitality to them and they recognised the kinship between their own religion and way of life and that of the Scots. The eventual but long-delayed result of their visit was the Cosmography and Tables of Ptolemy, only completed some four hundred years later in the time of the Roman emperor Hadrian (Chambers and Batho, 1938, 68–69). It is not so much that Boece has confused Ptolemy the geographer and astronomer (fl. 127–48) with one of the earlier royal Ptolemies (perhaps Ptolemy II Philadelphus, founder of the Museum and Library of Alexandria), as that he is determined to adduce his work as evidence for the antiquities of the Scots in the pre-Christian era. Thus the castle of Berigon in Lochaber, where Fergus I established his seat, has its origin in Ptolemy's *Rerigonion*, probably situated somewhere in the vicinity of Loch Ryan in Galloway (Rivet and Smith, 1979, 138–9).

One purpose of all this may be to explain how information was preserved about the early stages of a non-literate society, a point later much stressed by Buchanan, but Boece does no more than hint at this, nor is he always consistent with himself. An interest in Egyptian antiquities, incidentally, is characteristic of many humanists in Italy and elsewhere. Names which come readily to mind include Ficino, Pico della Mirandola and Bruno (Yates, 1964).

The most remarkable instance in Boece of antiquarian flair is his realisation (Chambers and Batho, 1938, 165–6) that Inchtuthil on the Tay had earlier been a place of some importance. He makes it a town abandoned and destroyed by the Picts as part of their scorched-earth policy against the Roman invasion. It was only realised in this century that Inchtuthil was a legionary fortress evacuated by the Romans before completion (Salway, 1981, 149–52; Rivet and Smith, 1979, 499).

As a humanist, Boece is well aware that literary, philosophic and scientific achievement is part of the historical record. Thus in II.6 and 7 (Chambers and Batho, 1938, 68, 70–71) he discusses the development of medicine as an art in early Scotland, perhaps with the Beaton family tradition of later times in mind (Bannerman 1986). In V.5 he places the death of King Dardanus (allegedly 85 A.D.) in a highly intellectual context (I have made an obvious correction in the printed text of the translation):

'Eftir the deth of Dardanus in to thir dayis wer mony excellent clerkis in sindry partis of the warld: as Quintiliane, oratour; Serapio, medicinar; Philo Jew, philosophoure & oratour; Cayus

Plenius Secundus, that wrait the Historie Naturall; Cornelius Tacitus, historicien, quhom we haif followitt in this werk; Cecilius Plenius Secundus, oratour; Suetonius Tranquillius, historicien; Claudius Ptolomeus. maist excellennt in methamatik, quhilk brocht the Cosmografy of Ptolomeey afoir rehersit to ane bettir knawlege with mony addicionis. And in thai days wer excellent poeittis: as Iuuenaill, Silius Italicus, Marcialis, with mony vtheris.'

(Chambers and Batho, 1938, 193)

The passage, incidentally, shows clearly enough that Boece did not confuse the geographer and astronomer Ptolemy with the king of the same name.

One of Boece's ambitions was to reconcile the sequence of events in first-century Britain as given in *Scotichronicon* and in the recently recovered works of Tacitus. At the end of Book IV he makes the claim explicit:

'This history that I haif schewin of Caratak, Corbreid, and Galdus, Kingis of Scottis, is drawin sum part oute of oure wlgair cornikillis, bot maist is drawin oute of Cornelius Tacitus, and hes insertit nocht only his sentence, bot oftymes his wourdis, that it may be patent to thaim that redis baith oure historijs and the Romanis sall fynd the sentence nocht far discordand'.

(Chambers and Batho, 1938, 183)

The crudity of his method is not perhaps surprising when allowances are made for the early date of his work and his strong national prejudices. He mistakes *Mona*, 'Anglesey', for the Isle of Man, and as a consequence sets up a college of Druids there (Chambers and Batho, 1938, 73–74). He identifies Conaire Mor, the Irish 'peace-king' who figures in the earlier stages of the Scots royal genealogy and in the historical tale, *The Destruction of Da Derga's Hostel*, with Caratacus (Caratac), the redoubtable British opponent of the Emperor Claudius, who was eventually brought captive to Rome. Caratacus' seat of power he places in the Ayrshire Carrick, influenced no doubt by the distant similarity of name. Voada, the sister of Caratacus, is made the neglected wife of Arviragus, king of the Britons; she and her younger daughter Vodicia form, as it were, a gemination of Boudicca or Boadicea, warrior queen of the Iceni, now adorned with the benefit of Scots ancestry. Calgacus or Galgacus, defeated by Agricola at Mons Graupius, becomes Galdus nephew of Caratacus, defeated in battle among 'the montanis of Granyeben, quhilk rynnis fra the fute of Dee to Dounbritan'. The Scots royal line is thus brought into direct and violent contact with the Romans, and Boece demonstrates to his own satisfaction that the classical record enhances rather than contradicts the native tradition (Chambers and Batho, 1938, 104–83).

The inadequacy of Boece's historical method is obvious. Like many other humanist exercises of the time, his *History* is an extended rhetorical elaboration on a historical theme, dependent for its effect on stylistic flair and the extensive citation of authorities not necessarily studied in any depth, and who may even on occasion be fictitious. For this reason it is more appropriate to place Boece in the tradition of panegyric oratory than history. For a humanism more thoroughly based on source and textual criticism one must look to his successor George Buchanan (1506–82) and his *Rerum Scoticarum Historia* first published in Edinburgh in the year of his death. Buchanan's mind is instinctively and incisively critical, as may be seen from much of his satirical writing in verse and prose, Latin and Scots – *Franciscanus*, for instance, or *Chamaeleon*. He was unfortunate however in the application of this critical faculty to some matters of science and scholarship. His didactic poem on astronomy, *De Sphaera*, attacked the Copernican system of the planets for what must at the time have seemed excellent reasons; unfortunately, he was wrong, and although the poem remained in esteem for many years after his death, it was eventually discredited and as a consequence, despite its beauties and virtues, ignored (J. MacQueen, 1982, 9–17). Almost the same fate has befallen *Rerum Scoticarum Historia*. Buchanan cleared away a good deal of rubbish and established new ways of investigation. His summary dismissal of Brutus and Gathelus alike (II.7–12) is well in advance of its time (Milton, it will be recollected, still accepted the historicity of Brutus, and made a serious translation of the oracle of Diana with which, half a century earlier Buchanan had had so much philological fun), as, in a more positive way, is his reconstruction of the movements of early Celtic peoples by place-name and other linguistic evidence (II.24–36). He ignores the ancient Egyptian religion, but allowed himself (II.23) some brief discussion of the Druids. He removed many excrescences from Boece's account of the first forty kings, and strengthened, so far as that was possible, the rational grounds for belief in their existence. The name Caratacus, for example, he retains (IV.23) as that of his eighteenth monarch, but deliberately abandons the attempt to equate him with the Caratacus of Tacitus. 'Hector (Boece),' he remarks earlier (II.47), 'attributes the actions of others against the Romans to his Scots.' Buchanan concedes the possibility that the twenty-first king, Galdus, may be the same as Galgacus; the phrase which he uses (IV.26) is 'Some think he is the same who is called Galgacus by Tacitus' (*Sunt qui hunc Galgacum a Tacito apellari existiment*). Here at least it is unquestioned fact that Galgacus was a native of the area later called Scotland. In general his treatment of the earliest kings is more succinct, less rhetorical, than anything in Boece. I am not even certain that he felt much interest in them. His sole crime, much denounced in recent years, is that he did not actually abolish them as a group, for whose existence he had what appeared to him and many others plausible evidence.

One relevant factor is that Buchanan was a Gaelic-speaking Highlander, who recognised the kinship between Boece and the traditions preserved by the senachies (*seneciones*) for which he expresses (II.2) a modified contempt, not on the grounds that it is worthless, but rather that it is likely to be biased, distorted in favour of a patron, and because it has not been safeguarded by preservation in writing.

Buchanan's closeness to the Gaelic tradition may also be illustrated from *De Iure Regni apud Scotos Dialogus*, the dialogue, ultimately modelled on the *Republic* and *Laws* of Plato, which in 1579 he dedicated to James VI. The theme is the proper relationship between justice, the law, the monarchy, and the will of the people, a theme given particular urgency by the forced abdication in 1567 of Mary I, who fled the country to endure a long imprisonment and finally execution at the hands of her cousin, the English Queen Elizabeth. In many ways the dialogue is a more abstract consideration of the general theme underlying the detailed narrative of events in *Rerum Scoticarum Historia*. The many cross-references to events in the as-yet-unpublished *Historia* are backed by illustrations drawn from classical and modern European sources. Buchanan however obviously sets a particular importance on the authority of the Gaelic society of which he was by birth himself a member. The appointment of clan chiefs is evidence for the way in which monarchs were once elected:

*Etiam in antiquis familiis vetusti moris quaedam vestigia remanent. Scoti enim prisci, ad nostram usque aetatem, suos eligunt Phylarchos, & electis concilium seniorum adhibent: cui concilio qui non parent, honore privantur.*

('In the ancient clans, some traces of the old custom still remain. Right up to our own time, Scots who speak Gaelic choose their own Chiefs and appoint a council of elders to advise those elected. Those who do not obey the council are deprived of office.')

(Ruddiman, 1715, 25)

This may be a somewhat idealised version of Gaelic custom, but at least it shows that a scholar, widely versed in European institutions from ancient times to the present, saw the relevance of native culture to his studies as a whole. It is almost a paradigm of Buchanan's humanism that the literary vehicle used for the expression of such insights is the Platonic dialogue.

The humanistic approach to Scripture, which formed part of the Protestant reformation, is also visible in the *Dialogus*. Biblical authority formed an important part of the doctrine of absolute monarchy usually advanced in the sixteenth and seventeenth century. Buchanan questioned the validity of this approach in his discussion of the preliminaries to Samuel's choice of Saul as king of Israel (1 Samuel, 8.11–18), the advice given to Israel to obey the foreign king Nebuchad-

nezzar (Jeremiah, 27), and the advice given by Paul to the early
Christians to subject themselves to the civic authorities (Romans,
13.1–8, 1 Timothy, 2.2, Titus, 3.1). His attitude is notably detached
and analytic; his principal concern is with the question of whether
they are to be read as examples of universal application or simply
in their historical context. He comes down heavily in favour of the
latter. His remarks on the circumstances under which Paul and
Jeremiah wrote are full of insight. The illustration – contemporary
Christians under Turkish rule (MacNeill, 1964, 80–81) – is striking
and appropriate, the application convincing in a way quite different
from that of the medieval theologian, both in itself, and also as
forming part of a work written in a primarily classical tradition.

Christian humanists who were also Reformers tended to have a
particular interest in the presentation and interpretation of the
Psalms for their contemporaries. Professor McFarlane (1981, 248–50)
gives many continental examples, but they are also reasonably
frequent in the British Isles. Sir Thomas Wyatt, for instance, makes
the Penitential Psalms (6, 32, 38, 51, 102, 130 and 143) dramatic
monologues in the context of David's repentance for his adulterous
love of Bathsheba. Surrey and Alexander Scott are more concerned
with courtly lyrical and musical effects appropriate to the tastes of
the time. Buchanan differs from all three. The Psalms he sees as
Hebrew equivalents of classical literary works, more especially the
*Odes* and *Epodes* of Horace, directed towards issues with a historical
as well as a universal relevance. He attempts to find a classical form
appropriate to the content of the Hebrew poem. His versions are
deliberately paraphrases rather than translations and superimpose
their own context. One instance must suffice. He draws a parallel
between Psalm 19, 'The heavens declare the glory of God' and,
rather unexpectedly, Horace, *Odes* I.34, *Parcus deorum cultor et
infrequens*, a poem traditionally accepted as Horace's account of a
conversion from Epicurean to Stoic beliefs brought about by thunder
from a clear sky. The Epicureans held that thunder was caused by
the clashing of two clouds; the obvious inadequacy of this brings
the poet to belief in the Stoic Heimarmene, which he realises
involves a paradoxical harmony between stable God and fickle
Fortune. The wisdom of Epicurus which he once cultivated has
become madness, *insanientis dum sapientiae/consultus erro* (2–3).

Buchanan begins his paraphrase with a variation on these words,
and offers the spectacle of the heavens, rather than a peal of
thunder, as evidence of universal harmony. The metre of his
version, like that of the ode, is Alcaic:

> *Insanientis gens sapientiae,*
> *Addicta mentem erroribus impiis,*
> *Tot luce flammarum coruscum*
> *Cerne oculis animoque coelum.*

*Hinc disce, prudens quam fuit artifex,*
  *Qui templa Olympi fornice flammeo*
  *Suspendit, et terrae capacem*
    *Et pelagi sinuavit arcum.*

*Dies tenebras et tenebrae diem*
  *Semper prementes perpetua vice*
  *Non fortuito res caducas*
    *Ire monent per inane lapsu*

*Sed tota concors fabrica personat . . .*

(Buchanan, 1686, 33)

Only in the sixteenth century could a humanist have undertaken to paraphrase all the Psalms on such terms, and, even then, only if he had achieved Buchanan's pre-eminence as poet and scholar. Three-quarters of a century later Arthur Johnston (1587–1641), a physician who in 1637 became rector of King's College, Aberdeen, introduced his own Latin verse-rendering of the Psalms, with an admiring reference, which contains just a hint of adverse criticism. Buchanan's version is magnificent, but more appropriate to David as king than as prophet. Johnston's will aspire to the latter level:–

*Cinxit Iessiaden Buchananus veste, pyropis*
  *Quae simul et cocco nobiliore nitet,*
*Haec, ego quam dono, nec gemmis picta nec ostro est,*
  *Tota sed, ut cernis, stamine texta rudi.*
*Rex erat et vates hic cui servimus, amictus*
  *Et regi et vati non satis unus erat.*
*Apta paludato Buchanani purpura regi est,*
  *Regibus aut si quid grandius orbis habet.*
*Nil mihi cum sceptris; ego do velamina vati;*
  *Hunc decuit cultu simpliciore tegi.*

(Geddes, 1895, 170)

The bejewelled purple robes are the Horatian metres and verbal reminiscences which Buchanan works into his text. Save in Psalm 119, Johnston limits himself to plain translation and the elegiac couplet. This may involve a further complication. Johnston was an Episcopalian, several of whose complimentary poems are directed to bishops, including Archbishop Laud, much hated by Presbyterians. He was also a royalist, to whom the principles of *De Iure Regni* were not acceptable. His general position indeed was close to that of Thomas Innes, already mentioned. Buchanan was not himself a Calvinist, but his version of the Psalms was especially popular among Presbyterians, and it may be that the Stoic insistence on Heimarmene, an absolute Providence, imposed by the Horatian pattern, was attractive to Presbyterians, less so to Episcopalians. It

is at least curious that the Episcopalian advocate of ceremony and
tradition in the church should offer a plain version of the Psalms in
opposition to the more gaudy ornamentation of Buchanan's.

Johnston shows some interest in contemporary courtly poetry in
the vernacular. He produced a version, for instance, of Thomas
Carey's 'Ask me no more where Jove bestows' (Geddes, 1895, 202).
More significantly, one of his epigrams (Geddes, 1895, 47) compares
the poetic merits of the vernacular humanist Drummond of Hawthornden with the Latinist Buchanan. It is some indication of changing
priorities in the seventeenth century that final supremacy is awarded
to the vernacular – in a form, too, which to modern ears may seem
English rather than Scots. Johnston seems to regard it as entirely
Scots, a point of view which modern critics of Drummond may find
of some relevance.

## REFERENCES

ALDIS, H.D. (1970), *A List of Books printed in Scotland before 1700*,
reprinted with additions, Edinburgh: National Library of Scotland.
ANDERSON, M.O. (1980), *Kings and Kingship in Early Scotland*, 2nd
ed., Edinburgh and London: Scottish Academic Press.
BANNERMAN, J. (1974), *Studies in the History of Dalriada*, Edinburgh
and London: Scottish Academic Press.
—— (1986), *The Beatons: a medical kindred in the classical Gaelic tradition*,
Edinburgh: John Donald.
BAWCUTT, P. (1976), *Gavin Douglas: a critical study*, Edinburgh:
Edinburgh University Press.
BROTHER KENNETH (1962), 'The Popular Literature of the Scottish
Reformation.' In McRoberts, D. (ed.) *Essays on the Scottish Reformation*,
Glasgow: Burns.
BUCHANAN, G. (1686), *Poemata in tres Partes Digesta*, London: Griffin.
CARPENTER, S. (1988), 'Early Scottish Drama.' In Jack, R.D.S. and
Craig, C. (eds.) *The History of Scottish Literature* vol.1, Aberdeen:
Aberdeen University Press.
CHAMBERS, R.W. and BATHO, E. (eds) (1938), *The Chronicle of
Scotland Compiled by Hector Boece Translated into Scots by John Bellenden
1531*, Edinburgh and London: Scottish Text Society.
CONSTABLE, A. (ed.) (1892), *A History of Greater Britain as well
England as Scotland*, Edinburgh: Scottish History Society.
CRAIGIE, J. (ed.) (1955), *The Poems of James VI of Scotland*, vol.1,
Edinburgh and London: Scottish Text Society.
CRAIGIE, W.A. (ed.) (1901, 1903), *Livy's History of Rome The First Five
Books Translated into Scots by John Bellenden 1533*, 2 vols., Edinburgh
and London: Scottish Text Society.
DONALDSON, W. (1988), *The Jacobite Song, Political Myth and National
Identity*, Aberdeen: Aberdeen University Press.
DURKAN, J. and ROSS, A. (1961), *Early Scottish Libraries*, Glasgow:
Burns.

GEDDES, W.D. (ed.) (1895), *Musa Latina Aberdonensis Arthur Johnston*, vol.2, Aberdeen: New Spalding Club.

GILMORE, M.P. (1952), *The World of Humanism*, New York and Evanston: Harper and Row.

HALL, F.W. (1913), *A Companion to Classical Texts*, Oxford: Clarendon Press.

HENDERSON, I, (1967), *The Picts*, London: Thames and Hudson.

INNES, T. (1879), *A Critical Essay on the Ancient Inhabitants of the Northern Parts of Britain or Scotland*, Edinburgh: Paterson.

JACK, R.D.S. (1988), 'Poetry under King James VI.' In Jack, R.D.S. and Craig, C. (eds.) *The History of Scottish Literature*, vol.1, Aberdeen: Aberdeen University Press.

KERMACK, W.R. (1967), *The Scottish Borders (with Galloway)*, Edinburgh and London: Johnston & Bacon.

MACDONALD, R.H. (1971), *The Library of Drummond of Hawthornden*, Edinburgh: Edinburgh University Press.

—— (1976), *William Drummond of Hawthornden, Poems and Prose*, Edinburgh and London: Association for Scottish Literary Studies.

MCFARLANE, I.D. (1981), *Buchanan*, London: Duckworth.

MACNEILL, D.H. (1964), *The Art and Science of Government among the Scots*, Glasgow: MacLellan.

MACQUEEN, J. (1967), 'Some Aspects of the Early Renaissance in Scotland', *FMLS* III, 201–22.

—— (1982), *Progress and Poetry*, Edinburgh and London: Scottish Academic Press.

MACQUEEN, J. and MACQUEEN, W. (1988), 'Latin Prose Literature.' In Jack, R.D.S. and Craig, C. (eds.) *The History of Scottish Literature*, vol.1, Aberdeen: Aberdeen University Press.

MACQUEEN, J.G. (1988), 'Scottish Latin Poetry.' In Jack, R.D.S. and Craig, C. (eds.) *The History of Scottish Literature*, vol.1, Aberdeen: Aberdeen University Press.

O'BRIEN, M.A. (1962), *Corpus Genealogiarum Hiberniae*, vol.1, Dublin: Dublin Institute for Advanced Studies.

RIVET, A.L.F. and SMITH, C. (1979), *The Place-names of Roman Britain*, London: Batsford.

RUDDIMAN, T. (ed.) (1715), *Georgii Buchanani Scoti, Poetarum sui seculi facile Principis, Opera Omnia*, vol.1, Edinburgh: Freebairn.

SALWAY, P. (1981), *Roman Britain*, Oxford: Clarendon Press.

SKENE, W.F. (ed.) (1871), *Johannis de Fordun Chronica Gentis Scotorum*, Edinburgh: Edmonston and Douglas.

YATES, F.A. (1964), *Giordano Bruno and the Hermetic Tradition*, London: Routledge and Kegan Paul.

## Humanism in The Visual Arts, *c.* 1530–*c.* 1630

MARTIN KEMP, with the assistance of CLARE FARROW

On his embassy to Scotland in 1435, Aeneas Sylvius Piccolomini expressed more interest in curiosities of nature and the beauty of Scots lassies than the visual culture of his hosts.[1] There was little in Scottish art and architecture at this time to satisfy the standards of this Sienese humanist who as Pope Pius II was to sponsor the construction of Pienza, that most delightful piece of Renaissance town planning. To Renaissance eyes, the residences of the Scottish kings and nobles would have appeared austere and defensively-minded, with no trace of the Latinising grace which was gaining favour in central Italy.

By contrast when Mary Stuart returned to assume power in 1561, she was able to inhabit a number of royal buildings that provided congenial settings for Renaissance courtly activities of the kind she had come to expect as a matter of course in Henri II's French court. The transformation between 1435 and 1561 may be attributed to the great building campaigns of James IV and James V, and the most overtly Renaissance features to the desire of James V to emulate the aristocratic ambiance enjoyed by his royal and noble relatives in France.

However, if we look again at Scotland in 1603, the year of James VI's accession to the English throne, the general situation would have appeared puzzling to someone who regarded James V's buildings and Mary's Renaissance trappings as the dawn of a fully-fledged Scottish Renaissance in the visual arts. Far from having aped the Renaissance style initiated at the court, the local lairds, the nobles and successive Regents had developed a nationally individual form of castellated architecture, the baronial style, in which any Renaissance motifs were limited to a series of quotations within overall compositions which remained obstinately vernacular. Even an educated, travelled laird, such as Sir John Scott of Scotstarvet, who felt at home in Latin literature, considered it appropriate to inhabit a severe, upright baronial tower in which only a few of the decorative motifs in the uppermost storey made passing reference to the principles of Renaissance design.

If, by the strictest definition of 'humanist' style in the visual arts

– namely the systematic adoption of motifs from classical antiquity, according to the grammatical principles of ancient Roman architecture and sculpture – we ask whether we can legitimately describe any indigenous buildings, sculptures, paintings or artefacts as incontestably humanist in design, the answer is 'no', even if a qualified 'no'. However, this negative answer conceals a pattern of great interest and diversity. If we adjust our definition to the rather more flexible formulation which is appropriate for Northern Europe – namely the selective development and refining of the indigenous style according to the lessons of the ancients, particularly as transmitted through Italianate intermediaries – we will find much of value that can be appropriately grouped under the humanist heading. This is particularly true in the applied arts, in which objects, decorative patterns and even craftsmen proved to be relatively mobile, and exercised a marked impact on Scottish products.

The following review of humanism in the visual arts in Scotland takes its main shape from the architecture of the period, and will be organised around four phases. The first concerns the precocious 'Royal Renaissance' of the first half of the sixteenth century, particularly under James V. The second deals with the Marian Renaissance, in which attention will be directed particularly to the figurative and applied arts, including non-indigenous objects. The third phase relates to the extraordinary efflorescence of the baronial style after 1570, in which a number of highly individualistic incidents under patrons such as Regent Morton, the Setons and the Lindsays make unexpected if unconsolidated references to different aspects of the humanist style. The final phase represents the beginning of the full-scale naturalisation of a Renaissance style after 1620 in the hands of such recognisable architects as William Wallace and William Ayton. For the purposes of this review, the generation of buildings contemporary with George Heriot's Hospital (begun 1628) will mark a suitable point of termination, before the idiosyncratic 'baroque' of Drumlanrig later in the century.

The decision to concentrate upon the period following the accession of James V should not be taken to mean that earlier monarchs were not considerable patrons in their own right nor that clear links did not exist with the most advanced work in Europe. Indeed Linlithgow, a palace which was to figure prominently in the building campaigns of James V and James VI, took its main shape from the large-scale rebuilding by James I, following a fire in 1424. If more has been claimed for the patronage of James III than the evidence sustains, the activities of his successor have been somewhat underrated. James IV was responsible for substantial amounts of work at Stirling, Falkland and Edinburgh – all buildings that are to feature later in this essay – and with his queen, Margaret, was responsible for the importation of Continental religious manuscripts.[2] The corbels supporting the wooden roof he built in the Great Hall in Edinburgh Castle, apparently datable between 1496 and 1511, exhibit precocious Renaissance features.[3]

This early period also saw the importation by Sir Edward Bonkil of the two magnificent painted panels of the *Trinity 'Altarpiece'* by Hugo van der Goes probably in the late 1470s.[4] Scottish coinage had already exhibited some Renaissance features, above all in the striking portrayals of James III on his groats (6d. and 14d.). Later in the century, Archbishop William Schevez of St Andrews was the subject of a fully fledged Renaissance medal (plate 1), probably executed in Louvain in 1491 by Quentin Metsys.[5] However, these and other individual episodes remained unconsolidated, and it was only with James V and his Queens that the ambition to create a humanist style in the visual arts became established in something approaching a programmatic manner.

The first phase of James V's building activities as a bachelor king testify to the scale of his ambitions, though not at first to the achieving of a particularly Renaissance style. The first phase of building at Holyrood between 1528 and 1532 involved work on the North-West tower at considerable expense and in a style that made some reference to Tudor work in England.[6] Much the same is true of the Gate House at Falkland, which may be associated with the master mason John Brounhill, who had worked on the Holyrood tower.[7] The other work at Falkland, however, declares a radically adjusted set of artistic ambitions, reflecting the circumstances of his two French marriages. His travels in France in 1536, at the time of his marriage to Madelaine, daughter of the 'Renaissance King' Francis I, introduced him first-hand to the latest Italianate fashions of the French Court. The influence of the French style was consolidated by his later marriage to Mary of Guise. It was hardly surprising that they should look to bring French masons to Britain when he conceived the remodelling of Falkland as a modernised palace.

In 1537 Nicholas Roy arrived from France to establish the basic articulation of the inner facade of the South range, and (after his death?) in 1538 he was succeeded by his countryman, Moses Martin, who was responsible for the East range (plate 2), which has survived in rather better condition.[8] The vocabulary of the French classical style has been used with some skill in such details as the attached columns, broken cornices, inverted consoles and above all in the vigorous, high-relief roundels containing Roman-style heads. However, the overall grammar of the facade retains much in common with the late gothic system of wall, windows and buttresses, as seen on the street facade of the Falkland chapel, for which Peter Flemisman was carving '5 gret stane imagis' in 1538–9.[9]

The contemporaneous work at Stirling Castle on the adornment of the 'King's House' or palace within the fortifications reflects similar Renaissance ambitions (plate 3), and some of the French masons may again have been employed, though the stylistic characteristics are rather different.[10] The elements in the architectural articulation may be described as a form of stripped late Gothic, but the sculptural detail makes a bold attempt to speak in a more up-to-date voice. A series of overtly secular figures (plate 4) stand on candelabrum-style balusters, which combine acanthus leaf motifs in the Renaissance manner with Gothicising capitals. Each 'candelabrum' is supported by a corbel figure of a quite unclassical kind. The effect is not such as to suggest direct acquaintance with classical exemplars but rather an inventive mingling of motifs known through prints and the decorative arts.

James's comparable ambitions for architectural interiors can best be judged from the remaining fragments of what must have been a magnificent wooden ceiling in the Great Hall at Stirling.[11] The surviving elements come from a series of 56 roundels in high relief, depicting figures and 'portrait' busts of classical and contemporary characters. Some of the reliefs depict narrative subjects, as in the nude man wrestling with a lion (plate 5), who may be identified either as Hercules or Samson. Perhaps the former should be preferred, since the story of Hercules was figured prominently in James's tapestries at Stirling. Other roundels may represent more generalised evocations of ancient and modern nobility, without specific identities. One head has sometimes been recognised as James himself (plate 6), but this tempting identification cannot be supported by firm evidence. Although similar in their basic conception, the various roundels show clear signs of different hands at work, which is hardly surprising given the scale and speed of the enterprise. The overall responsibility may have rested with Robert Robertson, 'carvour', who was given general charge over 'all werkis concernyng his craft and utheris' in 1541.[12]

The medallic heads at Stirling are the finest and largest examples of what became a widespread fashion in Scottish decorative woodwork and furniture.[13] Similar motifs had made an early appearance at Cardinal Wolsey's Hampton Court, and depended ultimately on North Italian examples, but the Scottish fashion drew more of its strength from French models. The taste would have been reinforced even after James's death by the continued importation of French products, such as the elegant book-binding of the Greek *Works of Synesios* published in Paris in 1553 and owned by William Ramsay (plate 7), whose latinised name is stamped on the front and back covers.[14]

In one sense, James's death in 1542 marked the aborting of his precocious phase of the Scottish Renaissance in the visual arts, and it is certainly true that the architectural and sculptural ambitions at

Falkland and Stirling did not find immediate successors. However, the elements of continuity represented in the applied arts were probably stronger than the very incomplete survivals suggest. In the mid-1550s, a French mason, John Roytell, was in the Royal service, in succession to his countrymen at Falkland and Stirling. Edinburgh goldsmiths, particularly James Gray, whom we will encounter later, were capable of achieving work of Renaissance elegance. A succession of Edinburgh printers from the late 1530s onwards, including Thomas Davidson and Robert Lekpreiuk, were publishing books in which the Latin texts were set in Roman typefaces and laid out in imitation of Italian and French models.[15] And professional calligraphy, exemplified by John Geddy's superb mathematical manuscript, written in 1586 for presentation to James VI, and by the accomplished work of the French-born Esther Inglis, progressively exhibited the modern italic hand in preference to the old Gothic 'black-letter' script.[16]

When Mary Stuart returned from her French exile on a wave of optimism in 1561 all seemed set fair for the re-adoption of her father's Renaissance. She had spent her formative years from 1548 in the French court, becoming naturalised in its environment of Renaissance stylishness and chivalric courtesy. Behind her lay a rich fabric of court existence: of poetry, philosophy, music, sculpture, painting and decorative interiors; of richly ornamented textiles and elaborate masques; of embroidered costumes, of jewels containing mythological allusions and decorated with linear designs of grotesques and arabesques. As the inspiration of writers, Ronsard and Brantôme, and of artists – most importantly, of François Clouet – Mary had herself become the subject of works of art.[17] Her virtual 'deification' as a classical goddess is exemplified by the suave bronze bust (plate 8), executed in an accomplished Mannerist style and attributed to Ponce Jacquio who had returned from study in Italy in 1559.[18] Her court existence found expression, above all, in the art of the masque, in which the mythological past became merged with the present. Mary was viewed simultaneously as a contemporary monarch and as embodying a humanist ideal of womanhood – as a Venus, Diana, Flora or Minerva.

On her departure from France, Ronsard lamented that the court was '. . . Like a beautiful meadow stripped of all its flowers, Like a painting of its colours all deprived . . .'[19] While contemporary inventories reveal the visual richness that Mary was to bring to the Scottish court, our visual image of her has tended to lack colour. The dominant image has been of a rather formalised, even abstract beauty: an icon whose origins lie in the chalk drawing by Clouet, 'En Deuil Blanc' (plate 9).[20] By its very nature, this study of Mary 'in white mourning' makes no visual reference to the kinds of costumes, jewels, textiles and personal effects transposed to the Scottish court and described by Bishop Leslie in 1561:

'Attour the Quenis hienes fornitour, hingingis, and appareill,
was also in hir awin cumpanye, transportit with her Majestie
in Scotland, many costlye jewells and golden wark, precious
stanis, orient pearle, maist excellent of any that was in Europe,
and mony coistly abilyeamentis for hir body with meikill silver
wark of coistlye cupbordis, cowpis, plaite.'[21]

It is through the medium of these decorative and largely ephemeral
art forms, rather than those of drawing, painting, or sculpture, that
the thread of humanism in the Scottish arts can be traced from
France.

Contemporary inventories, written by Mary's 'valet de chambre',
Servay de Condé, provide a rich source.[22] A list of the 159 jewels
brought from France is contained within the inventory of 1561.
These were predominantly designed in the latest Renaissance style:
settings of oriental pearls, balas rubies, diamonds and emeralds,
decorated in brightly-coloured enamels. Among them were fashionable pendant jewels, such as the 'Great Harry' (a large, faceted
diamond with pendant cabochon ruby, in the form of an 'H'). Some
were shaped as roses, musical instruments and antique-style vases.
One enseign (hat-jewel) was adorned with the mythological figures
of Venus and Cupid. Within a year of her arrival at the Scottish
court, Mary had commissioned a further 21 jewels, including 'one
carkane of perle and of gold, contenand 220 pearls', as recorded in
the Treasury Accounts with the names of Scottish goldsmiths, James
Mosman, James Gray, Peter Riche, William and John Gilbert (an
Edinburgh craftsman from whom 264 large pearls were bought in
1562).[23] In the inventory of 1566, details of 'stones that the Queen
has bought recently' include 'an emerald finger ring' and 'a large
hanging jewel with an emerald, sapphire and 8 small diamonds'.

An important form of Renaissance jewellery was the portrait
cameo, and one example, among the few extant jewels associated
with Mary, is the heart-shaped pendant (plate 10) incorporating a
continental cameo, crafted with French ornamental designs, and
enclosed within a Scottish setting: a jewel that reveals the visual
contrast in sophistication between continental and Scottish Renaissance craftsmanship. The cameo depicts the profile portrait of Mary,
in contemporary costume yet recalling the heads of Minerva and
Venus on antique gemstones. On the reverse of the cameo, a refined
French 'grotesque' pattern is painted in gold and coloured enamel.
In contrast, the Scottish setting, crowded with floral ornament and
precious stones, is a somewhat coarsened reworking of fashionable
French forms.[24]

A comparable Scottish translation of Continental motifs is visible
in the gold enamelled locket with miniature portraits thought to
represent Mary and James VI (plate 11). Its frame of twisted gold
interwoven with pearls, its rough texture and irregular form trans-
forms the nature of the raw materials less completely than the

ornamental abstraction of French technique. Among the remaining
jewels of Scottish craftsmanship, there is nothing to rival in its
Renaissance conception the double-sided cameo, (plate 12), which
seems to have passed to Mary from James v's collection. A perfect
oval agate conceals within its constricted shape two sculptured
cameo reliefs, the Scourging of Christ and the Crucifixion.

Another inventory of 1561 contains details of the now faded
textiles and costumes of Mary of Guise, to which Mary Stuart was
to add a wealth of Renaissance examples, embroidered with cyphers,
flowers, birds and animals. Tapestries, particularly rich in mythological allusion, were supplied by the court 'tapissiers', Pierre
Martin, Nicholas Carbonier and David Liages. The earlier tapestries
of Mary of Guise had themselves embodied the latest taste, incorporating images from nature ('a tapestry of great leaves and flowers')
and from popular myth ('a tapestry of the history of hunting the
great unicorn'). To these, Mary added cloths of state in brightly-
coloured velvets and cloths of gold and silver, ornamented with gold
thread, precious stones and figurative embroidery; bed valances
embroidered with flowers, leaves, animals, birds, mythological
figures, cyphers and grotesques: 'crimson velvet enriched with gold
phoenixes and tears', embroidery work of gold 'of the history of
Hercules', 'cloth of gold and silver, made in the shape of vases of
flowers, with embroidery work of long round shapes called ovals,
wherein the histories are contained'. Tapestries 'of all sorts' include
'histories' of 'the Triumph of Truth', 'the Judgement of Paris', 'the
history of the sailing of Aeneas' and 'the works of Hercules'. Some
were embroidered with images from nature, not infrequently incorporating mottos and Renaissance conceits. A complementary style
of ornamentation is reflected by items in the inventories of costumes
by the court tailors, Jacques Foulis, Johnie Decumpaise, Johnne
Pailyeatt and the 'furior' Constantyne Cursalis. The rich amalgam
of late Gothic exuberance and subjects drawn from ancient history,
classical mythology, emblematics and the sciences was typical of the
effortless mingling of humanist learning and chivalric values in
Renaissance courts.

The impact of Mary's appurtenances on the visual style of the
Scottish court must have been very considerable, but her lack of
access to substantial funds and the relatively short duration of her
period of real power largely prevented the undertaking of enduring
works in architecture, sculpture or painting. The emphemeral
nature of her works has meant that few tangible signs of her
Renaissance remain, and the possibility of a more sustained, court-
lead Renaissance in the visual arts disappeared with Mary's capture
in 1567. The compensation for the historian of Scottish art and
architecture is that the centrifugal nature of subsequent political

1. Quentin Metsys(?), *Medal of Archbishop William Schevez of St. Andrews*, 1491, private collection.

2. Moses Martin(?) *Falkland Palace Courtyard, East Range, 1539–42.*

3. *Stirling Castle, Inner Facade of the Palace Block, c.1540.*

4. *Allegorical or Mythological Figure (Venus?) from Stirling Castle,
Palace Block, c.1540.*

5. Robert Robertson(?) *Hercules with the Nemean Lion(?)*, *c*.1541, Stirling Castle (formerly on the ceiling of the Great Hall).

6. Robert Robertson(?) *Portrait Medallion James V(?).*, *c*.1541, Stirling Castle (formerly on the ceiling of the Great Hall).

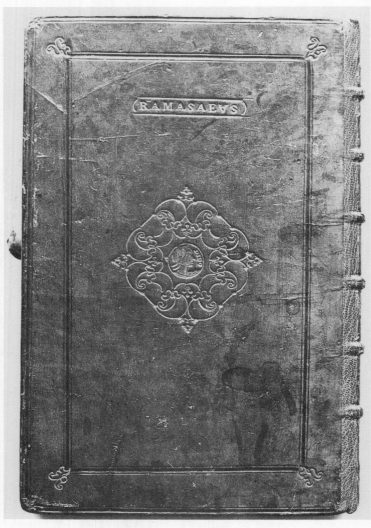

7. *Rear Cover of Senesii Episcopi Cyrenes (the Works of Synesios),
with Medallion of Dido, c.*1553–5, made for William Ramsay,
University of St Andrews, Library.

8. Ponce Jacquio, *Bronze bust of Mary as Queen of France*, c.1560, Edinburgh, Scottish National Portrait Gallery.

9. Francois Clouet, *Mary Stuart ('En Deuil Blanc')*, red and black chalk, *c.*1559–60, Paris, Bibliothèque Nationale.

10. *Pendant with Cameo of Queen Mary*, *c*.1561–3, Edinburgh, National Museums of Scotland.

11. *Gold Enamelled Locket with Miniature Portraits (Mary, Queen of Scots and James VI?)*, *c*.1566, Edinburgh, National Museums of Scotland.

12. *Italian Double-sided Bloodstone Cameo of the Scourging of Christ
and Crucifixion with Pendant Pearl and Agate set with Gold and
Rubies*, c.1535–40, Edinburgh, National Museums of Scotland.

13. James Gray, *The Galloway Mazer*, 1569, Edinburgh,
National Museums of Scotland.

James Gray, *Bronze Funerary tablet for the Earl of Moray* (with George Buchanan's epitaph), 1569, Edinburgh, St Giles Cathedral.

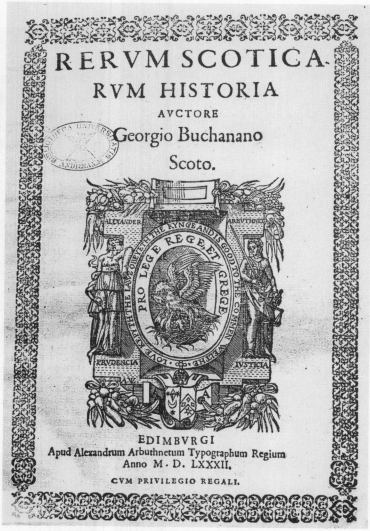

15. *Title Page of George Buchanan's 'Rerum Scoticarum Historia'*,
Edinburgh, Alexander Arthbuthnet, 1582.

16. Arnold Bronckhorst(?), *James VI Holding a Hawk*, *c.*1574, Edinburgh, Scottish National Portrait Gallery.

17. Unknown artist, *George, 5th Lord Seton as Master of the Household*, *c.*1558 (with later modifications?), Scottish National Portrait Gallery.

18. *Edinburgh Castle, Portcullis Gate, 1577–84.*

19. *Mar's Work, c.*1572, Stirling.

20. *Crichton Castle, Courtyard*, 1581–92, Aberdeenshire.

21. *Fyvie Castle, Entrance Front, c.1597–9*, Aberdeenshire.

22. *Edzell, Walled Garden, c.1604*, Forfar.

23. *Relief of Saturn, from the Walled Garden, Edzell.*

24. *Cullen House, Astral Ceiling* (destroyed), 1603, Banffshire.

25. *Painted Ceiling* (from Rossend Castle, Burntisland, Fife), *c.*1620, Edinburgh, National Museums of Scotland.

26. *Craigevar, Plaster Ceiling in Withdrawing Room*, 1626, Aberdeenshire.

27. *Stirling Castle, Chapel Royal, Porch, 1594.*

28. *Linlithgow Castle, North Range, 1617–20.*

29. William Wallace (and William Ayton), *Heriot's Hospital, Edinburgh*, 1628–39 and 1642–c.1650.

30. William Wallace, *Heriot's Hospital, Entrance Porch, c.*1628–39.

31. Monuments to (left to right) *John Byres of Coates*, *c*.1629 (by William Wallace), *Thomas Henryson* (1636) and *George Foulis* (1636) (by William Ayton), Edinburgh, Greyfriars Churchyard.

32. *Argyll's Lodging, c.*1632, Stirling.

33. *Monument to Sir Robert Montgomerie and Margaret Douglas,* 1636–9, Largs, Skelmorlie Aisle.

power proved conducive to the highly individualistic and varied flowering of the baronial style in architecture.

Even immediately after Mary's fall, the climate in Edinburgh was not so unsympathetic as to prevent a continued exploration of Renaissance motifs in the applied arts. Two works by the great Canongate goldsmith, James Gray, will give some idea of the most advanced Scottish design at this time.[25]

The Galloway Mazer of 1569 (plate 13), made for Archibald Stewart (later Lord Provost of Edinburgh) is one of a remarkable series of Mazers with stems, including Gray's own Tulloch Mazer of 1557, which are especially characteristic of Scottish design. Although the Galloway Mazer shows affinities with Tudor metalwork, and some of the motifs can be closely paralleled in Nuremberg silverware, Gray has achieved a classic piece of design on his own account, integrating fashionable details, such as the acanthus-leaf baluster and the late gothic strawberry-leaf frieze below the rim, with a sense of proportion which is altogether Renaissance in feeling. One likely source of inspiration was the magnificent sword of state which Pope Julius II had sent from Rome in 1507. The inscription on the mazer – 'Proverb 22. Ane good name is to be chosen above great riches and loving favour Is above silver and most fyne gold. 1569' – exploits a sense of irony appropriate to its formal sophistication.

The other work by Gray demonstrates a direct involvement with literary humanism. In 1569 the masons John Roytel (son of one of James V's French masons) and Murdoch Valker were commissioned to carve the stone monument to Regent James Stewart, Earl of Moray. Gray, for his part, was charged with the 'ingraving of one platt of bras upoun my Lordis sepulteur'.[26] The tablet on which Gray engraved George Buchanan's Latin funerary inscription has survived (plate 14), albeit set within a monument which is a nineteenth-century reconstruction of the original. Comparable humanist aspirations are reflected in Scottish typography. The title page of Buchanan's *Rerum Scoticarum Historia* (plate 15) published (with many typographical errors) in 1582 by Alexander Arbuthnet the king's printer exhibits a somewhat laboured emulation of Northern European Renaissance design.

The politically variable years of the Regency were also marked by the first sustained invasion of the continental-style painted portraits. These served what may loosely be described as humanist functions: as a formal record of individuals, serving as 'visual inventories' of features, costume and jewellery; and as painted surrogates, embodying authority and presence, and, as such, suitable for reproduction and distribution in the form of engravings, coins, miniatures or painted copies.

The new style of portraiture in Scotland depended largely on the Netherlandish tradition, above all through the practice of Arnold Bronckhorst (active 1565/6 or earlier–1583) and Adrian Vanson (active 1581–c.1602). It was primarily mimetic in function, relying upon the detached, detailed observation for which Netherlandish masters were famed. Bronckhorst is recorded as court painter in the Treasury Accounts, from 1580, when 'certane portratour is paintit be him to his grace', until 1583. In 1584, Adrian Vanson appears in the record 'in place of Arnold Bruckorst', as portrait painter and decorative artist.[27]

In the *Portrait of James VI, holding a hawk* (plate 16), attributed to Bronckhorst (in spite of problems about the sitter's apparent age), the viewer is confronted by a lively depiction of an individual that succeeds, to some extent, in evoking the young king's personality. Although the portrait conforms to conventional standards of composition, it fulfils its courtly function with some skill and alludes effectively to one of James's favoured pursuits.

The very fact that the portraits attributed to Bronckhorst (and later to Vanson) exist as sharply characterised records of individuals in a reasonably up-to-date style suggests that the art of portraiture in Scotland can be regarded at least in part within a humanist framework. While few portraits of court figures contain classicising references, the naturalistic portrayals testify to the power of painting to sustain the individual's existence in defiance of time and place. As the humanist Alberti had written in 1435, recalling classical portraiture: 'Painting has a divine power, not just because it makes absent ones present, but it makes the dead seem to live, after centuries . . .'[28]

It is difficult to know how many Scottish sitters would have been conscious of the humanist connotations of the new portrait style, but Buchanan, who was portrayed by Bronckhorst according to the records, would hardly have missed the point, and we may assume the same for a few ambitious patrons like *George, Lord Seton* (plate 17) whose portrait is exceptionally polished, with its classicising architecture and inscription. The dating and attribution of this portrait of Seton as Master of Mary's Household are problematical. It may have been painted by a French master in 1558, when he attended Mary's wedding to the Dauphin, in which case the inscription on the pedestal would have been added later. Seton's family in exile, including the young Alexander who was to become an important patron of architecture, was later to be the subject of a painting probably by Frans Porbus the Elder (1572, Scottish National Portrait Gallery), which confirms the unusually advanced nature of Seton's taste.

However, any esteem the portraitists' art may have gained was limited in a court that generally continued to recognise the material and aesthetic value of the decorative arts more readily than the intellectual potential of painting as an autonomous art form. It is revealing that, in December 1601, Vanson – who was succeeded as court painter by his son, Adam de Colonne – was paid £20 for a miniature of the king, attached to a gold chain commissioned from an Edinburgh craftsman for over £600.[29]

In architecture, the years following Mary's fall were not conducive to large-scale royal work. However, Regent Morton did make contributions of an importance which suggest that his role as a patron needs reassessment. At Edinburgh Castle he was responsible for the enlargement of the Portcullis Gate (plate 18), the lower stage of which was commenced by William McDowell in 1577, while the upper level, including a neat classical aedicule adorned with Morton heraldry, was added by William Schaw in 1584.[30] Schaw, whom we will encounter again, may also have been responsible for one or both of Morton's own castles, Drochil and Aberdour. Drochil exhibits a self-consciously symmetrical plan in the form of a 'double tenement', possibly derived from a plan in Jacques Androuet du Cerceau's *Les plus excellents bastions de France* (1576–9), while Morton's additions at Aberdour began to transform the old castle into something closer to a domestic palace with Renaissance detailing.[31]

During the years 1570 to 1620 Scotland witnessed an astonishing burst of regional castle construction, on grand and domestic scales. While the majority of the castles may best be described as idiosyncratic elaborations of a Scottish Gothic tradition of castellated tower-houses, each decade saw notable individual instances of homage to Renaissance fashions. The most remarkable example from the 1570s is the elaborately decorated though ruined facade of Mar's Work, below Stirling Castle (plate 19). Rich aggregations of Renaissance details are picturesquely composed in the manner of the title page of a book, rather than with the architectural logic of a classical building. The effect is of a Latinised late Gothic composition. The most startling piece of design from the next decade is the diamond rustication of the courtyard facade at Crichton Castle (plate 20). The patron, the Earl of Bothwell, had returned from exile in Italy in 1581, and may have been inspired directly by Italian examples of decorative rustication, such as the Palazzo dei Diamanti at Ferrara, but the actual details and general disposition of the rusticated wall over an arcade is closer to a German example, the Rathaus at Lubeck of 1570.

Knowledge of continental (especially French) precedents is also important in understanding the ambitions behind the great symmetrical facade at Fyvie (plate 21), constructed in the late 1590s by Alexander Seton, Lord Fyvie and Earl of Dunfermline, who was to become Chancellor of Scotland in 1604. It is likely that the architect was William Schaw, whose epitaph at Dunfermline Abbey was composed by Seton. We learn that Schaw 'in his eagerness to improve his mind . . . travelled through France and many other kingdoms'.[32] This perfectly complements Seton's own background; he was described as 'a great humanist in prose and in poecie, Greek and Latine, well versed in the mathematicks and had great skill in architecture and herauldrie'.[33] However, it is perhaps surprising that Fyvie is not more openly Renaissance in its overall style. The fact that a cosmopolitan patron and well-travelled mason should work so hard to create one of the masterpieces of the baronial style – characterised by verticality, decorative corbelling and coronas of capped turrets, with only touches of Renaissance detail – demonstrates a positive and knowing element in the Scottish resistance to a total adoption of the Latinising style. Seton and Schaw clearly felt that the castellated style represented the proper statement of a laird's status in the area under his domination, as well as continuing to serve the needs of low-grade fortification against local skirmishing.

The most notable piece of Renaissance individualism from the first decade of the seventeenth century was the walled garden at Edzell built by Sir David Lindsay, Earl of Crawford (plate 22). The garden wall is punctuated by small aedicules, chequer patterns and low relief carvings of the cardinal virtues, liberal arts and planetary gods. The style of the carvings is relatively crude – the amusing image of the peg-legged Saturn (plate 23), for example, is a stiff translation into stone of a German engraving by the Master IB – but the intellectual conceit is entirely in keeping with the Renaissance taste.

This taste was also expressed in emblematics. James Hamilton, Earl of Arran, had been the dedicatee of a French edition of Alciatus's *Emblemes* as early as 1549,[34] and Queen Mary had herself spent many hours during her English captivity making needlework hangings of arcane emblems with allusive Latin mottos.[35] In Scottish design this enthusiasm featured prominently in painted ceiling decoration – perhaps the most characteristic aspect of Scottish decorative art of the late 16th and early 17th centuries. These ceilings – painted in robust if unpolished styles by decorative artists such as Walter Bynning, John Anderson and Valentine Jenkins – derived much of their vocabulary from continental textiles, prints and books, drawing upon a repertoire of Renaissance and traditional subjects.

The few remaining painted ceilings, ranging chronologically from Prestongrange of 1581, to Skelmorlie Aisle of 1638, consist of rich aggregations of derived motifs. Colourful fruits and flowers, exotic birds and animals are adapted from such printed material as Conrad Gesner's *Icones animalium* of 1560, with its parade of real and fantastic creatures, and Claude Paradin's emblem book, *Symbola heroica* of 1557, in which the metaphysical meanings of natural images are expounded through Latin mottos. Mannerist decorative motifs such as French strapwork, 'antique' grotesques and knot designs are mingled with personal emblems, coats-of-arms, musical instruments, mythological figures, and personifications of the senses and the liberal arts.[36]

We may suspect that the language of the ceilings was not specifically underpinned by any consistent humanist programme, but more generally inspired by the fashionable potential of the decorative motifs and a taste for heraldic allusion. Their layout was determined by the formal construction of the timber ceilings: long flat panels of painted boards, interspersed with wooden beams, or coved ceilings providing an open timbered surface for ornamental designs. One of the coved ceilings was at Cullen House (1603, now destroyed) and was devoted to an unusually coherent astral fantasy (plate 24). The central field was flanked by narratives of a *Boar Hunt* and the *Siege of Troy* in a sophisticated style probably based on imported tapestries. The astral design exhibits personifications of the abstract concepts of time, truth, antiquity, and liberal arts ('musica' with a lute; 'geometria', with a compass and ruler), and figures from classical mythology labelled with their Latin names, 'Mercurius', 'Luna', 'Neptunus' and 'Flora'. The figures betray their origins in printed sources – above all William Cunningham's *Cosmologicall Glasse* (1559) – and lack the refined articulation, modelling and colour that characterises continental Renaissance painting.

The ceiling of Rossend Castle of c.1620 (plate 25) is an example of the more common flat, open-timber construction, and contains the customary abundance of emblems and patterns. The individual designs, compounding fantasy, symbol and nature, are again drawn from printed sources. A number of the emblems, including the star surrounded by a snake with a crown, and the beehive with poppies, are derived from Paradin. Other motifs, such as the lion with the sword at its feet, may depend on Geffrey Whiteney's *A Choice of Emblemes, and other Devises*, 1556, and yet others on Gabrielle Rollenhagen's *Nucleus emblematum selectissimorum*, 1611.

During the first half of the 17th century, plaster reliefs of more disciplined design came to rival painting as the most prestigious form of ceiling decoration. The 1626 ceilings at Craigievar (plate 26), for example, make obvious reference to the English Jacobean style, though the ever-popular medallic heads stand in line of descent from the decorative motifs of the James V era.[37] By contrast, the exterior architecture at Craigievar, together with the related castles of Glamis and Crathes, remains resolutely Scottish in its unclassical composition, and represents the supreme flowering of the Baronial style – of an inventiveness and quality that needs no apology.

However, the accession of James VI to the throne of England led progressively to the dominance of what may be called 'Scottish Jacobean' design. James's own works in Scotland show strong classicising tendencies. The entrance porch to the Chapel Royal at Stirling Castle in 1594 (plate 27) with its paired columns of a broadly

Tuscan type, is a notable piece of sober literacy in Latin design, and his remodelling of the North Range at Linlithgow (plate 28) using triangular and arched pediments over paired rows of similar windows goes some way towards achieving a classical articulation of the wall surface. This range, dating from 1617 to 1620, may be the work of William Wallace, the king's Master Mason and one of the earliest figures in Scotland who can be justifiably described as an 'architect' in the Renaissance sense of the term.

Wallace's masterpiece is George Heriot's Hospital, Edinburgh (plate 29), commenced in 1628 and continued after 1631 by William Ayton (or Aitoun).[38] Some indication of how Ayton (and, we may suppose, Wallace) worked as an architectural designer can be gained from a document in which Ayton receives payment 'for drawing the form of the House on Paper'.[39] Wallace's design for Heriot's Hospital depends in a sophisticated way on a range of foreign sources. The plan appears to be based on an example in the seventh book of Serlio's *L'Architettura*, while details of the entrance porches (plate 30) indicate a knowledge of Vignola's published designs. Although the building retains a certain sense of baronial display, it exploits Italian, North European and Jacobean motifs in an accomplished manner within an impressive, symmetrical and coherent ensemble. Ayton's independent skill as an architect can be seen at Innes House and Castle Gogar, and was demonstrated on a smaller scale in his tomb for George Foulis of 1636 in Greyfriars Churchyard, amongst an impressive group of monuments to which Wallace also contributed. (plate 31)

By the 1630s the Scottish Jacobean style was becoming firmly established beyond Edinburgh. Argyll's lodging in Stirling (plate 32), built for Sir William Alexander of Menstrie using money from ventures in Nova Scotia, is a fine example of the new type of smaller-scale domestic palace in which the Jacobean details and balanced fenestration do not entirely dispel the continued Scottish feel of the building. Probably the most spectacular pieces of Jacobean design in this period are the series of grand funerary monuments, especially those to the Earl of Dunbar (after 1611), the Earl of Kinnoull, Sir Robert Montgomerie (1636), and the Lauderdale Monument at Haddington.[40] The Montgomerie monument in the Skelmorlie aisle, Largs (plate 33), is an elaborate architectural structure, comprising a triumphal arch, articulated in the manner of a Palladian window, over a tomb chamber, which is entered by a sunken door. The Latin inscription – 'I was dead before myself. I anticipated my proper funeral, alone of all mortals, following the example of Caesar' (i.e. the Emperor Charles V) – perfectly captures the humanist tone of the enterprise. In a complementary manner, the ceiling makes accomplished play with antique 'grotesques'. The attractive Jacobean profusion of classicising detail has often been attributed to an

English designer, but the contemporaneous work of Wallace, Ayton, John Mylne and Richard Doby suggests that Scottish masons were capable by this date of such advanced design.

The period we have been considering is one that resists ready generalisation and the description of consistent developments – other than the sophisticated elaboration of the baronial style after 1560. The sheer variety and individualism, verging on perverseness if viewed in the light of Italian and French developments, comprises much of the interest of Scottish design in this period – mirroring the political vagaries of the monarchs' fortunes, vagaries which give such excitement to the narrative of Scottish history. Humanism in the visual arts of Scotland during the Renaissance speaks over the years in a variety of accents that are both confusing yet deeply fascinating and not infrequently impressive.

## NOTES AND REFERENCES

1. *The Commentaries of Pius II* (1942–57). Trs. F.A. Gregg, *Smith College Studies in History*, 25, 30, 35 and 43.
2. See particularly, Caldwell, D. (1982) *Angels, Nobles and Unicorns*. Exhibition catalogue. Edinburgh, National Museum of Antiquities.
3. Gifford, J., McWilliam, C. and Walker, D. (1984) *The Buildings of Scotland, Edinburgh*. Harmondsworth, 97.
4. Thompson, C. and Campbell, L. (1974) *Hugo van der Goes and the Trinity Panels in Edinburgh*. Edinburgh.
5. Hill, G.F. (1920) *Medals of the Renaissance*. Oxford, 123–4 and plate XXII no.1.
6. Gifford et al. (1984) 143; and Dunbar, J. (1963) 'The Palace of Holyrood House during the First Half of the Sixteenth Century' *Archeological Journal*, 110, 243–4; and Dunbar, J. (1984) 'Some Aspects of the Planning of Scottish Royal Palaces in the 16th Century', *Architectural History*, 27, 15–24.
7. Royal Commission on Ancient Monuments (Scotland) (1933) *Inventory of Fife*. Edinburgh; Gifford, J. (1988) *The Buildings of Scotland. Fife*, Edinburgh, 212–7; MacGibbon, D. and Ross, T. (1887–92, reprinted 1971) *The Castellated and Domestic Architecture of Scotland*. 5 vols. Edinburgh, 5, 536. See also more generally Dunbar, J. (1966) *The Historic Architecture of Scotland*. London; and Cruden, S. (1960) *The Scottish Castle*. Edinburgh and London.
8. *Accounts of the Masters of Works for Building and Repairing Royal Palaces and Castles* (1957). Ed. H. M. Paton. Edinburgh, I (1529–1615) xxxiii–iv, with references to Martin, Roy and Brounill; Girouard, M. (1959) 'Falkland Palace, Fife', *Country Life*, 135, 118–21 and 178–81; and Bentley-Cranch, D. (1982) 'An Early Sixteenth-Century French Architectural Source for the Palace of Falkland.' *Rosc*, 2, 85–95.
9. *Accounts of the Masters of Works* (1957). Edinburgh, 256.

10. Royal Commission on the Ancient and Historical Monuments of Scotland (1963) *Stirlingshire*. Edinburgh, 1, no.192; *Accounts of the Lord High Treasurer of Scotland* (1907). Ed. J. Balfour Paul. Edinburgh, 7 (1538–41), 48 and 184 (for the French craftsmen imported by James V); and Dunbar, J. (1985) in *Building Chronicle*, 1, 121.

11. Dunbar, J. (1975) *The Stirling Heads*. Edinburgh.

12. *The Register of the Privy Seal of Scotland*. (1921) Ed. D. Hay Fleming. II (1529–42), no. 4191; and *Accounts of the Masters of Works* (1957). 1, xxvi.

13. *Renaissance Decorative Arts in Scotland, 1480–1650* (1959). Exhibition catalogue. Edinburgh, Scottish National Portrait Gallery; and Richardson, J.S. (1925–6). 'Unrecorded Scottish Wood Carvings', *Proceedings of the Society of Antiquaries*. 60, 384–408, nos. 28–34.

14. Doughty, D. (1975) 'Renaissance Books, Bindings and Owners in St Andrews and Elsewhere; the Humanists'. *The Bibliothek*, 7, 117–33; and Mitchell, W.S. (19) *The History of Scottish Bookbinding*. Edinburgh and London, 27–70.

15. Dickson, R. and Edmond, J. (1890, reprinted 1957) *Annals of Scottish Printing*. Amsterdam. Note particularly Thomas Bassadyne's ed. of Henryson's *Morall Fabilis* in 1571 (Edinburgh, N.L.S.).

16. Geddy, J. (1586) *Methodi sive compendii mathematici*, University Library, St Andrews; and Simpson, G. (1973) *Scottish Handwriting, 1150–1650*. Edinburgh, 30 and fig. 11. See also the Maitland Quarto MS., Magdalene College, Cambridge.

17. *Les Oeuvres de Pierre Ronsard* (1970). Washington, VIII, 5–31; *Les Oeuvres complètes de Pierre Brantôme* (1823). Paris, V, 83 and 86; and Smailes, H. and Thomson, D. (1978) *The Queen's Image*. Exhibition catalogue. Edinburgh, Scottish National Portrait Gallery, no. 13 (see also nos. 14 and 15); and more generally Cust L. 1903 *Notes on the Authentic Portraits of Mary Queen of Scots*. London.

18. Smailes and Thomson (1987), no.12.

19. Ronsard (1970), VIII, 27.

20. Smailes and Thomson (1987), no.13.

21. Leslie, J., Bishop of Ross (1830) *The History of Scotland*. Edinburgh, Bannatyne Club, 299.

22. *Inventaires de la Royne Descosse Douairiere de France (Catalogues of the jewels, dresses, furniture, books and paintings of Mary, Queen of Scots, 1556–69)* (1863). Ed. J. Robertson, Bannatyne Club. Edinburgh.

23. *Accounts of the Lord High Treasurer of Scotland* (1916). Ed. J. Balfour Paul. Edinburgh, XI (1559–66), indexed under craftsman's name.

24. Scarisbrick, D. (1982) 'Mirror of Tragedy. The Jewels of Mary Stuart, I' and 'Treasured in Adversity: the Jewels of Mary Stuart, II'. *Country Life*, 171,1632–4 and 1740–2; and Marshall, R.K. (1978) 'Jewellery in Scottish Portraits 1500–1700', *The Connoisseur*. 197, 283–91.

25. Howe, G. (1934) 'Scottish Standing Masers'. *The Connoisseur* 92, 313–19; and more generally Findlay, I. (1956) *Scottish Gold and Silver Work*. London.

26. Laing, D. (1864–6), 'Notice Respecting the monument of the Regent Earl of Moray.' *Proceedings of the Society of Antiquaries of Scotland* 6, 49–50.

27. *Accounts of the Lord High Treasurer of Scotland* (1978). Ed. C.T. McInnes. 13 (1574–80), 413; and biographical entries with reference

to MSS sources in Apted, M.R. and Hannabus, (1978) *Painters in Scotland 1301–1700*. Scottish Record Society, n.s.7 Edinburgh. See also Thomson, D. (1975) *Painting in Scotland*. Exhibition catalogue. Edinburgh, Scottish National Portrait Gallery, 22 (and more generally for portraits attributed to Bronckhorst and Vanson).

28. Alberti, L.B. (1972), *'On Painting'* and *'On Sculpture'*. Ed. C. Grayson. London, 60–1.
29. *Accounts of the Lord High Treasurer of Scotland,* cited by Thomson (1975), p. 22.
30. Gifford et al (1984), 91.
31. Gifford (1988), 60–3.
32. Emerson, R. (1985) 'The Building of Fyvie Castle'. *Treasures of Fyvie*. Exhibition catalogue. Edinburgh, Scottish National Portrait Gallery, 11; and Stirling, A.M.W. (1928), *Fyvie Castle, its Lairds and its Times*. London.
33. Maitland, R. and Kingston, A. (1829) *The History of the House of Seytoun*. Glasgow, Maitland Club, 63.
34. Alciatus (1549) *Emblemes de nouveau tra[n]slatez en Fra[n]cois*. Translated by B. Aneau. Lyons, published by G. Rouille, printed by M. Bonhomme.
35. Swain, M. (1986) *The Needlework of Mary Queen of Scots*. Edinburgh; and Zuleta, F. de (1923) *Embroideries by Mary Stuart and Elizabeth Talbot at Oxburgh Hall*. Norfolk.
36. Apted, M.R. (1966) *The Painted Ceilings of Scotland*. Edinburgh; and Apted, (1980) 'Two Painted Ceilings from Rossend Castle, Burntisland, Fife', *Proceedings of the Society of Antiquaries of Scotland,* 104, 222–35.
37. Simpson, W.D. (1980) *Craigievar Castle*. Aberdeen; and Beard, G. (1969) 'Plasterers in 17th-Century Scotland', *Country Life,* 145, 909–12.
38. Gifford et al. (1984), 179–82.
39. MacGibbon and Ross (1982), 5, 537, referring to Ayton's work on Innes House. See also the entries for Ayton and Wallace in Colvin, H. (1978) *Biographical Dictionary of British Architects, 1660–1840*. London.
40. Graham-Campbell, D. (1982) *Scotland's Story in Her Monuments*. London.

*Photographic credits*
National Galleries of Scotland 8, 16, 17.
National Museums of Scotland 10, 11, 12, 13, 25.
Paris, Bibliothèque Nationale 9.
Royal Commission on Ancient and Historical Monuments of Scotland 2, 4, 5, 6, 19, 20, 21, 22, 23, 24, 26, 28, 32, 33.
Martin Kemp 1, 3, 7, 14, 15, 18, 27, 29, 30, 31.

Legal Humanism and the History of Scots Law:
John Skene and Thomas Craig
JOHN W. CAIRNS, T. DAVID FERGUS
and HECTOR L. MACQUEEN

*(i) Introduction*

It was to their native law that sixteenth century Scottish jurists
applied most successfully the humanistic methods first developed
on the continent in the study of Roman law. These had grown from
the use of two principal techniques; first, the application of philological methods and analysis of grammar and style to the language of
the texts; and second, the use of other historical sources to elucidate
the texts with reference to their social and historical background.
These studies started in Italy, associated initially with the names of
Lorenzo Valla (1407–57) and Maffeo Vegio (1407–58); but the movement developed in Germany and, most powerfully, France, where,
as the *mos docendi gallicus*, it was especially associated with the
university of Bourges. Particularly influential individuals included
Guillaume Budé (1467–1540), Andrea Alciato (1492–1550) and Ulric
Zasi (1461–1535). Broadly speaking the initial aims had been to
recover the uncorrupted Justinianic text; but this led on to the view
that that text itself was a Byzantine corruption of classical material
which could also be reclaimed in the same way [Kelly, 1970; Osler,
1983, 1985; Percival, 1985; Robinson, Fergus and Gordon, 1985: 284–
300; Stein, 1986; 297–301]. While continental legal humanism was
closely associated with university study (which still centred on the
civil and canon laws), there is little evidence of sustained law teaching
in Scottish universities between 1450 and 1650 [Rait, 1895: 26; Stein,
1968: 40–45; Durkan and Kirk, 1977: 127–31, 330–1; Macfarlane, 1985:
319–22, 377–82]. So it was perhaps inevitable that there should have
been no major contribution in Scotland to this movement in Roman
law studies. Recent work has demonstrated that the most significant
Scottish contributions to contemporary Roman law studies were
made by scholars working on the continent – Henry Scrymgeour,
Edward Henryson and William Barclay. Scrymgeour, a graduate of
Bourges, had charge of the Fugger library at Augsburg and later
taught at Geneva, while Henryson taught at Bourges and Barclay at
Paris. Scrymgeour's 1558 edition of the Novels was printed at
Geneva, Henryson's *De Testamentis* at Paris in 1556 and Barclay's

commentaries on the Digest's titles *De rebus creditis* and *De jurejurando* at Paris in 1605 [Durkan, 1978; also Baird Smith, 1914: 136–63].

The new learning nevertheless had an impact in Scotland through the continental education of many leading lawyers [Durkan, 1986], and there is clear evidence of a humanistic legal culture in sixteenth century Scotland. In the 1550s royal lectureships in the laws and other sciences (including Greek) were established in Edinburgh [Durkan, 1983]. These were patronised by, amongst others, Robert Reid, second president of the College of Justice and owner of a copy of the *Opera* of Alciato. The lecturers included Edward Henryson [Durkan and Ross, 1958: 46; Durkan, 1983: 74]. A bequest for the purpose by Reid led ultimately to the establishment of the Town's College in Edinburgh; his intention may have been to establish a strong law school in Scotland, but this was not realised [Grant, 1884: i 1–16; Horn, 1966: 216–17]. It may be significant that a stress on legal education, particularly in Roman law, seems to have been an aspect of the Scottish Reformation, evidenced by provisions in the *First Book of Discipline* for instruction in municipal and Roman law at the universities of St Andrews, Glasgow and Aberdeen [Cameron, 1972; 140, 143, 144]. These schemes bore little fruit, except perhaps at St Andrews, where William Skene, John Arthur and William Welwood, author of not only *The Sea Law of Scotland* (1590) and *Abridgement of all Sea-Lawes* (1613) but also *Juris Divini Judaeorum ac Juris Civilis Romanorum Parallela* (1594), may have brought humanistic techniques to bear upon instruction in the civil law [Durkan and Kirk, 1977: 330–1; Durkan, 1986: 25–7]. In the 1590s there was a further abortive scheme for a chair of law at the new Town's College in Edinburgh [Grant, 1884; i 184–9; Dickinson, 1926]. Many tantalising but elusive figures demand further research in connection with legal humanism. For example, Master Archibald Whitelaw, humanist and king's secretary in the later fifteenth century, is known to have worked on Roman law materials [Durkan, 1953: 5; Lyall, 1985: 69]. John Sinclair, fourth president of the College of Justice, owned a copy of Budé's study of Roman coinage, *De Asse* (1514), which exemplified 'the principle of "controlling" sources by external criticism' [Durkan and Ross, 1958: 60; Kelley, 1970: 57, 65–6]. David Chambers or Chalmers and Archibald Crawford were both lords of session in the 1560s with evident humanist interests [Baird Smith, 1933; Durkan and Ross, 1958: 85; Williamson, 1979: 118–20]. Alexander Sym was a royal lecturer in Greek and the laws in the 1550s [Durkan, 1983: 73–4].

The backdrop to this humanist culture was a process of radical if gradual change in the Scottish legal system. In the medieval period before 1450, it had been heavily influenced by the developing English common law [Sellar, 1988]. This owed much to Anglo-Normans who, under royal patronage, began to settle in Scotland from early in the twelfth century. They brought with them forms and habits of government and land tenure from which developed a Scottish common law very similar in basic content and technique to that of England. The nature of the parallel was reflected in the composition sometime between 1318 and 1400 of *Regiam Majestatem*, which was very largely based upon and copied from the twelfth century English book *Glanvill* [Duncan, 1961; Stein, 1969]. It is indicative of the conservatism of Scots law that *Regiam* remained its principal text until near the end of the seventeenth century [Cooper, 1936: 80]. Whereas the English system became highly centralised with a secular profession trained in the Inns of Court, Scots law was administered mainly in local courts and, while there may have been men who acted regularly as pleaders, they did not form a secular legal profession akin to that of England [Donaldson, 1976: 1–3; MacQueen, 1986: 420–1]. By the end of the fifteenth century, however, a central court, the Session, was emerging from the regularisation of the judicial business of the king's council, and its reconstitution in 1532 as the College of Justice gave it jurisdiction in all civil matters, contrasting with its earlier, relatively limited powers [MacQueen, 1984]. The court had a body of permanent paid judges, fifteen Senators headed by a President.[1] A secular profession of pleaders and writers evolved to serve litigants, becoming increasingly conscious of themselves as a distinctive group defined by function, training, and a growing number of privileges arising from their association with the Session [Hannay, 1933: 135–64; Hannay, 1936].

The process of change was not immediately reflected in legal writing. There is some evidence that this caused difficulties from early in the fifteenth century, when the Scottish parliament initiated a series of largely unsuccessful attempts to revise, 'codify', and publish legal texts and the considerable body of legislation attributed more or less reliably to the reigns of kings from the eleventh century onward. In 1425, a commission was appointed to 'se and examyn the bukis of law of this realm that is to say Regiam Maiestatem and Quoniam Attachiamenta and mend the lawis that nedis mendment' [APS ii 10 c 10]. Nothing substantial was produced, however [cf O'Brien 1980], and similar commissions appointed in 1469 and 1473 were equally unfruitful [APS ii 97 c 19; APS ii 105 c 14]. While further efforts of this kind were not made until the mid-sixteenth century, the project was not forgotten, because in 1507 Chapman and Millar, the first Scottish printers, received exclusive rights to print 'the Bukis of our Lawis [and] Actis of Parliament' [RSS i no 1546].

Much more was achieved after the Reformation by a series of commissions. The first was appointed in 1566. Notable among its members were Sir James Balfour of Pittendreich, Lord Clerk Register, and Mr Edward Henryson, 'doctour in the Lawis' [APS i 29]. In 1566 Henryson published the 'Black Acts', an edition of post-1424 legislation, acknowledging in his preface the 'sinceir afald and glaid concurrance to perfyte this wark' of Balfour. A commission was appointed in 1575 to look not only at the books of the law and the acts of parliament but also at 'Decisiouns befoir the Sessioun' in order that 'thair may be ane certaine writtin law . . . to juge and decyde be' [APS iii 89]. Balfour was also a member of this commission, and his *Practicks*, an integration under chapter headings of legislation, treatises and cases, were possibly one result [McKechnie, 1933; McNeill, 1962].[2] He is said to have been assisted by Mr John Skene, who from this period is prominent in commission work. Yet another commission appointed in 1578 included Mr Thomas Craig, advocate, who was later to write *Jus Feudale* and a number of other works, all of which were concerned, at least in part, with the legal, political and historical relations between Scotland and England [Levack, 1975, 1980].[3]

Skene was a member of another commission appointed in 1592, of which the outcome was his *Lawes and Actes* published in 1597, a new edition of the post-1424 legislation [APS i 31–3]. The published editions show that, as a source, Scottish legislation presented some historical difficulties, related to the state of the parliamentary records, which probably did not go back beyond 1424 [Murray, 1974: 129; Duncan, 1984: 1–3]. There was little doubt of the authenticity of post-1424 statutes, therefore, but opinions varied about the earlier material. To the *Lawes and Actes* Skene appended a commentary entitled *De Verborum Significatione* [Donaldson, 1962]. This took the form of a dictionary of 'the difficill wordes and termes conteined in the foure buikes of *Regiam Majestatem*', and considered both post-1424 and earlier material in great detail. It is apparent that the publications before 1600 were only part of a larger project by Skene. It culminated in 1609 with the publication of *Regiam Majestatem* in Latin and Scots editions, which also included other texts and pre-1424 legislation.

This activity in collecting and publishing native legal material is reminiscent of the directions which humanism took in contemporary France and England. Historical analysis of the *Corpus Iuris* increasingly suggested that Roman law was the product of a particular time and place, the relevance of which to the modern world could be doubted or even, as in the work of François Hotman (1524–90), rejected altogether [Baird Smith, 1916: 328; Kelly, 1974a]. From this arose a nationalistic, Gallican approach to legal studies, which placed indigenous law and custom above Roman law. An emphasis on native law also led to greater concentration on the *Libri Feudorum*, as an embodiment of customary law still of significance throughout Europe. A prominent figure in this was Jacques Cujas (1522–90) whose edition of the *Libri Feudorum* (1567) was important and influential [Pocock, 1987: 72–7; Kelley, 1970: 185, 187–8; Robinson, Fergus and

Gordon, 1985: 291–3]. Some scholars now rejected a Roman historical origin for feudal law [Stein, 1986: 303]. In England, humanistic study of English law and its history [Kelley, 1974b; Brooks and Sharpe, 1976; Kelley, 1976; Knafla, 1977: 39–74; Baker, 1979: ii 28–46; Baker, 1985; Prest, 1986: 184–208] opened the way for the spectacular developments of the seventeenth century in legal history [Pocock, 1987; Levack, 1975; Rodgers, 1985, 1986]. Civilians such as Sir Thomas Smith provided a comparative background [Levack, 1973; Stein, 1978; Dewar, 1982]. William Lambarde published texts of the Anglo-Saxon laws in his *Archaionomia* (1508) [Terrill, 1985], while others, whose identity remains uncertain, published editions of medieval texts like *Glanvill* (1554 and 1604) and *Bracton* (1569) [Hall, 1965: preface, lxii; Yale, 1981: 385–7].

The activities of the Scottish commissions also recall the codification of the customs of France in the fifteenth and sixteenth centuries [Dawson, 1940; Filhol, 1971]. Although it has not hitherto been suggested that these events in France had any direct connection with the contemporaneous developments in humanist thinking about customary law, the aims of both movements had some common ground. An examination of the intellectual background and methods of the leading members of the Scottish commissions strongly suggests that their work was inspired by the ideas of French humanism. It is hardly necessary to argue this for Edward Henryson. But the case for John Skene and Thomas Craig as humanists primarily concerned with the native law of Scotland requires elaboration.

### (ii) Sir John Skene of Curriehill (c.1543–1617)

In the dedication to the king prefacing his Latin edition of *Regiam*, Skene states that he had been at the university of Wittenberg. In *De Verborum Significatione* [sv ADJURNATUS], he refers to his 'praeceptor' Matthew Wesenbeck, who taught at Wittenberg and carried the *mos docendi gallicus* into Germany from the Netherlands [Cont LH 1912: 397].[4] In 1575 he passed advocate and, as well as pursuing a legal career, he served the crown in a number of capacities, principally as Lord Clerk Register from 1594 to 1612. It is important to note that in this capacity most of the records of central government were under his supervision [Murray, 1971; 1974]. Skene was also admitted as a barrister of the Middle Temple c.1605 [Bedwell, 1920: 100, 103]. The dedications of his Latin edition of *Regiam* provide evidence that Skene had at least a passing acquaintance with humanist learning. He quotes both from the Digest and from the lay authors of antiquity. His prose is that of one concerned with elegance of style – the occasional Greek phrase makes a self-conscious appearance. *De Verborum Significatione* is a work of a characteristically humanist type: the title, taken from Digest 50, 16, was employed by Valla,

Vegio and Alciato [Kelley, 1970: 42, 89, 94; Robinson, Fergus and Gordon, 1985: 287; Percival, 1985]. His citations in both works include references to Budé, Zasi, and Alciato, and, frequently, to Cujas' commentary on the *Libri Feodorum*, as well as to the work of the English humanists, Sir Thomas Smith and William Lambarde. Citations alone, however, do not demonstrate Skene's humanism, for he refers most often to the works of the late medieval commentators, Bartolus and Baldus. To show that Skene's methodology was essentially humanist, we must turn to the contents of his work.

His task was essentially that of the textual scholar and critic and, if his own account can be trusted, its genesis lay firmly in the traditions of continental legal humanism [Fergus, 1988]. He claims to have based his research on primary sources, the surviving MSS: 'As much as I could I have followed the best and most ancient manuscripts in their integrity.' Like many humanists he makes much of the difficulties of using these sources: their poor physical condition together with frequent obscurities of meaning have resulted in a task similar to that of Hercules in the Augean stables. Nevertheless, despite their intrinsic problems, he has clung to his sources 'as to a holy refuge'. Humanist techniques demanded critical emendation of the text to purge it of errors and additions and to restore it to its original state. Skene claims that his texts have been 'cleansed of blunders and restored to former brilliance', and that he has restored them 'to an intact state by what one might call a law of *postliminium*'.[5] The result has been the excision from the texts of later intruding glosses and additions, the restoration of rubrics to their proper place (some confusion being apparent in the sources), and the retention of the *ipsissima verba* of the originals, even if this offends against the 'elegance of the Latin tongue' and requires the appending of notes to explain obscure and outdated terms. Skene informs us that he has emended many things, but always by reference to the evidence of the MSS themselves. [See RM (Latin), Epistles Dedicatory, passim.]

Much of this also comes through in Skene's annotations of the Latin text of *Regiam* and in *De Verborum Significatione*. He refers to variant MS readings in order to criticise his text [RM (Latin) ff 67v, 71v]. His work on the early MSS allowed him on occasion to doubt the authenticity of passages in later ones. Thus of RM II, 33, 10, he states that 'these are not found in any of the old books [i.e. MSS] nor in the books written in English [i.e. the later MSS containing texts of RM translated into Scots]. They seem from the context to have slipped in by accident' [RM (Latin) f 52r]. He also realised that II, 45 came from a thirteenth century English source, the *Prerogativa Regis* [see Maitland, 1891; Sayles, 1939: preface, lii; Thorne, 1949; Bean, 1968: 70; Richardson and Sayles, 1981: xxv, 41[6]], but noted (correctly, so far as can now be said [Duncan, 1961: 202–3]) that the chapter was not found in the old MSS [RM (Latin) f 57v]. Chapter

23 of *Quoniam Attachiamenta* refers to the davoch which, as Skene rightly notes, was an ancient fiscal measurement of land [Easson, 1986: 45–100], and he then comments that later MSS substituted the words 'Bovatae terrae', a step 'against the faith of the authentic codexes' [RM (Latin) f 112v; cf DVS sv BOVATA TERRAE]. He has even left evidence of his doubts on the MSS themselves: in the Bute MS he put a note saying that a particular text 'seems corrupt' because it was different from texts of the same name in other MSS [APS i 182].

Skene's humanism is also apparent in the many philological notes in *Regiam Majestatem* and *De Verborum Significatione*. Often these are trite in nature: for example his reference to the shift from G to W between French and Scots [RM (Latin) f lv], his derivation of 'pactum' from 'pax' [RM (Latin) f 27r], and some of his observations about the roots of particular words [eg RM (Latin) ff 3v, 8v, 11r, 16v, etc; DVS passim]. He can be more original, in particular when he is discussing words in his text which derived from the Celtic or Gaelic strand in Scotland's legal history. Thus 'colpindach' is an Irish (ie, Gaelic) word formerly used by the Scots now corrupted to 'quyach' [RM (Latin) f 4r; DVS sv COLPINDACH]; 'toscheoderach' is a barbarous name used by the early Scots and Irish for the sergeant who serves citations [DVS sv TOSCHEODERACHE; RM (Latin) f 13r]; 'croo' means composition or satisfaction for a homicide or delict according to an act of parliament [RM (Latin) f 100v]; 'culreach' is an Irish word for a pledge or security[7] [DVS sv CULRACH; RM (Latin) f 108r]; 'enach' amongst 'our' Irish means satisfaction given to another for any delict or injury [RM (Latin) f 103v]. Sometimes Skene cheerfully admits to ignorance or doubt as to a derivation. Thus of 'yburthananseca' he says: 'This word, unknown and unused amongst us, is found in all the codexes; what its etymology may be I do not know'. He then offers a possible French derivation about which he clearly had doubts [RM (Latin) f 98v; DVS sv BERTINSEK, YBURPANANSECA]. Similarly he confesses ignorance about the meaning of 'galnes', but suggests that it is a kind of satisfaction or emends for a delict or killing payable to the relatives of a deceased [RM (Latin) f 100v; DVS sv GALENES]. He was also doubtful about 'kelchyn' but notes that he had been told by the earl of Argyll that in the early Scots tongue 'gailchen' meant a pecuniary mulct inflicted for a delict against another [RM (Latin) f 104r]. All this suggests a lively and not uncritical interest in language and its origins of a characteristically humanist nature.

Skene was also capable of criticising the text itself as 'more obscure than useful' [RM (Latin) f 48r], and he did not put a blind faith in his texts as statements of current law. Some of his notes to *Regiam* make this clear, as, for example, when he commented that the system of appeals described in I, 13, was out of date: 'by the law of this realm as now used civil litigations decided by an inferior judge or by an assize can be resuscitated and in the second instance annulled and reduced by the Lords of Council and Session' [RM (Latin) f 20v; see also ff 84v–85r]. On the other hand, he did annotate some obsolescent passages of the texts with an eye to current use. In the chapters on the brieves of novel dissasine and mortancestor, for example, remedies which had fallen into desuetude early in the sixteenth century [MacQueen, 1983], he states that the modern equivalents to the former are the actions of ejection and spuilzie, and to the latter, the brieve of inquest [RM (Latin) ff 86v–89r, 93r; also DVS sv BREVE].[8]

Also significant in Skene's work was his use of the historical records under his supervision as Lord Clerk Register to illuminate points in the texts. Thus, in his discussion of the toscheoderach, he notes a great seal charter of the fourteenth century granting the office of sergeant of the earldom of Carrick: 'which office is called Toschaderech, vulgarly, a mair of fee' [RM (Latin) f 13r]. Again, discussing a *Regiam* passage which mentions the lands of Dalginch as the chief place of Fife, he observes that the lands of Dalginch formerly belonged to James Cockburn in the time of James II, but their name has now changed to Brunton, and they are owned by Wardlaw, laird of Torrie, being next the lands of Markinch [RM (Latin) f 24r]. This information seems likely to have come from the great seal register [see RMS ii nos 226, 791, 3642, 3738; iv nos 3, 1415; vi no 1658]. He was aware of the value of history in assessing the authenticity of his materials and often cites the work of Hector Boece: for example, to establish the truth of the story at the beginning of the *Leges Malcolmi Mackenneth* about King Malcolm II (*c*.1005–1034) granting Scotland to be held of him by his knights by the feudal service of ward and relief [RM (Latin) f 1r].

In his preface, Skene claims, and his notes in *Regiam* and *De Verborum Significatione* bear him out, that he has compared Scots law with Roman law – and indeed with English, feudal and canon law as well as the customs of Normandy and Burgundy.[9] This comparative technique, into which the French humanists had been led by their study of customary law, enables Skene to show, amongst other things, the close link between *Regiam* and *Glanvill*. Sometimes his general knowledge of comparative legal development leads him to question the authenticity of parts of his texts. He comments, for example, that the final chapters of RM, though found in all the old MSS, 'do not seem to be authentic'. He offers two reasons: first, they seem to be congruent with the old English laws, as appears from the book by William Lambarde (this is presumably the *Archaionomia*) and with the old Norman laws; and second, he has seen some MSS where these chapters are entitled 'Leges inter Brettos et Scotos' and appear in French rather than in Latin [RM (Latin) f 103r].[10] Skene's point (which has recently been echoed by A.A.M. Duncan [1961: 204]) seems to be that these chapters are most likely interpolations distinct from the rest of the text.

### (iii) Thomas Craig of Riccarton (1538–1608)

In contrast to Skene, Craig had more the career of a busy and successful private practitioner than of a man of political ambition. It is perhaps a clue to his character that he served his king loyally as a scholarly redactor of the laws, and as a lawyer-commissioner for union with England, rather than in any great office of state, though he did hold a number of minor appointments [Tytler, 1823; Irving, 1839: i 147–60]. Craig commenced his studies in arts at the university of St Andrews. He continued them in Paris, for in the manuscripts of *De jure successionis*, he twice referred to the time when as a young man he there studied letters [EUL MS Dc. 3.48, 38 and 81. Cf Craig, 1695: 136; Craig, 1909: 161, 419]. It is likely that he also studied law at a French university, as his works contain many references to the leading humanist legal scholars of sixteenth century France. His praise of, and identification with, these men in *Jus Feudale* suggests that he viewed them as his intellectual, if not his actual, mentors. In particular, he cites Hotman more than any other writer, and is familiar with his *Francogallia* (1573) and *De Feudis Commentatio Tripertita* (1573). Hotman's influence on *Jus Feudale* is pervasive. Especially notable is Craig's adoption of Hotman's Bartolist distinction of the respective interests of superior and vassal in a single piece of ground as *dominium directum* and *dominium utile*. This he favoured as more consonant with Scottish practice than Cujas' association of the feu with Roman emphyteusis, a type of long lease [JF 1.9.9–14, esp. at 11; see Cairns, 1989].

Craig's legal writings were all composed towards the end of his life. They are accordingly the distillation of the busy professional career demonstrated in *Jus Feudale* by many anecdotes from his observations of the court and less frequent allusions to his own practice [See e.g. JF 1.10.11; 1.12.38; 1.16.47; 2.7.8]. The chronology of composition of his works is complicated and needs to be studied further, but from internal evidence, and some remarks in his *De hominio*, we can deduce that he probably started serious research for *Jus Feudale* sometime in the 1590s, had started writing it after 1597 at the latest, was certainly working on it in 1600, and was still revising it as late as after July 1606 [JF 2.3.34; 2.7.11; 2.20.23; Craig, 1695: 1]. We need not assume that Craig had a single purpose in writing *Jus Feudale*, nor that his aims in working on it did not change, but it is worth noting his statement, in the dedication to King James, that he had compared Scottish forensic usage with the written feudal law so that Scots law, which many considered vague and uncertain, could be given a structure and a method [JF viii]. He likewise said in the text that he intended to show the relationship between Scots law and the feudal law [JF 1.4.1]. It may plausibly be suggested that this was Craig's initial and primary aim in composing the book. Craig alludes, in a passage reminiscent of the proemium to Justinian's *Institutes*, to the possibility that his work might please young men desirous of administering the commonwealth, and three times explained a point or followed a certain structure in order, so he said, to please young men and further their studies [JF, dedication, viii; 1.8.6; 1.9.33; and 2.13.9]. This would not be inconsistent with a later revision in connection with the union project [Levack, 1975, 1980; Galloway, 1986; 146–7]. Supporting this is his statement in *De hominio* that he started work on the Scots feudal law before being impelled by intellectual curiosity to study that of England [Craig, 1695: 1–2].

Conventional humanist traits are apparent in all Craig's work, in particular a concern with language and style befitting one who composed Latin poetry. He wrote clear, even elegant, Latin and in his dedication of *Jus Feudale* states: 'If anyone was here missing the purity of the Latin language, he should remember that we are engaged in forensic matters, and compelled to use legal words, lest over anxious about words, we sometimes abandon the matter in hand' [JF viii]. Despite this robust apology, Craig later considers it necessary to explain, in parenthesis, that in using the verb 'providere' in discussing the effect of marriage provisions he is using it as a term of art, not in its Latin meaning [JF 2.14.10], and also that he will retain the words 'introire', 'adire', and 'intrare' in discussing non-entry, as being technical legal words, though scarcely Latin in this meaning [JF 2.19.3]. The same consciousness of classical Latin style leads Craig to comment that the *Libri Feudorum* are written in Latin except for legal terminology, but with Lombardic rather than Latin grammar: the forensic style was – he says – that of the uneducated age in which they were written [JF 1.6.4]. Craig is manifestly proud of his knowledge of Greek when, in discussing the *Ius Protimesios*, he writes that it is wrongly written 'protomeseos' by those unskilled in Greek. He goes on to discuss the derivation of this Greek word [JF 3.4.21] and later notes that a constitution of a medieval Roman Emperor does not follow correctly its Greek model, probably 'because of ignorance of the Greek language, which in that century was not perfectly known by very many people' [JF 3.4.21]. Greek words are used from time to time in *Jus Feudale*, and there are references to many Greek authors including Aristotle, Plutarch, Xenophon and Plato as well as, among others less obvious, Josephus, Philo, Demosthenes and Menander. He quotes Homer on the benefit of there being a single monarch [JF 2.13.32]. Craig's elegant learning in the Latin classics is frequently displayed in his references to Livy, Virgil, Sallust, Pliny, Ovid, Suetonius, Tacitus and, above all, Cicero.

Given his aims, Craig does not deal to any extent with the history of Roman law; but his discussion is typically humanistic. Thus he alludes to the *Litera Florentina*, the earliest and best manuscript, as the text of the Digest now used to correct other texts or dubious readings, and once refers to it himself to explain that it shows that the labials 'b' and 'v' are interchangeable [JF 1.2.11; 1.12.15]. He sets out the history of Roman law, dividing it fairly uncontroversially into the periods of the Twelve Tables, of the praetorian development, of the jurists, of the Emperors, and of Justinian, relating the history to the varying sources of the law [JF 1.2.1–10]. More specifically, he deals with the history of various areas of Roman law according to this scheme. [See, e.g., JF 2.13.8–14; 2.13.17; 2.13.41; 2.15.2–8.] He mentions the Codex Theodosianus, once using it to explain the term 'Canae' [JF 1.10.28; 1.12.12]. He recognised Roman law as having been a dynamic system, influenced by history, politics and personality; for example, his references to the – for him – malign influence of Theodora over the legislation of her husband Justinian is particularly instructive [JF 2.14.2; 2.15.4; 2.16.7; 2.16.11]. In his account of the subsequent history of Roman law, he recognised that institutions fell out of use because they were not understood [JF 2.15.9]. He lists the school of jurists starting with Irnerius as far as Decio, the teacher of Alciato [JF 1.2.11]. That he mentions none of the sixteenth century humanists in this list suggests that he recognised those of the feudists and Romanists who were among the '*Neoterici*' – with whom he obviously identified himself – as being somehow qualitatively different from their predecessors. The only writers of the schools before the humanists whom he mentions with any significant frequency are Bartolus and Baldus – though he cites each of them almost as many times as he cites Hotman. Nonetheless he clearly drew a contrast between '*novi interpretes*' such as Cujas and Schoener (dates unknown to us) and '*veteres interpretes*' such as Decio (1454–1536) [JF 1.9.4]. Though he may sometimes prefer the view of the '*veteres*', he was obviously predisposed to think that the '*novi*' had greater understanding, for he commented that Gratian was 'not unlearned' but only for 'those times' [JF 1.3.8]. He could accuse the glossators of torturing themselves in attempting to untie the knot posed by the apparent contradiction of prohibiting alienation while permitting subinfeudation, a knot which Craig himself unties easily by reference to Scottish practice and the nature of alienation and subinfeudation [JF 3.3.22].[11]

The study of words was obviously an important part of historical research for Craig, which meant that to understand a topic the etymology of the key words had to be discussed. Craig typically starts a new area of his subject with etymological discussion. At the very beginning of his discussion of the introduction of feudal law into England, for example, he examines English legal terminology to demonstrate that feudalism was introduced at the Norman

Conquest [JF 1.7.2]. Elsewhere he embarks on a lengthy discussion of the etymology of 'feu', before rejecting the various derivations to suggest that it is a word, originally in use among the northern peoples, preserved in its pristine form, meaning a fee or reward [JF 1.9.1–4]. This view may well be original to Craig – it is certainly not that of either Cujas or Hotman – and it also links with one of the general themes of *Jus Feudale*. He likewise introduces his account of charters with a discussion of the derivation of 'charta' [JF 2.3.3]. In considering the origin of Pontifex he disagrees with Varro, and quoting Virgil and citing Livy, derives it – quite wrongly – from 'posse' and 'facere' [JF 1.13.3]. On etymology, he sometimes cites Hotman's dictionary of feudal terms [JF 1.13.8; 1.16.7; 1.16.34], or Skene's *De Verborum Significatione* [see, e.g., JF 2.3.13] and he refers to Budé's annotations on the *Pandects* for the etymology of 'brieves' [JF 2.17.24].[12]

Craig's accuracy as an historian has been questioned [Robertson, 1974], but he approached law with a lively historical sense [Cairns, 1988], generally relating it to the nature of particular societies. He used the Twelve Tables, for example, to make a general point about early law [JF 2.13.4]. Not only did he pay attention to sources, but he could also conceive of history as a broad sweep of development. In his account of the introduction of feudalism into England, he makes sensitive historical evaluations of the evidence he had, surpassing anything that had hitherto been said in England on the topic, and anticipating the work of Henry Spelman (?1564–1641) [Pocock, 1987: 84–90]. Weighing up the statements of classical writers and the evidence of the Bible, he decides that Moses is the earliest lawgiver who certainly published laws [JF 1.1.10–13]. He borrows from Hotman the *'non inelegans'* term *'feudastrum'* to describe the new type of feu which he saw as having developed in the 'degeneracy' of the feudal system [JF 1.9.6; 1.9.27; 2.1.5; 2.1.6]. It is by no means clear, however, to what extent this was a recognition of the modern historian's 'bastard feudalism' [see Wormald, 1985: 12], or rather a reflection of Craig's view that in the modern world mores are decaying so that anything is possible [JF 1.12.18; 1.13.1; 1.14.1]. He certainly noticed with regret a departure from the simplicity of the ancients, and the decline of military glory in the modern world [JF 2.10.14; 2.18.29]. This may even just reflect Craig's view that the anti-Christ was active in the world [JF 1.3.23].

Craig follows Hotman very closely in claiming that feudalism originated in Germany, and devotes a whole title to demonstrating that it did not have a Roman origin [JF 1.5; cf. Hotman, 1573b: 6–9]. Perhaps here influenced by the *De Republica* (1576) of Jean Bodin (1530–96), Craig relates different racial characteristics to different climates, arguing that the northern races were more warlike and less servile than the southern [JF 1.4.2–3]. All kinds of aspects of feudalism are related by Craig to its military origin among the

Germanic peoples who overran the Roman empire: the preference for males over females in succession [JF 2.14.2]; the use of symbols in delivery of land, 'for the northern races were always accustomed to interpose a sign or symbol of possession or ownership' [JF 3.1.8]; and deprivation of a feu for failure to provide military service, because among the northern peoples it had been very dishonourable to desert one's prince [JF 3.5.23]. He also describes the ancient practice in deciding controversies, so that posterity should know that the early mores of the northern races had not been so barbarous as sometimes represented [JF 3.7.1].

### (iv) Humanism and the sources of Scots Law

The aim of the post-Reformation commissions – and the achievement of Craig, Skene and Balfour – was to order and make more accessible the material used by Scots lawyers. This prompted reflection on the authority of these sources, resulting in the identification of at least three closely related problems: the broad, essentially political question of the justification of law's authority; the question of the historical authenticity of what were alleged to be the laws; and, finally, the explanation of strictly legal theories about the relative authority of the various sources. In their approach to these problems, the Scottish lawyers entered a European debate which went to the heart of the humanist enterprise.

### (a) Roman law

As for the French humanists, a primary issue was the authority of Roman law as a source for contemporary practitioners. Skene and Craig united in their relegation of Roman law to a place below that of native Scottish sources, without going as far as (in their different ways) Cujas and Hotman in rejecting its relevance to modern practice. Skene is critical of what he perceives as a growing preference for Roman over Scots law in contemporary legal circles.[13] He claims that lawyers tend to devote all their energies to acquiring a knowledge of Roman law and thereby neglect the law of Scotland, which ought to be their first and proper concern, a point elegantly driven home with a quotation from the Digest. Primacy of place is to be given to *lex scripta*, followed by [native] custom and, finally, 'the customs of foreign peoples', among which he includes Roman law [RM (Latin), Dedication to the King]. Craig, however, appears readier to recognise that Roman law has been used by Scots lawyers and will continue to be used in cases of difficulty; but, agreeing with Skene, only where there is no written or customary Scottish source [JF 1.2.14; 1.8.16].

### (b) Sovereignty and the sources of Scots law

The principal problem then becomes one of ascertaining the authentic, native sources of Scots law. Though humanist techniques could be applied to determine the authenticity of legal material, the problem went deeper. What was the ultimate justification for treating these sources as law at all? Of the lawyers, only Craig dwelt on this point. He viewed society as resulting from the combination of individual family groups for mutual protection, and wrote that 'when society between men first was contracted, and laws (*leges*) were not yet written down, practice (*consuetudo*) and the tacit consent of the citizens resolved all controversies'. He explained that 'among all peoples, practice (*consuetudo*) claims for itself the name of law (*jus*), and law (*jus*) is said to have been created by customs (*mores*): and practice existed on the contrary before written law' [JF 1.8.13]. The appointment of magistrates was then necessary to resolve disputes. Citing Homer, Craig argues that all such early magistrates were kings, and that, although originally elective, kingship soon became hereditary to avoid disputes over succession [JF 1.1.2–7]. By the initial election, however, the people had irrevocably alienated their power to the king and his successors [Craig, 1703: 185].

Much of this has obvious affinities with the ideas of George Buchanan (1506–82), notably as expressed in the *De Jure Regni* (1579) [McFarlane, 1981: 392–415, 430–33]. Buchanan was not a lawyer, and 'spent remarkably little time examining the specific elements which composed Scottish positive law' [Williamson, 1979: 110–11]; but the important role of law in his theories of politics related in part to his perception of the historical operation of the Scottish constitution [Sellar, 1985: 18–19 and references there given]. He too cites Homer for the condition of early man, and argues that law is the product of social expediency. Kings were originally appointed for the resolution of disputes, and laws were the means by which this function was carried out [DJR, cc VIII–IX]. Buchanan went on to argue for the people's continuing right to depose the king who failed to fulfil his kingly function, a right which he founded on the notion of a mutual contract [DJR, c LXXXVI]. On this point we know that Craig would have disagreed, even though he talked about the partnership (*societas*) of king and people and stressed the mutuality of the obligations of lord and vassal in the feudal law. He argued that evil kings were a judgment of God who alone might judge them, though using human instruments in the execution of his will. Furthermore, the law of royal succession was ordained by the law of God, the law of nature, and the law of nations, and to depart from it was to invite the ruin of the nation by divine retribution [JF 1.1.4; 1.12.1; 2.1.17–18; 3.3.34; Craig, 1695: 165–6, 267, 279, 363–8; Craig, 1703: 144–5, 151–3, 161, 167–83, 187–9, 191–7, 206].

*(c) Legislation, and the problem of the early laws*

When Craig describes Scottish legislation as 'the constitutions and statutes of the three estates of the kingdom with the consent of the prince' [JF 1.8.9], further differences with Buchanan become apparent. 'As is almost our custom', wrote Buchanan, 'selected people of all the estates (*ordinibus*) should meet with the king in council. Then when a preliminary decree has been made by them, it should be referred to the judgment of the people' [DJR c XXVII]. It has been persuasively argued that Buchanan is here referring to the Scottish practice whereby legislation was drafted and presented to parliament for enactment by the Lords of the Articles, and that he saw 'the people', not as the populace at large, but rather as the politically responsible part which gathered in the legislature [Mason, 1982: 19–20]. While, therefore, Buchanan may have accepted the current operation of the Scottish constitution, his interpretation of the roles of the actors in it, emphasising the consent of the people rather than that of the king, was precisely opposed to that of Craig.

It would seem that, despite lodging ultimate sovereignty with the people (however defined), Buchanan saw law-making as essentially legislative rather than customary in nature.[14] He attacked the view that 'the force of daily custom was such that it had the strength of law' [DJR c LX], speaking of the 'tyranny of custom', which he contrasted with reason [DJR c LXI]. Though the lawyers did admit a role for custom, they too regarded written law as the pre-eminent source of contemporary Scots law. [For Skene and Craig, see above, 60.] Written law meant legislation: so, for example, Balfour comments that if a question arises on which there is 'no cleir writtin law', it should be referred to parliament for the making of a law [McNeill, 1962: i 1–2]. Any view of written law, however, had to deal with the uncertain status of the pre-1424 texts and statutes. The resolution of these uncertainties in varying ways demonstrates how the lawyers viewed sovereignty as essentially vested in the king.

Craig argues that, as societies developed beyond primitive simplicity, there was an inevitable tendency for law to be written down for the greater security of judges and litigants against prejudice [JF 1.1.11–12]. This he links with the appointment of kings, as he is certain that only popes and princes who acknowledge no superior have the power and right to make statutes [JF 1.6.7]. He cites Bodin, and sometimes specifically his *De Republica*, a number of times, and has grasped the idea that legislation was very much an aspect of sovereignty [JF 1.1.8; 1.2.13; 1.3.6; 1.7.3; 1.12.6; 2.2.2; 2.13.38; 3.5.16]. Skene also identifies the sovereign power with the king [RM (Latin), Dedication to the King]. In his *Lawes and Actes*, he lists the main works which he considers to be 'authentic' sources of Scots law. His reasons for excluding some texts as not authentic are not made clear, but in one case it seems to be connected with his opinion that the work is the production of a 'private man' [*Lawes and Actes*, last folio]. This may be contrasted with his acceptance that *Regiam* had been written at the command of David I (1124–53), even though, as his notes show, he was aware that it was closely parallel to *Glanvill*, which was known to have been composed during the reign of Henry II (1153–89). In the Scots edition of *Regiam*, he further explains that, despite the doubts of 'sundrie learned men', he regards its contents as having authority because the post-1424 legislation referred to them [RM (Scots), Epistle to the Reader, vii]. The link between inauthenticity and private men may therefore be that the private man cannot be a law-giver and so, while his work may be 'profitabill', it is not authentic law – in modern terms, it is a secondary rather than a primary source.

While Skene and, so far as can be told, Balfour accepted all the legislation attributed to kings from Malcolm II to Robert III (1390–1406), Craig doubted much of it on historical grounds – particularly the *Leges Malcolmi Mackenneth* [JF 1.8.1–2; 2.8.9–10; 2.20.3–4; 2.20.30; 3.5.4]. Craig approached the early texts with the same historical perspective from which he had learned to approach Roman law, and which he had seen applied by, for example, Hotman in works such as *Francogallia* [JF 1.12.9]. Close attention to, and criticism of, texts helped to establish the history of the development of the law and to identify which texts were authoritative. Just as Craig adopts the detailed textual and historical arguments of Cujas and Hotman on the date and authorship of the *Libri Feudorum* [JF 1.6.3–4], so he applies the same techniques to *Regiam Majestatem*. Craig's treatment of *Regiam* is apparently contradictory, in that, while denying it the status of a source of Scots law, he also appears, both overtly and covertly, to use it as one [Sellar, 1981: 144–45]. Careful study, however, shows that, while there may be minor inconsistencies, he gives a coherent account of the possible use of *Regiam* in achieving a historical understanding of Scots law.

Craig's best-known discussion of *Regiam* is where he claims it to have been copied from *Glanvill* and denies that it is a formal source of Scots law. He states that law should be perfect and complete in all its parts, so that *Regiam* should be purged from the public acts of the kingdom and 'corrected by learned men'. He warns that the books of *Regiam* have no authority, contain nothing from which a decision in a case could be sought, and must never be taken in court as authentic customs [JF 1.8.11]. He explicitly rejects the authority of *Regiam* in five instances where it sets out English institutions which he thought could not otherwise be traced in Scots law – socage, villeinage, mortgage, acquisition of possession by use, and the claim of the paternal uncle in succession, [JF 1.11.1; 1.11.32; 2.6.25–27; 2.6.30; 2.7.3; 2.13.39].[15]

The key to understanding Craig's view of *Regiam* is found in a passage on terce. He there supports a proposition by stating: 'This is proved by our written law.' He is evidently referring to *Regiam*.

He next remarks that: 'Because the law of the English and of the Normans moreover concurs, and, above all, equity urges this view, I accordingly bring it forward as correct, although I have not seen a precedent' [JF 2.22.27]. Though Craig argued that feudalism as a form of social organisation reached Scotland before England, he was perfectly aware, and frequently said directly, that many institutions and terms of Norman law had reached Scotland through England after the conquest [See, e.g., JF 1.11.33; 2.8.23; 2.8.40; 2.15.16; 2.16.1; 2.17.25; 2.20.2; 2.20.32; 3.5.2]. He occasionally states that certain rules were derived from England [JF 2.3.6; 2.13.47]. In the passage where he argues that the practice of sasine came from France to England, and from England to Scotland, he seems explicitly to rely on *Regiam* for historical evidence of ancient Scots custom. He comments that delivery of property was sometimes given by handing over keys, and states that the writer of *Regiam* indicates it to have been in use in his time. Passing no remark on the authority or otherwise of *Regiam*, he says that, since in that place little was said on the topic, he will explain it. This he does, finally referring to a deed in the muniments of the laird of Rires as an illustration [JF 2.7.1].

Craig seems to consider *Regiam* as authority for Scots law where what it states has been accepted into the customs of Scotland. He does not regard it as having in itself any authority as statute because, having been copied from *Glanvill*, and hence not ordained by David I, it must have been the unauthorised work of a private man [JF 1.8.11]. He distinguishes between historical and formal sources of law. Where accepted into Scots customary law *Regiam* was an historical source; but this would always have to be established by examination of customary practices. This may well explain what Craig meant when he called for the 'correction' of *Regiam* by learned men. Comparative and historical studies could determine which parts of *Regiam* contained Scots law.

### (d) Custom and the Session

It is apparently paradoxical, that, on the one hand, Buchanan attributed ultimate sovereignty to the people, yet was deeply suspicious of the role of custom [see above, 62], while, on the other, the lawyers stressed native custom above all sources other than written law, but gave sovereignty to the king. Buchanan's position may have derived from his view that law should emerge from the rational deliberations of the politically responsible members of society. The lawyers' analysis of custom may be explained from their opinion that custom was determined, not by actual social beliefs and behaviour, but by the decisions of the king's court. The emergence of the Session meant that, like other European countries in this period, Scotland had a court whose institutional origins lay in the king's council, and it may have been this link with the sovereign power of the king which was seen as giving it an authority above that of other courts to determine custom [Maitland, 1901: 19–20, 69–70; Baker, 1985: 54–6].

From early in the sixteenth century, some at least of the judges of the Session kept personal records of their cases, presumably for use in subsequent decision-making. To judge from the number of surviving MSS of these 'decision practicks', they were much copied, perhaps by entrants to the profession learning 'practick' [Murray, 1980: 91, 104]. The 1575 commission was instructed to examine the decisions of the Session [APS iii 89]. Balfour's *Practicks* is notable for its use of these decisions as sources, despite its own assertion that only parliament could make law [McNeill, 1962: i 1–2]. Balfour used a two-volume digest of decisions, known as the register, which went back to 1469 [McNeill, 1962: i, preface, lxi–ii]. Skene included 'decreetes given be the Lordes of the Session and Councell' amongst the sources of Scots law [*Lawes and Actes*, last folio], and cited many cases in *De Verborum Significatione* and in his notes to *Regiam Majestatem*. Sometimes these are cited as '*in registro*', presumably the same as Balfour's register [McNeill, 1962: i, preface, lxi], but at least once it can be shown that Skene's citation was directly from the decision practicks of John Sinclair [MacQueen, 1984: 62–3].

Craig is apparently the first to state explicitly that the settled course of judicial decisions manifests the custom of Scotland. He writes: 'Whenever we lack our own statute law,[16] then the practice (*consuetudo*) in what has constantly been so decided is followed, which we call practick (*praxin*): although on the pretence of this practice (*consuetudo*) very serious errors may be made in judicial decisions' [JF I.8.13]. Craig mentions almost ninety cases by name in *Jus Feudale*,[17] while citing or alluding to a great many more without naming any of the parties involved. He refers frequently in more general terms to the practice of the court. Most cases appear to be cited by Craig from personal recollection, and no doubt many of them formed part of a fund of knowledge held in common by the bar. He regularly notes discussions with colleagues, or arguments he has heard them present [JF 1.10.11; 1.10.36; 1.16.47; 2.2.24; 2.6.29; 2.15.9; 3.5.9].

Craig obviously considers that, in certain circumstances, the Court of Session, but not inferior courts, can change the law, as he remarks that 'inferior judges are not permitted to introduce in some other way law or custom contrary to express rules of law, nor are their opinions able to have the force of law' [JF 2.13.47]. There are examples of cases which he considered to have changed the law [See, e.g., JF 2.7.15–16; 2.8.34; 2.19.17]. On the other hand, the authority of the Court of Session was not thought to be unlimited, since he notes a case which was referred to parliament because it was so novel (in line with the recommendation in Balfour's *Practicks*) [JF 1.11.17; see APS iii 214 c 9 (1581) and above, 62]. Decisions helped define practice in uncertain areas [JF 1.16.32]; that the settling of disputed and uncertain custom was a primary function of judicial decisions appears from his noting in one area that a number of decisions were pending before the court which would settle the point at issue [JF 2.22.19], and his occasional regrets that there was no decision, and speculation as to what the court would decide [JF 2.5.7; 2.5.10]. He comments of one decision that it must be seen as turning on its own special facts, and hence not as a guide for the future [JF 2.6.6], while he also points out that, for a decision to be useful, it must have been based on a contested argument [JF 1.8.15]. This all obviously reflects his view that 'practick' formed law.

### (v) Conclusions

The humanistic movement in legal studies had a fundamental impact on the development of Scots law. Its influence on the work of the post-Reformation commissions to revise and restate the law was plainly substantial. The core of these commissions was a small group of humanist scholars, in which the leading figure was John Skene, but which also, from time to time, included Edward Henryson, James Balfour and Thomas Craig. These men and their assistants – such as Habakkuk Bisset, Charles Lumsden and James Carmichael[18] – formed a closely-knit group with broadly similar aims, although it is apparent that they did not always agree with each other. It is hard to overstate their importance – and therefore the importance of legal humanism – in the history of Scots law. Their essentially Renaissance notions of sovereignty enabled them to explain, justify, and rationalise the materials used by Scots lawyers. Thus Henryson, Balfour and Skene assembled the written sources of the law from the medieval period on, and provided the raw material from which later lawyers were to erect the structure of modern Scots law. Balfour and Skene were themselves the first to attempt such a critical structure, albeit not in particularly sophisticated ways. Skene's humanist techniques were of French inspiration, though he was aware of work in England and refers to Germany as 'the seat and home of good letters' [RM (Latin) Dedication to the King]. Skene's humanist outlook enabled him to identify, if not to solve, many of the problems of Scottish legal history [Fergus, 1988].

The most profound achievement of this humanist movement in Scotland was Craig's *Jus Feudale*. Craig sought to systematise Scots law using a model derived from feudal law, which he claimed as the law of Scotland [JF 1.8.16]. This might seem to challenge the thesis presented here, that the lawyers explained sovereignty as the basis of law's binding force in terms of the ultimate political authority of the king. Understanding Craig in his humanist context again provides an explanation. He argues that 'all the law which we use today in court, and all the custom and practick have flowed down from the springs and fountains of that law' [JF 1.8.16]. What is important for him is that feudal law is the historical source of Scots law [Cairns, 1989: 77]. He accordingly argues that in cases of doubt it is better to refer to the feudal law than to Roman or canon law. When feudal law is an authoritative source of Scots law it is because it has been adopted as local law. Craig notes, for example, that feudal law varies from one country to another [JF 2.22.7]. He notes Scots and English departures from the general feudal law [JF 1.10.7; 1.10.9; 2.12.26; 2.13.31]. He regularly stresses that feudal law is local law [see eg JF 1.8.16; 1.11.19; 2.12.3; 2.22.7; 3.3.32]. Where feudal law has been rejected, it is because this had seemed better to our people [JF 2.12.26]. Where it has been adopted, it is because of the customs and practices of the region [JF 2.22.7].[19] As Craig puts it: 'When these feudal customs first began to have the force of law in the court, the European peoples, as each judged suitable for its state of affairs, borrowed for themselves a particular part and transplanted it to themselves with some restriction' [JF 3.5.10].

Craig's success was due to his following methods and approaches learned from the humanist scholars of France. Their work and methodology provided him with a means of developing an historical critique of the supposed sources of Scots law to reach a definition of what was truly Scottish and authoritative. He vigorously pursued this work by means of textual and historical criticism, and thus provided a firm intellectual foundation for the further development of modern Scots law. It is a mark of Craig's achievement that his was the only humanist Scottish legal work to gain a European audience.

NOTES

1. The use throughout Europe of the Roman term 'Senators' for judges and the description in Latin texts such as Craig's *Jus Feudale* of a court as the 'Senatus' is worthy of fuller study: see e.g. John P. Dawson, (1968) *The Oracles of the Law*, Westport, Connecticut, 189; Louis A. Knafla, (1977) *Law and Politics in Jacobean England*, Cambridge, 64.
2. Balfour's *Practicks* circulated in MS until its publication in 1754.
3. See Craig's *De Unione Regnorum Britanniae Tractatus*, Edinburgh (1909), *The Right of Succession to the Kingdom of England*, London (1703), and *Scotland's Sovereignty Asserted* London (1695); also B.R. Galloway and B.P. Levack (eds) *The Jacobean Union: Six Tracts of 1604*, Edinburgh (1985).

4. In the preface to the Latin edition of *Regiam*, Skene refers to his seven years of travel before his return to Scotland in 1575. Evidence for some of his journeys is to be found in *De Verborum Significatione*. 'I have seene the like in the countrie of Helvetia, in the yeir of God 1568, amangst the Zuitzers' [sv MENETUM]; 'the Scottesmen in the realme of Polonia, quhairof I saw ane great multitude in the town of Cracovia, anno Dom 1569' [sv PEDE PULVEROSUS].

5. 'A Roman citizen who had been caught by an enemy as a prisoner of war became a slave of the enemy, but he regained freedom and "all his former rights through *postliminium (iure postliminii)*," when he returned to Roman territory.' A. Berger, *Encyclopedic Dictionary of Roman Law*, Philadelphia (1953) 639.

6. We are grateful to Dr P.A. Brand for some of these references.

7. Skene correctly translates 'culreach' as 'back borgh': see W.D.H. Sellar, 'Celtic Law and Scots Law: Survival and Integration', *Scottish Studies* 29 (1985) 1–27 at 15–16.

8. See also Balfour, *Practicks* ii 420–3 and 465, and Craig, *Jus Feudale*, 2. 17. 22–42, for a similar approach.

9. A process made easier by the availability of published editions of *Glanvill*, the *Corpus Juris Canonici*, the customs of Normandy and the commentary of Barthelemy Chasseneux (*c.*1480–1541) on the customs of Burgundy (1517), all of which are cited by Skene, as well as by his ownership of a 1518 Paris edition of the Digest: T. Miller, 'The Skene Library at Mar Lodge, Braemar', *Juridical Review* 39 (1927) 446–57. It is also known that Skene had read John Cowell's *Interpreter* (1607): see G. Neilson, *Skene's Memorabilia Scotica 1475–1612 and Revisals of Regiam Majestatem*, Glasgow (1923) 27, 30 and plate 2.

10. In the oldest surviving Scottish legal MS, the Berne MS, these chapters do indeed appear in French but not under the heading 'Leges inter Brettos et Scotos'. The MS is now in the Scottish Record Office, call no. PA 5/1.

11. Subinfeudation is to transfer land while retaining a superior interest; alienation is an outright transfer.

12. Mr. W.D.H. Sellar has drawn our attention to W.F. Skene's approval of Craig's etymology of the Gaelic word 'cain': *Celtic Scotland*, Edinburgh (1886–90) iii 231 note 50.

13. For contemporary observations on the Roman element in Scots law see P.G. Stein, 'Roman law in Scotland', *Ius Romanum Medii Aevi*, Milan (1968) pars V, 13b, 49–50; B.P. Levack, 'The proposed union of English law and Scots law in the seventeenth century', *Juridical Review* 20 (1975) 97–115 at 99–104.

14. Note also that in Sir David Lindsay's mid-16th century *Satyre of the Thrie Estaitis* [edition in *Four Morality Plays* ed. P. Happe, Harmondsworth (1979)] the realm is finally reformed for 'the Commonweill and equitie' by a series of 'Nobill Actis of our Parliament': see lines 3810–981.

15. Craig was actually mistaken on a number of these points – for example, socage and villeinage.

16. '*Verum ius proprium*' has been translated as 'statute law' because from *Jus Feudale* 1.8.9 and 12 it may be deduced that this is what Craig meant.

17. Craig, *Jus Feudale* trans. J.A. Clyde, Edinburgh (1934) vol. i, pp. xxxiii–xxxiv, contains an incomplete list.
18. See *Habakkuk Bisset's Rolmentis of Courtis* ed. P.J. Hamilton Grierson (Scottish Text Society 1920–26) i 70–85 and A.H. Williamson, *Scottish National Consciousness in the age of James VI*, Edinburgh (1979) 65–6 for Bisset and Carmichael. Lumsden was the copyist of MSS of Skene's *Regiam* and Craig's *De hominio* and *De Jure Successionis* (National Library of Scotland, Adv MSS 7.1.10; 25.5.8 and 16.2.25 and Edinburgh University Library MS Dc. 3.48).
19. Baird Smith (in 'Sir Thomas Craig, feudalist', *Scottish Historical Review* 12 (1915) 271–302 at 293) is wrong to universalise the passage where Craig states that local custom and statute should be strictly interpreted when they depart from the feudal law, *Jus Feudale* 3.3.32, as Craig is there dealing only with such customs and statutes as permit alienation of the feu.

## BIBLIOGRAPHY

### Manuscript sources

Adv. MS 7.1.10: National Library of Scotland Advocates' MS. Skene. *Regiam Majestatem*.
Adv. MS 16.2.25: National Library of Scotland Advocates' MS. Craig. *De hominio disputatio*. See Craig 1695.
Adv. MS 25.5.8: National Library of Scotland Advocates' MS. Skene. *Regiam Majestatem*.
Berne MS: Scottish Record Office PA 5/1.
Bute MS: Now purchased by the National Library of Scotland.
EUL MS Dc.3.48: Edinburgh University Library, Craig. *De Jure Successionis*. See Craig 1703.

### Printed sources

APS: *Acts of the Parliaments of Scotland, 1124–1707*, ed. T. Thomson & C. Innes 12 vols. Edinburgh (1814–75)
D. Baird Smith, 'William Barclay', *Scottish Historical Review* 11 (1914) 136–63.
D. Baird Smith, 'Sir Thomas Craig, Feudalist', *Scottish Historical Review* 12 (1915) 271–302.
D. Baird Smith, 'François Hotman', *Scottish Historical Review*, 13 (1916) 328–65.
D. Baird Smith, 'Archibald Craufurd, Lord of Session', *Juridical Review* 45 (1933) 166–78.
J.H. Baker, ed. *The Reports of Sir John Spelman*, 2 vols. Selden Society, London (1977).
J.H. Baker, 'English Law and the Renaissance', *Cambridge Law Journal* 44 (1985) 46–61.
J.M.W. Bean, *The Decline of English Feudalism*, Manchester (1968).

C.E.A. Bedwell, 'Scottish Middle Templars 1604–1869', *Scottish Historical Review* 17 (1920) 100–17.

A. Berger, *Encyclopedic Dictionary of Roman Law*, Philadelphia (1953).

*Habakkuk Bisset's Rolmentis of Courtis*, ed. P.J. Hamilton Grierson, Scottish Text Society, Edinburgh (1920–26) 3 vols.

J. Bodin, *Les Six Livres de la République*, Paris (1576) (*De Republica*).

H. Bracton, *De legibus et consuetudinibus Angliae libri quinque, in varios tractatus distincti, ad diversorum et vetustissimorum codicum collationum, ingenti cura, nunc primum typis vulgati*, London (1569).

C. Brooks and K. Sharpe, 'History, English Law and the Renaissance', *Past and Present* 72 (1976) 133–42.

DJR: G. Buchanan, *De iure regni apud Scotos, dialogus*, Edinburgh (1579) trans. D.H. McNeill, *The Art and Science of Government amongst the Scots*, Glasgow (1964).

Budé 1508: *Annotationes Gulielmi Budaei Parisiensis secretarii regii in quatuor et viginti pandectarum libros ad Ioannem Deganaium cancellarium franciae*, Paris (1508).

Budé 1514: *De asse et partibus eius libri quinque Guillielmi Budaei Parisiensis secretarij regij*, Paris (1514).

J.W. Cairns, 'The *Breve Testatum* and Craig's *Jus Feudale*', *Tijdschrift voor Rechtsgeschiedenis* 56 (1988) 307–29.

J.W. Cairns, 'Craig, Cujas and the Definition of Feudum: Is a Feu a Usufruct?' in P.B.H. Birks, ed. *The Roman Law of Property*, Oxford (1989) 75–84.

J.K. Cameron, ed. *The First Book of Discipline*, Edinburgh (1972).

*Commentaria Bartholomei de Chasseneuz, . . . in consuetudines ducatus Burgundiae principaliter et totius fere Galliae consecutive*, Lyon (1517).

Clyde 1934: See Craig 1934.

*A General Survey of Events, Sources, Persons and Movements in Continental Legal History*, various authors, Continental Legal History Series, vol. 1, London (1912)

T.M. Cooper, '*Regiam Majestatem* and the Auld Lawes', *An Introductory Survey of the Sources and Literature of Scots Law*, Stair Society, Edinburgh (1936) 70–81.

*Corpus iuris canonici. Editio Lipsiensis secunda post A.E. Richteri curas. Ad librorum manu scriptorum et editionis Romanae fidem recognovit et adnotatione critica instruxit Aemilius Friedberg*, Graz (1959).

C J C: Justinian I, Emperor of the East, *Corpus iuris civilis* 3 vols., ed. T. Mommsen, P. Krueger, G. Kroll Berlin (1904–6).

J. Cowell, *The Interpreter: Or, Booke Containing the Signification of Words* Cambridge (1607).

T. Craig, *Jus Feudale*, Edinburgh and London (1655); Leipzig (1716); Edinburgh (1732).

T. Craig, *Scotland's Soveraignty Asserted*, trans. Ridpath, London (1695).

T. Craig, *The Right of Succession to the Kingdom of England*, trans. Gatherer, London (1703).

T. Craig, *De Unione Regnorum Britanniae Tractatus*, ed. Sanford Terry, Scottish History Society, Edinburgh (1909).

T. Craig, *Jus Feudale* trans. J.A. Clyde, Edinburgh (1934) including trans. *Libri Feudorum*.

J. Cujas, *De feudis, libri V, quorum primus est Gerardi Nigri, secundus et tertius Oberti de Orto* etc., Lyon (1566) and others.

J.P. Dawson, 'The Codification of the French Customs', *Michigan Law Review* 38 (1940) 765–800.

J.P. Dawson, *The Oracles of the Law*, Ann Arbor (1968).

M. Dewar, ed., *De Republica Anglorum by Sir Thomas Smith*, Cambridge (1982).

W.C. Dickinson, 'The Advocates' Protest Against the Institution of a Chair of Law in the University of Edinburgh', *Scottish Historical Review* 23 (1926) 205–12.

R. Donaldson, 'A "Mixed Edition" of *De Verborum Significatione'*, *The Bibliotheck* 2–3 (1959–62) 219–20.

G. Donaldson, 'The Legal Profession in Scottish Society in the Sixteenth and Seventeenth Centuries', *Juridical Review* 21 (1976) 1–19.

A.A.M. Duncan, '*Regiam Majestatem:* a Reconsideration', *Juridical Review* 6 (1961) 199–217.

A.A.M. Duncan, *James I King of Scots 1424–1437*, 2nd ed., Glasgow University, Scottish History Department (1984).

J. Durkan, 'The Beginnings of Humanism in Scotland', *Innes Review* 4 (1953) 1–24.

J. Durkan, 'Henry Scrimgeour, Renaissance Bookman', *Edinburgh Bibliographical Society Transactions* 5 (1978) 1–31.

J. Durkan 'The royal lectureships under Mary of Lorraine', *Scottish Historical Review* 62 (1983) 73–8.

J. Durkan, 'The French Connection in the Sixteenth and Early Seventeenth Centuries', *Scotland and Europe 1200–1850*, ed. T.C. Smout, Edinburgh (1986) 19–44.

J. Durkan and J. Kirk, *The University of Glasgow 1451–1577*, Glasgow (1977).

J. Durkan and A. Ross, 'Early Scottish Libraries', *Innes Review* 9 (1958) 5–167.

A.R. Easson, *Systems of Land Assessment in Scotland Before 1400*, Edinburgh University Ph.D., (1986).

T.D. Fergus, *Quoniam Attachiamenta*, Glasgow University Ph.D., (1988).

R. Filhol, 'The Codification of Customary Law in France in the Fifteenth and Sixteenth Centuries', *Government in Reformation Europe*, ed. H.J. Cohn, Glasgow (1971).

B.R. Galloway, *The Union of England and Scotland, 1603–1608*, Edinburgh (1986).

B.R. Galloway and B.P. Levack, eds., *The Jacobean Union: Six Tracts of 1604*, Scottish History Society, Edinburgh (1985).

R. de Glanvill, *Tractatus de legibus et consuetudinibus regni Angliae etc.*, London (1554) and others.

R. de Glanvill, *Tractatus de legibus et consuetudinibus regni Angliae . . . Qui nunc imprimitur post 50. annos a priore et prima impressione, quia in pluribus concordat cum antiquo libro legum Scotiae vocato Regiam majestatem precipue in locis hoc signonotatis*, London (1604).

A. Grant, *The Story of the University of Edinburgh during its first three hundred years*, 2 vols, London (1884).

G.D.G. Hall, ed., *The treatise on the laws and customs of the realm of England commonly called Glanvill*, London and Edinburgh (1965).

R.K. Hannay, *The College of Justice: Essays on the Institution and Development of the Court of Session*, Edinburgh and Glasgow (1933).

R.K. Hannay, 'The Early History of the Scottish Signet', *The Society of Writers to His Majesty's Signet*, Edinburgh (1936).

D.B. Horn, 'The Origins of the University of Edinburgh', *University of Edinburgh Journal* 22 (1966) 213–25, 297–312.

Hotman 1573a: F. Hotman, *Francogallia* (Geneva 1573) and others.

Hotman 1573b: F. Hotman, *De Feudis Commentatio Tripertita*, Lyon (1573).

D. Irving, *Lives of the Scotish [sic] Writers*, Edinburgh (1839) 2 vols.

D.R. Kelley, *Foundations of Modern Historical Scholarship*, New York (1970).

D.R. Kelley, 'History, English Law and the Renaissance', *Past and Present* 65 (1974) 24–51.

D.R. Kelley, *François Hotman*, Princeton (1974).

D.R. Kelley, 'A rejoinder', *Past and Present*, 72 (1976) 143–6.

L.A. Knafla, *Law and Politics in Jacobean England*, Cambridge (1977).

Lambarde 1568: *Archaionomia, sive de priscis Anglorum legibus libri . . . Gulielmo Lambardo interprete*, London (1568).

B.P. Levack, 'The Proposed Union of English Law and Scots Law in the Seventeenth Century', *Juridical Review* 20 (1975) 97–115.

B.P. Levack, 'English Law, Scots Law and the Union, 1603–1707', *Law Making and Law Makers in British History*, ed. A. Harding, Royal Historical Society, London (1980) 105–19.

*Libri Feudorum*, Many editions. See under Cujas or Hotman 1573b or Craig 1934.

R.J. Lyall, 'Scottish Students and Masters at the Universities of Cologne and Louvain in the Fifteenth Century', *Innes Review* 36 (1985) 55–73.

I.D. McFarlane, *Buchanan*, London (1981).

L.J. Macfarlane, *William Elphinstone and the Kingdom of Scotland*, Aberdeen (1985).

H. McKechnie, 'Balfour's Practicks', *Juridical Review* 43 (1944) 179–92.

P.G.B. McNeill, *The Practicks of Sir James Balfour of Pittendreich*, 2 vols, Stair Society, Edinburgh (1962, 1963).

H.L. MacQueen, 'Dissasine and Mortancestor in Scots Law', *Journal of Legal History* 4 (1983) 21–49.

H.L. MacQueen, 'Jurisdiction in Heritage and the Lords of Council and Session after 1532', *Miscellany II*, ed. W.D.H. Sellar, Stair Society, Edinburgh (1984) 61–85.

H.L. MacQueen, 'Pleadable Brieves, Pleading and the Development of Scots Law', *Law and History Review*, 4 (1986) 403–22.

F.W. Maitland, 'The Praerogativa Regis', *English Historical Review* 6 (1891).

F.W. Maitland, *English Law and the Renaissance*, Cambridge (1901).

T. Miller, 'The Skene Library at Mar Lodge, Braemar', *Juridical Review* 39 (1927) 446–57.

A.L. Murray, 'Sir John Skene and the Exchequer 1594–1612', *Miscellany I* by various authors, Stair Society, Edinburgh, (1971).

A.L. Murray, 'The Lord Clerk Register', *Scottish Historical Review* 53 (1974) 124–56.

A.L. Murray, 'Sinclair's Practicks', *Law Making and Law Makers in British History*, ed. A. Harding, Royal Historical Society, London (1980) 90–104.

G. Neilson, *Skene's Memorabilia Scotica 1475–1612 and Revisals of Regiam Majestatem*, Glasgow (1923).

I.E. O'Brien, *The Scottish Parliament in the Fifteenth and Sixteenth Centuries*, Glasgow University Ph.D., (1981).

D.J. Osler, 'Graecum Legitur: A Star is Born', *Rechtshistorisches Journal* 2 (1983) 194–203.

D.J. Osler, 'Budaeus and Roman Law', *Ius Commune* 13 (1985) 195–212.

W.K. Percival, 'Maffeo Vegio and the Prelude to Juridical Humanism', *Journal of Legal History* 6 (1985) 179–193.

J.G.A. Pocock, *The Ancient Constitution and the Feudal Law*, Cambridge (1957); reissued with a retrospect, Cambridge (1987).

W.R. Prest, *The Rise of the Barristers: A Social History of the English Bar 1590–1640*, Oxford (1986).

R.S. Rait, *The Universities of Aberdeen: a History*, Aberdeen (1895).

H.G. Richardson and G.O. Sayles, *The English Parliament in the Middle Ages*, Hambledon Press (1981).

RMS: *Registrum Magni Sigilli Regum Scotorum, 1306–1668* II vols, Edinburgh (1862–1914).

J.J. Robertson, 'The Illusory *Breve Testatum*', in G.W.S. Barrow, ed., *The Scottish Tradition*, Edinburgh (1974).

O.F. Robinson, T.D. Fergus and W.M. Gordon, *An Introduction to European Legal History*, Abingdon (1985).

C.P. Rodgers, 'Humanism, History and the Common Law', *Journal of Legal History* 6 (1985) 129–56.

C.P. Rodgers, 'Legal Humanism and English Law – The Contribution of the English Civilians', *Irish Jurist* 19 (1984) 115–36.

RSS: *Registrum Secreti Sigilli Regnum Scotorum, 1488–1584*, 8 vols, Edinburgh (1906–1984).

G.O. Sayles, ed., *Select Cases in the Court of King's Bench under Edward I vol. III*, Selden Society, London, (1939).

W.D.H. Sellar, 'English Law as a Source', *Stair Tercentenary Studies*, ed. D.M. Walker, Stair Society, Edinburgh (1981) 140–50.

W.D.H. Sellar, 'Celtic Law and Scots Law: Survival and Integration', *Scottish Studies* 29 (1985).

W.D.H. Sellar, 'The Common Law of Scotland and the Common Law of England', in R.R. Davies, ed., *The British Isles 1100–1500*, Edinburgh, (1988).

J. Skene, *The Laws and Actes of Parliament (1424–1597)*, Edinburgh (1597).

J. Skene, *De Verborum Significatione*, Edinburgh (1597).

(Latin): J. Skene, *Regiam Majestatem Scotiae, Veteres Leges et Constitutiones, ex Archives Publicis, et Antiquis Libris Manuscriptis collectae recognitae, et notis Juris Civilis, Canonici, Normannici auctoritate, confirmatis, illustratae, opera et studio Johannis Skenae . . .*, Edinburgh (1609).

(Scots): J. Skene, *Regiam Majestatem. The Auld Lawes and Constitutions of Scotland. Faithfullie collected furth of the Register and other auld authentick Bukes . . . and trewlie corrected in Sindrie Faults and Errours, committed be ignorant Writers. And translated out of Latine in Scottish Language . . . Be Sir John Skene*, Edinburgh (1609).

T.B. Smith, *Studies Critical and Comparative*, Edinburgh (1962).

P. Stein, 'Roman Law in Scotland', *Ius Romanum Medii Aevi*, pars V, 13b, Milan (1968) 1–58.

P. Stein, 'The Source of the Romano-Canonical part of *Regiam Majestatem*', *Scottish Historical Review* 48 (1969) 107–23.

P. Stein, 'Sir Thomas Smith, Renaissance Civilian', *Acta Juridica* (1978) 79–89 (no volume number).

P. Stein, 'Legal Humanism and Legal Science' *Tijdschrift voor Rechtsgeschiedenis* 54 (1986) 297–306.

R.J. Terrill, 'William Lambarde: Elizabethan Humanist and Legal Historian', *Journal of Legal History* 6 (1985) 157–78.

Samuel E. Thorne, *Prerogativa Regis Tertia Lectura Roberti Constable de Lyncolnis Inne Anno II Henry VII*, New Haven (1949).

P.F. Tytler, *An Account of the Life and Writings of Sir Thomas Craig of Riccarton*, Edinburgh (1823).

W. Welwood, *The Sea-Law of Scotland, shortly gathered and plainly dressit for the reddy use of all seafaringmen*, Edinburgh (1590).

W. Welwood, *An abridgement of all sea-lawes*, London (1613).

A.H. Williamson, *Scottish National Consciousness in the Age of James VI*, Edinburgh (1979).

J. Wormald, *Lords and Men in Scotland: Bonds of Manrent 1442–1603*, Edinburgh (1985).

D.E.C. Yale, 'Of no mean authority': some later uses of Bracton', in Morris S. Arnold et al., eds., *On the Laws and Customs of England: Essays in Honour of Samuel E. Thorne*, Chapel Hill (1981).

# Philosophy in Renaissance Scotland: Loss and Gain
## ALEXANDER BROADIE

In sixteenth-century Scotland philosophical activity gradually came under the influence of classical works in the original languages, and inevitably that activity came to acquire a renaissance character. Plato and Aristotle and other philosophers were read for the first time in Greek. At the start of the century there was little sign of Greek scholarship among Scottish philosophers, but by its end the situation was greatly altered, to the extent indeed that the theologian Robert Rollock, first principal of Edinburgh University, gave to his under-graduates logic lectures which consisted of little more than a slow dictation of Aristotle's works in the newly edited Greek texts.

Additionally, close study of Roman authors, especially the orators, led to Scots adopting the widespread humanist prejudice against scholastic Latin, and using instead Ciceronian Latin in their philosophy books. A major reason for this linguistic change was aesthetic. The philosophers were enthralled by the language of the classical Roman authors. But another consideration must not be lost sight of, namely that over the centuries scholastic Latin had been gradually refined into a 'scientific' Latin which was intended to help logicians and philosophers communicate their ideas with the greatest possible precision, and accordingly with the greatest possible chance of not being misunderstood by their colleagues. But the renaissance thinkers were not interested in saying the kinds of things that the schoolmen had said. This is true especially of scholastic logic. Typically, renaissance logicians had little or no patience for the logic that had been developed over the previous few centuries; as already hinted they were much more interested in returning to the 'pure' logic of Aristotle (just as Biblical scholars were then primarily interested in returning to the newly retrieved Greek text of the New Testament). We shall observe that at the start of the sixteenth century Scottish logicians were contributing many interesting new ideas to the logic of the late-scholastics, but by the end of the century new ideas in logic were less forthcoming. Aristotle's logic had by then almost acquired the status of Holy Writ, and Scottish logicians were mainly concerned to expound Aristotle's system of logic, taking care to avoid any regression into the logic of their scholastic predecessors.

The situation is the same in other areas of philosophy. Much was lost as a result of the general disregard of the works of the schoolmen. But there was undoubtedly a gain also. The decks were cleared at the bright prospect of a fresh start being made in logic and philosophy – a fresh start, that is, with the newly edited classical texts, most especially, perhaps, those of Aristotle and Cicero.

We shall begin with a group of thinkers who dominated Scottish academic life in the first few decades of the sixteenth century. The leader of the group was John Mair (c.1467–1550), professor of theology at Paris, principal of Glasgow University, provost of St Salvator's College, St Andrews, colleague of Erasmus, and teacher of John Knox. Mair matriculated in Paris c.1491, joining a Scottish contingent of students which in the recent past had included such distinguished figures as James Liddell (= Jacobus Ledelh) from Aberdeen, whose *Tractatus Conceptuum et Signorum* (Paris, 1495) was the first work by a Scot to be printed while he was yet alive. Mair's circle included David Cranston (c.1479–1512), a priest of the Glasgow diocese and philosophy regent in Paris; George Lokert (c.1485–1547), prior of the Sorbonne, rector of St Andrews University, and dean of Glasgow; William Manderston (c.1485–1552), rector of the universities of Paris and St Andrews; Robert Galbraith (c.1483–1544), professor of Roman Law at Paris and senator of the College of Justice at Edinburgh; and the Aberdonian Gilbert Crab (c.1482–1522). Others associated with Mair were Hector Boece, first principal of Aberdeen University, and Robert Wauchope, archbishop of Armagh.[1]

Mair wished accurate versions of great works of masters of the previous three centuries to be available, and to that end he and a number of colleagues prepared editions of works by Aquinas, Duns Scotus, John Buridan, Adam Wodham, and André de Neufchâteau among others. The works thus edited either by Mair or at least under his supervision included writings on logic, metaphysics, moral philosophy and theology. But Mair, at least in the earlier part of his career, was particularly interested in logic, and he and members of his circle, which included several immensely able logicians, made important contributions to the late flowering of terminist logic, the last advance made before renaissance ideas about the job of the logician led to a change of direction in the art. Terminist logic is concerned primarily with the logical properties of terms. The property most closely investigated was that of supposition, which is the signification a term has in the context of a proposition. 'In the context of a proposition' is the crucial phrase here. 'Man' by itself signifies whatever it is truly predicable of, namely, Tom, Dick and Harry, and so on for all men. But in ' "Man" is a monosyllable' it does not signify any man; it signifies itself qua term in a proposition, and signifies anything else which is equiform with it (for the term 'man' in any proposition is monosyllabic). Likewise in 'Man is a species' the term 'man' does not signify individual men, for neither Tom nor Dick nor any other man is a species. In the context of that proposition what does 'man' stand for? Aside from small variations which need not concern us here, members of Mair's circle took the view that a species is to be identified not (as the realists held) with its members nor with any quality of its members, but with a quality of the mind, called a 'concept' or 'notion', which is truly predicable of every member of the species. This nominalist answer was not maintained uniformly among Scottish philosophers; as the century unfolded there was an increasing tendency to adopt the Aristotelian realist doctrine that a species exists in each of its members and not at all as a concept or notion.

However the attention of the logicians was primarily focused not on nouns but on terms such as 'every', 'some', 'no', that is, on quantifiers, and on propositional connectives such as 'and', 'or' and 'if'. A common criticism of pre-Fregean logic is that it is unable to account for the logical relations between propositions where several quantifiers are involved, and hence is unable to explain why, for example, 'Every man has a head' and 'There is some head that every man has' are not equivalent though the second implies the first. This is not the place to set out the details of the logical apparatus developed to deal with such problems, but it should be said that early sixteenth-century logicians, with John Mair and his associates at the forefront, were able to solve both this problem and also many others which are commonly held to be insoluble within the framework of pre-Fregean logic. Two particularly important works in this area are by Robert Galbraith[2] and William Manderston.[3] Galbraith's book in particular should be reckoned among the classics of late-scholastic logic.

Another area of logic in which members of the circle were interested was that of 'exponible terms', which interest logicians in view of the role they play in inferences. The terms in question include 'only', 'except', 'in so far as', 'immediately', 'begins' and 'ceases'. Comparative and superlative forms were also discussed under this heading. This field, which has recently been attracting the attention of philosophers such as Norman Kretzmann, E.J. Ashworth, and P.T. Geach,[4] provided Mair with the subject of his first book, *Exponibilia* (Paris, 1499); Lokert also wrote a book on the subject, *Tractatus Exponibilium* (Paris, 1522), by no means always expressing agreement with his former teacher. David Cranston and others also wrote on exponibilia, though not devoting entire treatises to the subject. Elsewhere I have indicated some of the connections between these various discussions,[5] but there is room for a systematic study of their relationships.

As already noted, the members of Mair's circle were not occupied solely with logic. They had a good deal to say about epistemology, in particular about what it is to know something. Indeed Liddell's book, mentioned earlier, on concepts and signs, deals with precisely this question, and Lokert, Cranston and Crab devoted treatises to the topic.[6] Issues raised by those philosophers place their work in an interesting relation, never properly explored, with concerns dominant in the philosophy of the Scottish Enlightenment. For example, it can be demonstrated that what we now think of as Thomas Reid's most distinctive contribution to philosophy is hardly distinguishable from theories worked out by Lokert, Crab, and others.[7] Their concept of 'notion' (= *noticia*) is particularly important in this context.

More than one definition of 'notion' was given. As Crab uses the term, a notion is a quality inherent in a cognitive faculty and representing a thing or things to that faculty.[8] When we see a desk we are changed by that experience, at least in the sense that something is now true of us that previously had not been, for we are now seeing a desk. This change, in Crab's view, is a modification (or a modifying) of our cognitive faculty. And the modification, which is our notion of a desk, is a representative within us of the external object. Likewise if we hear the utterance 'desk' we form a notion. It should be said here that for a person who understands the word, the utterance results in not one but two notions, one 'non-ultimate' and the other 'ultimate'. For there is a notion representing the utterance merely qua sound (that notion is non-ultimate) and there is a notion representing what the sound conventionally signifies, namely a desk (that is the ultimate notion). Mair explains the terminology by saying that when we hear the utterance the mind does not rest there but goes on to consider what the utterance signifies.[9]

There was in fact an important disagreement between Crab and Lokert concerning what can be classed as a notion. Crab classed as notions only those modifications of the cognitive faculty which represent some thing or things. Thus we can have a notion of a desk or of Gilbert Crab. Lokert added that modifications of a cognitive faculty which represent 'in some way' (*aliqualiter*) are notions.[10] He has in mind the modifications which correspond, for example, to 'every' in the utterance 'Every student is busy'. Plainly 'every' does not represent anything. But it does represent in some way, namely by affecting the way we take the adjacent term 'student'. For as a result of the presence of 'every' the term 'student' must be taken, in the context of that proposition, to stand for not one student, or a few, but for every student.

But Crab and Lokert agree with Mair on the central point that a notion is not an object of an act of understanding but is the very act itself.[11] Thus when we hear and understand 'Every student is busy' we form a notion, and the notion is our act of understanding the utterance. When we hear and understand the utterance 'desk' the notion we form is our act of understanding the term. This kind of representationalism does not lead to scepticism. For though it is true that the notion is a representative of something, we cannot say that though we apprehend the notion, what the notion is supposed to represent may not really exist. The point here is that we do not apprehend the notion. Our having the notion of X is our unmediated cognitive grasp of X itself.

Thomas Reid makes exactly the same point though he speaks of 'ideas', which for him are operations of the mind, where Mair and his associates speak of 'notions'. And Reid uses the point as his main weapon against the implicit scepticism of Locke and the explicit scepticism of Hume. A detailed study of the relations between the epistemology of Mair's circle and of the philosophers of the Scottish Enlightenment would be a valuable contribution to our understanding of the development of philosophy in Scotland.

Unfortunately the valuable gains relating to 'notions' that had been made by Mair's circle, were not reflected in the writings of the later sixteenth century Scottish philosophers. Indeed so little was said thereafter about notions that it is barely possible to say what the term did signify for the later philosophers. And certainly we cannot say whether Crab's concept rather than Lokert's was accepted, or even whether subsequent philosophers knew about that dispute.

Regarding moral philosophy the members of Mair's circle were engaged not only in editing writings of others, but also in producing works of their own. Mair himself wrote a commentary on Aristotle's *Nicomachean Ethics* (Paris, 1530), and Crab[12] and Manderston[13] wrote on moral philosophy, paying close attention to what Aristotle had said, but also venturing into territory which cannot be called Aristotelian. In particular, Manderston's *Bipartitum in Morali Philosophia* repays close study. It is in part a careful exposition with discussion of Aristotle's teaching on the nature of virtue and on the principal virtues. But Manderston was a Christian philosopher and was therefore bound to take seriously certain problems which could not be expected to occur to Aristotle. Manderston was especially interested in problems concerning the application of Aristotelian criteria of voluntariness to the acceptance of articles of faith. For Christian teaching on the role of grace in the acceptance of such articles could not be ignored, and the question naturally arose as to the relation between freewill and grace in the acquisition of faith. The starting point for Manderston's discussion is the thesis of the Oxford Dominican Robert Holkot that every act of believing is caused purely naturally by a motive that necessitates the belief. It is therefore not at all subject to our will whether we believe something or not. But Manderston noted that God commands us to believe, and yet only what can be brought under the will can be commanded.

Hence belief must be subject to the will. Additionally only a willed act can be demeritorious and infidelity is judged demeritorious. Hence infidelity is subject to will and is not due to natural necessity. In the light of these considerations Manderston constructs a subtle and detailed response to Holkot's thesis, accepting the thesis in part and rejecting it for a crucial class of cases, namely those beliefs by which we give willing assent to articles of faith. In the course of his discussion Manderston makes extensive use of the concept of grace, and in particular he makes considerable play with the concept of 'special grace', a kind of help by which God, preceding our will, moves it to produce a good act. Such grace greatly interested Scottish writers. John Ireland wrote a book on it (no longer extant, though we know something of its contents).[14] John Mair refers to it,[15] as does George Lokert,[16] and it even features in Robert Henryson's *The Prais of Aige*.[17] The Scottish interest in the concept of special grace is a curious phenomenon not as yet investigated.[18]

Before we take leave of Mair's circle the character of their writings should here be stressed. All were logicians, perhaps logicians first and foremost, and everything they wrote, even when not formal logic, bears clear evidence of their logical preoccupations. They argued every point, considering objections to their theses, and objections to the objections, and so on, till they were sure that they had provided a sound intellectual basis for their theses. Their writings are therefore discursive. Space was not a consideration; the point was to get at the truth however many pages it took. In this the members of Mair's circle showed themselves heirs to the scholastic tradition. Additionally the Latin they used was the Latin of the schoolmen, with no sign of adoption of the Ciceronian style. But changes were on the way. One pointer is that in 1512 Mair and David Cranston attended lectures on Greek given in the University of Paris by the humanist Girolamo Aleandro.[19] Mair at any rate had clearly come to recognise the advantage of studying Greek philosophers in the original language, and in his last work, the commentary on the *Nicomachean Ethics* of Aristotle, he frequently reveals familiarity with the Greek text.

A second sign of change should here be mentioned, and is more dramatic. It concerns the discursive, argumentative style typical of the schools. A clear example of the change is provided by William Cranston (*c*.1513–1562), a rector of the University of Paris, provost of Mair's former college, St Salvator's at St Andrews, and friend of George Buchanan. In 1540 William Cranston dedicated to Cardinal David Beaton a book *Dialecticae compendium Guilielmo Cranston Scoto authore*, just seven folios in length. In the *Compendium* Cranston offers a diagrammatic presentation of logic. On the first page we are told in a diagram that a term is a subject or predicate of a proposition, and that a term can usefully be brought under one or other of just five pairs of headings, namely, (1) univocal or equivocal,

(2) material or personal, (3) absolute or connotative, (4) common or singular, and (5) name of a name or name of a thing. All other divisions and definitions, Cranston adds, are omitted because they are of little use to philosophers. In this way he disposed of the many expositions by earlier philosophers on the nature of terms, for example David Cranston's very interesting account of a term as 'a part of a proposition from the signification of which part there partially arises the signification of the whole proposition'.[20] William Cranston also lightly dismissed many distinctions crucial to the logic of the previous three centuries, for example the distinction between categorematic and syncategorematic terms, that is, between those terms such as nouns and pronouns, which are fitted to signify something, and those which are fitted to signify in some way (*aliqualiter*), such as the terms in which logicians were particularly interested, 'every', 'some', 'no', 'and' and so on.

A further omission from the *Compendium* is any reference to supposition, and yet many important advances in logic in the high middle ages and the late-scholastic period had related to the concept of supposition. William Cranston is the first Scottish logician to make such a break with the logic of his predecessors and teachers, and he set an example duly followed by many others. An important aspect of this clean break is that Cranston did not merely return to positions won in the earlier middle ages; essentially he went right back to Aristotle's *Organon*. Some elements are not Aristotelian. For example he includes some phrases about the so called 'hypothetical syllogism', that is, a syllogism in which a premiss or the conclusion is not a categorical proposition but is instead a conditional proposition (i.e. of the form 'If P then Q') or is a conjunction or disjunction of propositions (i.e. of the form 'P and Q' or 'P or Q'). Among such syllogisms is the inference from a disjunction, plus the negation of a disjunct, to the affirmation of the other disjunct (i.e. it has the form 'P or Q. Not P. Therefore Q'). Another is the inference from a conditional, plus the negation of the consequent, to the negation of the antecedent (i.e. it has the form 'If P then Q. Not Q. Therefore not P'). On this matter Cranston relies on later writers, but not later than Boethius. In the 1540 edition Cranston makes no reference to Boethius, but five years later he published another edition and there he admits that Aristotle did not write on the hypothetical syllogism, and that on this topic he is relying on Boethius.

There are several interesting differences between the two editions. Cranston evidently came to see that his exposition of logic in seven folios was too terse for those for whom it was written, namely undergraduate arts students, and he greatly increased its length by giving numerous examples both of his various definitions and divisions of terms and also of the varieties of inference which he refers to.

A further distinction is that the discursive style is not entirely eschewed in the later edition. Most notably, before the first of his diagrams Cranston attends to the distinction between the grammarian and the logician. Both deal with language but not quite the same parts of language. The grammarian recognises four levels of complexity, letters, syllables, words (*dictiones*), and propositions (*orationes*). The logician, on the other hand, proceeds from terms to propositions (*enunciationes*) and then to forms of argument. Thus the logician deals with nothing more complex than arguments; nor with anything simpler than terms, and hence he ignores letters and syllables. Cranston does not here spell out the principle of distinction between the domains of logic and grammar. But it is plain that he is relying on the long established doctrine that the logician is interested in things only in so far as they have signification. Thus for the logician the simplest thing in which he has an interest has signification but lacks parts whose signification contributes to the signification of the whole. Thus though the word 'sparrow' has signification the letters and syllables out of which it is composed have no signification which contributes to the signification of the whole. The logician therefore ignores the fact that 'sparrow' contains two syllables. However much Cranston turned his back on the doctrines of his teachers he could not abandon the doctrine that it was signification and not spelling or pronunciation that mattered to the logician.

A further distinction between the two editions is that while the later, no less than the earlier, is essentially a compendium of Aristotle's logic, the later edition names other logicians who influenced Cranston. Porphyry is mentioned several times; Cicero is quoted; and most interestingly the great Italian humanist Rudolph Agricola is also invoked, as for example when Cranston criticises the common mistake of identifying logical separation (*diductio*, i.e. the separation of a 'greater' term into 'lesser' terms) with logical division (*divisio*). For logical separation is in fact of two kinds, division and partition. Division is of a superior term into its inferior terms, for example, the division of 'animal' into 'non-rational' and 'rational'. But partition is of a whole into its parts, whether essential parts (e.g. the partition of something into matter and form), or integral parts (e.g. the partition of a human body into head, chest, shins, and so on). The logically significant point that Cranston is concerned to make here is that in the case of division the greater term is predicable of each of the lesser ones, for example, a rational thing is an animal; but in the case of partition the greater term is not predicable of any of the lesser ones, for example, neither a head, nor a chest, nor a shin is a human body – hence Cranston's reference to Cicero's *Topica* where it is stated that a whole is unlike a genus, for a whole cannot be affirmed of any part taken individually whereas a genus can be affirmed of any member of a species falling under that genus. Cranston is therefore right to deny the identity of separation and division. What is to be noted here is that in support of his position he also refers us to that handbook of the humanists, Rudolph Agricola's *De Inventione Dialectica* (Cologne, 1539) I ch.7 and I ch.9.

The evidence is not sufficiently strong to support the conclusion that between 1540 and 1545 Cranston underwent a conversion to Agricola's assessment of logic. It is possible that his dissatisfaction with the logic of Mair's circle and his consequent acceptance of Agricola's position antedate the first edition of the *Compendium*, though the 1545 edition certainly differs from the earlier one in containing a public declaration of Cranston's humanist sympathies. But whatever the truth of the matter, it is plain that Cranston had a humanist conception of logic as primarily a tool for the orator. Indeed he remarks in the 1545 edition that the only difference between the logician and the orator is that the orator is eloquent. And the extreme brevity of his treatment of logic also indicates sympathy for Melanchthon's criticism of late-scholastic logic as 'wagonloads of trifles'. The many hundreds of rules of inference devised by previous generations of logicians, rules often designed to help logicians to cope with very fine differences of meaning between different terms, could not be expected to help the orator to persuade anyone of anything. The rules were therefore useless and could profitably be ignored. 'Profitably' because logic was a compulsory subject for arts students, and they (and their parents) were increasingly coming to think that much of the time spent on 'logic chopping' should be spent on other things which might better fit the student for the new age. In Scotland no-one moved faster than William Cranston to provide the new kind of textbook required in the changed climate of opinion.

Someone who moved almost as fast was Patrick Tod who in 1544 published *Dialecticae Methodus Patritio Todaeo Scoto authore* (Paris). This book says hardly more than the first edition of Cranston's *Compendium*, though Tod eschews the diagrammatic mode of exposition. Tod's humanist sympathies are clearly expressed in his preface to the reader. There he congratulates his era, in which liberal disciplines are handed down by the revived studies of languages, and very famous authors are brought from the shade to the school, and from darkness to light. The languages in question are of course Greek and classical Latin, and Tod's book is written in Ciceronian style with Greek terms used wherever necessary. He does not claim originality for his book, for his method of composition was to collect some of the more noteworthy things to be found in 'the prolix and excessively verbose commentaries of others'. And indeed there is little in the book that is not to be found in Aristotle himself. Tod discusses the nature of definition, division and argumentation, making Cranston's distinction between division and partition, the two varieties of separation. But whereas Cranston gives five divisions

of 'term' Tod offers six. The extra one is the division of terms into
simple and complex. The only other difference between the lists of
division is that whereas Cranston distinguishes between names of
names and names of things Tod speaks of terms of second intention
and terms of first intention. There is no conceptual distinction here,
but it is interesting to observe Tod using the language of the
schoolmen at a point where Cranston avoids doing so. Thereafter
Tod's *Methodus* provides very brief expositions of the ten categories,
of the kinds of proposition, of the various forms of valid syllogism,
and of other varieties of argument.

Not all of Scotland's renaissance logicians were as terse as William
Cranston and Tod, and here we should note the work of their
contemporary John Rutherford (d.1577)[21] from Jedburgh, friend of
George and Patrick Buchanan, pupil of Nicolas de Grouchy, tutor
in the Montaigne household, and successor to William Cranston as
provost of St Salvator's College, St Andrews. This is not the place
to detail Rutherford's debt to de Grouchy, under whom he and
Patrick Buchanan studied at Bordeaux and whom he followed to
Coimbra, though reference is apposite here to de Grouchy's return
to Ciceronian translation of Greek texts. Nor can we dwell on
Rutherford's opposition to certain Scottish reformers, such as Andrew
Melville of whose Ramist leanings Rutherford was bound to dis-
approve; though it should be noted that Ramus's work influenced
numerous Scots, including John Johnston, Charles Ferme, and the
theologian John Cameron. It is quite likely that, as an anti-Ramist,
Rutherford was in a minority among Scottish scholars.

In 1557 Rutherford published his *Commentariorum de arte disserendi
libri quatuor* (Edinburgh) and in 1577 there appeared a second
edition, this time with a preface containing an effusive reference to
the anti-Stoic Scottish lawyer Edward Henryson. Apart from revealing a friendlier attitude to Plutarch the second edition differs little
from the first. The book, written in Ciceronian Latin with a liberal
sprinkling of Greek, is a commentary on Aristotle's logic. Rutherford
reveals no knowledge of certain important advances gained by his
late-scholastic predecessors, for example, advances concerning the
ordering of terms in a proposition, and in particular the recognition
that it is of the first importance, logically speaking, whether terms
do, or do not, follow given quantifiers or negation signs. Attention
to the ordering of terms was crucial to the development of logic, and
nothing was more damaging for its development than the failure of
the renaissance logicians to hold that crucial advance. Late-scholastic
doctrines on the importance of ordering of terms, and therefore on
the scope of quantifiers and negation signs, were bound up with
their development of the theory of supposition. That latter doctrine
had few defenders among renaissance humanists. It was not, after

all, a doctrine developed or even hinted at by Aristotle. And Rutherford says no more about it than Aristotle does.

This is not to say that Rutherford never strikes out on his own; for example, he is distinctive in listing 'few', 'many' and 'often' (= 'many times') as signs of particularity along with 'some'. But the chief importance of the *Commentariorum* probably lies in its being a particularly fine example of the humanists' attempt to return to the pure thought of Aristotle, to understand him not through the categories provided by the scholastic commentators, but to understand him as Aristotle's own contemporaries might have done. Even Rutherford's examples, which usually have a moral content, unlike typical scholastic examples, follow the humanist pattern. The opportunity to commend civic virtue was not to be overlooked, even in the exposition of the Aristotelian syllogistic.

But Rutherford's respect for Aristotle was not so great as to prevent him criticising the *Prior* and *Posterior Analytics* for being often more difficult than useful, and for being hard to retain in the memory.[22] Rutherford refers several times to the importance of writing what the students can be expected to remember, and he was evidently as exercised by this consideration as William Cranston and Patrick Tod showed themselves to be. It may be speculated that it was through thinking about the philosophers' need to write memorable textbooks that Alexander Dickson came to make a philosophical examination of memory. The influence of Giordano Bruno's memory theories can be detected in Dickson's writings.[23]

One interesting contemporary of Rutherford was the Aberdonian John Dempster (writing under the name 'Johannes Themistor'), whose book *Dialogus de Argumentatione* appeared in Paris in 1554. The book reveals Platonic and Ciceronian overtones, the former because it is in the form of a Platonic-style dialogue, and the latter because of the Ciceronian examples used to illustrate the logical points. But Dempster certainly owes more to Aristotle than to any other classical author. Though the book is on argumentation, it starts by acknowledging that argumentation cannot be the first act of the mind, for an argument is itself a composite collated by the mind; which in turn implies that something had already been grasped by the understanding and recorded in the memory. Unfortunately Dempster does not pause to discuss these interesting matters in any detail, but launches quickly into an exposition of logic. The logic in question is not restricted to Aristotle's system. Dempster has, for instance, a discussion of molecular propositions, conjunctions, disjunctions, and conditionals, in itself an unaristotelian topic. He employs a rather wide concept of conditionality according to which 'if' and 'since' are both signs of conditionality. In fact those two signs have a different logical character, because 'P' follows from

'Since P, Q' but not from 'If P, Q'. However in bringing the two
signs under one heading Dempster was repeating standard medieval
teaching.

But his account of disjunction is more distinctive. A disjunction,
he tells us, is a molecular proposition only one of whose parts is
asserted, and it is asserted in a confused, not a definite fashion.
Thus where 'or' is a sign of disjunction of the kind Dempster
describes, if 'P or Q' is true then P is true or Q is true, but not both.
And additionally 'P or Q' does not give an indication as to which of
P and Q is true – this is what Dempster means by saying that the
part that is true is asserted in a confused fashion. This kind of
disjunction, now called 'exclusive disjunction' (in contrast to 'inclusive disjunction' where it is not ruled out that *both* P and Q are true)
is presented by Peter of Spain in his *Summulae Logicales*, one of the
most influential logic textbooks of the middle ages. But it has to be
said that Peter of Spain's account of disjunction was generally
disregarded by subsequent generations of logicians, in favour of the
inclusive variety of disjunction. It is therefore interesting to observe
this neglected concept re-emerging in Dempster's work.

Dempster's discussion on argumentation focuses on the syllogism.
There he shows independence of mind on two deeply entrenched
matters, one of them of considerable importance. This concerns the
number of figures of the syllogism. The best known syllogism is that
named Barbara by medieval logicians. It has the form 'Every A is B.
Every C is A. Therefore every C is B'. The premisses have a shared
term, the 'middle term' which occurs as subject in the first ('major')
premiss and predicate in the second ('minor') premiss. The predicate
of the conclusion (called the 'major term') also occurs in the major
premiss, and the subject of the conclusion (also called the 'minor
term') also occurs in the minor premiss. An inference whose terms
are arranged in the order just described is said to be a syllogism in
the first figure. A syllogism in the second figure answers to the
description just given except that the middle term is the predicate
in each premiss. For example, 'No A is B. Every C is B. Therefore
no C is A' is a second figure syllogism. A syllogism of the third
figure is like one of the first figure except that the middle term occurs
as subject in each premiss. For example, 'Some A is B. Every A is
C. Therefore some C is B' is a third figure syllogism.

In the *Prior Analytics* Aristotle makes a systematic study of those
three figures of the syllogism, but does not include there any study
of syllogisms of any other figure, nor gives any hint that he thinks
there are any other figures. And almost all medieval and renaissance
discussions of the syllogism follow Aristotle faithfully in this matter.
But there *is* a fourth figure. It is like the first except that the middle
term is predicate in the major premiss and subject in the minor
premiss. Thus 'Every A is B. No B is C. Therefore no C is A' is in

the fourth figure. Some commentators do mention this figure, but only to reject it as in some way or other unsatisfactory. For example, Zabarella complains that it is 'unnatural' to reason with the aid of a fourth figure syllogism, and others said that the figure is redundant, for it is merely a version of the first figure, being much the same as the first figure and differing from it only in that the order of premisses is reversed. But Dempster saw clearly that there is a fourth figure and that it is not simply the same as the first with the order of premisses reversed. He goes on to describe five kinds of valid syllogism in the fourth figure, including 'Every A is B. No B is C. Therefore no C is A', and 'No A is B. Every B is C. Therefore some C is not A'. There are in fact six kinds of valid syllogism in the fourth figure. The one Dempster omitted has the form: 'Every A is B. No B is C. Therefore some C is not A'.

As regards the minor matter on which Dempster did not take the the common line, for centuries the forms of valid syllogism had been given names which were mnemonics containing a rather large quantity of information about the syllogisms named, concerning both the forms of those syllogisms and also the standard way to prove them. These names were obviously invaluable aids to the students studying logic. But one weakness in the mnemonics is that they did not indicate the figure of the syllogism named. Dempster rectifies this state of affairs by constructing nineteen mnemonic names of kinds of valid syllogism. Names for first, second and third figure syllogisms have respectively the initial letters P (for 'prima'), S (for 'secunda'), and T (for 'tertia'); and finally those for fourth figure syllogisms have an initial vowel (the names Dempster gives are Amedes, Amacir, Esarcob, Imacis, and Esiscod). There is no doubt that Dempster's list is more informative than the standard list.

In contrast with the independent minded Dempster was the Aberdonian William Davidson. Active in Paris at the time of the Reformation in Scotland, he remained a Catholic unlike his brother John who became the first Protestant principal of Glasgow University. William Davidson, writing in fine Ciceronian style, gives a luminously clear exposition of the logical writings of the ancient masters, in particular Aristotle and Porphyry.[24] He departs from Aristotle in his choice of examples, where he shows the customary humanistic predilection for formulating arguments about virtue and vice. But the substantial logical points are in every case from Aristotle and Porphyry, whom Davidson had evidently read in Greek, if his liberal use of Greek words and phrases is a sound witness.

In terms of the Scottish tradition Davidson can probably best be classified as in the Rutherford mould. As such he is one of many. There were thereafter a number of Aristotelian purists carefully expounding Aristotle's ideas. Mention may be made in this context of Robert Boyd of Trochrague, Walter Donaldson, Arthur Johnston,

Gilbert Burnet, Andrew Aidie, and Scots associated particularly with Leiden such as John Murdison and Gilbert Jack.[25] At least as regards logic this was the age of Aristotle-as-guru. But despite the adherence to Aristotle there was at the same time a Ciceronian climate of thought. Cicero was frequently named as among the wisest of men, he served as the model for literary style, and logical examples used were of a moral and civic sort of which he could be expected to approve.

After the heyday of the circle of John Mair the dominance of Aristotle's system was increasingly tempered, even in ethical writings, by Ciceronian influences. Nevertheless Aristotelian teaching continued to run deep among even the most independent minded of the post-Mair moral philosophers. One such independent thinker, at least as much his own man in ethics as Dempster was in logic, was Florence Wilson from Moray who, significantly, studied under Hector Boece at Aberdeen before travelling to France. He was familiar with the writings of Erasmus, and of Melanchthon also who seems to have been an important influence on him. He was also familiar with the latest writings of the Italian humanists, and indeed any substantial assessment of Wilson's achievement must take into account the fact that he spent his last few years, from the late 1540s, within a circle of humanists, many of them Italian, at Lyons which then had the nearest thing in humanist France to Plato's Academy.

Two books by Florence Wilson should here be mentioned, on the face of it very different in character, though in fact saying rather similar things and certainly animated by the same insights and attendant passion. One, *Commentatio Quaedam Theologica* (Lyons, 1539), is an overtly devotional work, much of it in the style of a litany, laying stress on man's absolute dependence on God: 'O my mind, thou art indeed subject to God, thy salvation is indeed from Him, He is assuredly thy Father who possessed, made, and created thee' (p.6); we who are mortal and made from gross visible matter do not clearly discern the invisible God, powerful king of the ages – 'wherefore to You, immortal invisible king, God alone, let all the honour be and all the glory' (p.9). God's utter otherness is stressed. For example, Wilson repeats Boethius's doctrine, which subsequently received its classic formulation in Aquinas's *Summa Theologiae*, that there is neither past nor future in relation to God, but in a single eternal vision He sees all things which occur separately in the flux of time (pp.13–14).

This God is sometimes spoken of by Wilson in humanistic terms, as when he calls Him 'the highest Jupiter' (p.31) and 'ruler of immense Olympus' (p.8). But He is the Christian God, and in Wilson's main work, the *Dialogue on the Tranquility of the Mind (De Animi Tranquillitate Dialogus)* (Lyons, 1543) knowledge of Him is identified as the goal of man. The title is suggestive of Boethius's

*The Consolation of Philosophy*, and one might reasonably regard Wilson's book as a sixteenth century version of Boethius's master-piece. The problem Wilson addresses is that of securing a tranquil mind, that is, a mind steadfastly at peace and devoid of a tumult of passions. The efficient cause of this happy state is the 'sedation' of the passions (p.19). Here Wilson takes issue with the Stoics, though elsewhere their influence on him is strong. For he attributes to them the view that all passions are bad, and that view he thinks absurd. Tranquillity does not involve a total absence of the passions, but an absence of a 'tumult of passions'. On this matter he judges 'our Aristotle' to have 'by far the more humane' position, for he prescribes moderation of passions, not their privation (p.47), in which context Wilson invokes Plutarch's rhetorical question: the passions are part of our nature, and who except the impertinent would call nature the author of evil? (p.48).

All this is at a very high level of abstraction, and Wilson seeks to make the *De Animi Tranquillitate* a practical handbook by listing a number of classical precepts and discussing each in turn, for example: 'We should not judge to be proper to us, or to be ours, what are alien to us'; 'Shamefully and in vain do we seek rest in external things'; 'Vainglory disturbs the peace of human society and impels to every sort of injury'; 'Since you are the servant, not the master of providence, obey willingly and cheerfully', this last precept leading to the unclassical injunction to despise death. As the departure of the mind from the body, death is not an evil – a position that Wilson sets in the context of a Christian piety which endures hideous suffering unto death, and which thereby leads to a likeness to Christ. Not surprisingly, in the light of this last consideration, Wilson shows little enthusiasm for physical pleasures and none at all for those of touch and taste, since these do not contribute to the likeness to Christ which he enjoins. Pleasures of the mind are however another matter. Nevertheless we must not court suffering for its own sake. Suffering 'is not consistent with the happiness of life now or in the future. For it greatly impedes contemplation and the study of wisdom, in which happiness has been placed' (p.212).

It will be plain that Wilson writes as a theologian no less than as a philosopher, and in certain areas, such as the one I have just expounded, the resultant synthesis has strong Thomist overtones. But we must not forget that Wilson, though very much a renaissance figure, was not a reforming spirit. Theologically, at least, his sympathies lay with the old order.

The judgements of the previous paragraph do not so comfortably fit the last of the philosophers to whom I shall turn, Robert Balfour (d. *c.*1625) from Tarrie in Angus, who studied under Rutherford before going to the Collège de Guyenne in Bordeaux. Through Rutherford he is connected with Nicolas de Grouchy (whom he quotes) and he shares with both men a deep respect for the *ipsissima verba* of Aristotle. His two main philosophical works are both commentaries on Aristotle,[26] written in an exuberant rhetorical style. Balfour, who was as much at home with Greek as with Latin, quotes in Greek a wide range of Hellenic and Hellenistic authors from Homer to Philo Judaeus and Plotinus, and his numerous references to Latin writers include many to such important renaissance figures as Agricola, Valla, and Ramus.

Balfour had a good deal to say on the topic of the usefulness of logic, a topic on which renaissance philosophers laid great stress. The splendour of logic, Balfour affirms with a typical flourish, illuminates all parts of philosophy. When he considers the arts attentively there is just one, logic, which by the light of its doctrine sheds light on all the others. It informs, that is, gives form to the method of enquiry of the other disciplines, (a point on which Ramus had laid great emphasis), and it aids the making of sound connections and the exposing of 'monstrous and false connections'.[27] In certain areas Balfour goes beyond Aristotle's logic, as for example when he discusses, though unreliably, the fourth figure of the syllogism. Little of the important innovative work of the medieval logicians, particularly in the fields of supposition theory and exponibles, finds a place in Balfour's Commentary. He does however include brief discussion of the characteristically medieval ideas on ampliation, for example in his discussion of the convertibility of propositions when he speaks of valid inferences involving premisses which are not in the present tense; and indeed Balfour's illustrations had been in common use in medieval logic textbooks, e.g. 'Every harlot was a virgin. Therefore someone who was a virgin is a harlot'.[28] His discussion is however a pale reflection of the subtle and complex discussions on ampliation to be found in the writings of his medieval predecessors.[29] But it was a major aim of Balfour's to draw attention to Aristotle's text, and he no doubt judged that inclusion of substantial sections of innovative medieval material would have had the opposite effect.

The same desire to retain Aristotle's text as the focus of attention also helps to shape Balfour's *Commentary* on the *Nicomachean Ethics*, though there are nonetheless matters of interest to us in that *Commentary*. But first Aristotle's ethics have to be placed in the context of Aristotle's account of the four kinds of cause. The four are (1) the final cause, which is the end to which a thing is drawn by its nature, as the seed is drawn to the flowering plant that it will become by nature; (2) the efficient cause, which precedes its effect and pushes it into a changed state, as for example the falling raindrop bends the leaf it strikes; (3) the formal cause, which is the nature or essence of the thing, as for example a man's rationality is his formal cause, for he is essentially a rational animal; (4) the material cause, the matter out of which a thing is formed, as marble is the material cause of the statue. Balfour begins by stating that for Aristotle the final cause of good acts is happiness – that is what they aim at by nature. The efficient cause is right reason, or will governed by right reason. (It later becomes plain that Balfour wishes to say that it is will governed by right reason, and not right reason as such which is the efficient cause.) The formal cause is virtue, which is a disposition to act according to a principle given by right reason; and the material cause of good acts is desire or passion. Balfour evidently approves of this account of the four causes of good acts. It is to be noted that like Florence Wilson he is no despiser of passion. He regards it as a part of our nature and bad only if not moderated by reason. In its moderated state it takes its place along with reason in good acts. As regards this aspect of Balfour's philosophy a question can be raised, with which there is not space to deal here, concerning a possible influence on Balfour by the anti-Stoic lawyer Edward Henryson whom Balfour's teacher Rutherford so admired.

Balfour's interest in the utility of intellectual disciplines, which emerges in his *Commentary* on Aristotle's logic, re-emerges in his *Commentary* on Aristotle's ethics. His defence of moral philosophy is vigorous: no part of philosophy is more fertile or more fruitful than ethics, which supplies us with the idea (*ratio*) of living well (p.11). Its teaching, placed in us by nature, assists and increases the seeds of the virtues.

Many passages in Aristotle's *Nicomachean Ethics* which had attracted the close attention of previous generations of commentators go entirely unremarked by Balfour. Certain of these silences are surprising in view of the facts (1) that some of the passages in question have an immediate and important bearing on law, and (2) that in many places Balfour reveals a lively interest in legal writings (ecclesiastical as well as civil). I shall mention one example. Balfour attends to Aristotle's discussion (*Nicomachean Ethics* III 1) on excusing conditions. A person is excused if he is compelled by force to do something bad, as when someone, pushed by another, suffocates an infant. He is no more thought blameworthy than a person is thought meritorious if against his will he does good, as when someone falling from a height destroys a tyrant. Ignorance also can excuse. But Balfour accepts that if a person does wrong in ignorance and is the author of his ignorance then by law he should be punished. This is *ignorantia affectata* and it does not excuse. There are, then, two kinds of ignorance, (1) that of which we are the author, and (2) that of which we are not the author. As regards (2) we deserve mercy and pity rather than punishment if we perform a bad act in that state. As regards (1) we are not excused if our ignorance is due to drunkenness or passion that we have brought upon ourselves, or if it is due to our negligence as when we neglect to learn something we ought to have known. Balfour mentions the law as a case in point, but immediately adds that 'a scrupulous and curious knowledge of the law' cannot be demanded of everyone. Boys, soldiers, and women are excused if they are ignorant of laws (p.159) – presumably of some laws; even boys, soldiers, and women can be expected to know that murder and theft are illegal. Now, in the course of his discussion on this topic Aristotle distinguishes between acts which are involuntary and those which are non-voluntary. He argues that every act done by reason of ignorance is non-voluntary; it is only what produces pain and repentance in the agent that is involuntary (*N.E.* 1110b18–19). This passage led to important medieval discussion on the relation between knowledge and the will, and in this context we find Aquinas, for example, spelling out and applying a distinction between antecedent, concomitant, and consequent ignorance,[30] by which distinction he is able to display the strength of Aristotle's position (though weaknesses of Aquinas's own application of that three–fold distinction remained to be exposed).

Despite Balfour's failure to capitalise on these insights, it has to be said that in general his commentary, twice the length of Aristotle's *Ethics*, is a careful exposition and close analysis of the text. An additional merit in his commentary is that the great panache and elegance of the writing would be highly attractive to students and would draw them on to a study of the *Ethics* itself.

Balfour's work is an excellent representative of philosophy in renaissance Scotland in that an assessment of his philosophy can fairly be projected onto that wider canvas. The chief question to be asked is whether the renaissance was a time of gain or loss for philosophy in Scotland. I think the answer should be that it was a time of both these things. The loss lies in the fact that valuable advances made by scholastic philosophers were not only not capitalised on, they were in many cases ignored altogether. Some of these advances have had to wait till this century to be rescued from oblivion. On the other hand, the abandonment of so many good ideas was in part the outcome of the humanists' drive for the establishment of accurate editions of the writings of the Greeks and Romans. Identifying Aristotle as *the* philosopher, quite as much as the schoolmen did, they sought (unlike the schoolmen) to return to his system and see it in its pristine state uncluttered by the accretions of centuries of speculative endeavour. Hence, as I mentioned at the start, we find Robert Rollock, first principal of Edinburgh University, giving lectures which consisted largely of dictation of the newly edited Greek texts of Aristotle. The establishment of critical editions of the works of the classical philosophers has to be judged a good. I do not know how to measure the long term gain and loss. But as regards the period I have been covering, it seems to me plain that the early part of the sixteenth century, when John Mair and his circle were active, constitutes a period of valuable achievement in Scottish philosophy. But additionally there can be no doubting the immense debt owed to the humanists for their endeavours to give philosophy a fresh start by returning directly to the classical masterpieces. John Mair, a restless searching spirit if ever there were one, asked 'Has not Amerigo Vespucci discovered lands unknown to Ptolemy, Pliny and other geographers up to the present? Why cannot the same happen in other spheres?'[31] Mair could hardly be expected to approve of the content of much humanist philosophy – he was after all one of its chief targets. But the intellectual drive to get at the truth and the belief that Aristotle was an irreplaceable guide in that search, were things Mair shared with his humanist successors. Though I cannot say whether the gains of the humanists outweighed the loss of much marvellous work done by the scholastics, I hope at least to have shown that for the whole of the sixteenth century Scotland produced philosophers who are worth our close attention. A history of sixteenth-century Scottish culture that failed to take into account the contribution of the philosophers, would give a seriously misleading picture, as would a history of Scottish philosophy that did not place considerable emphasis on the achievements of that century. The Scots, a nation of philosophers, did themselves justice in the Scottish renaissance.

## NOTES AND REFERENCES

1. For bibliographical details on all these men see A. Broadie *George Lokert: Late–Scholastic Logician*, Edinburgh, 1983, ch.1, and *The Circle of John Mair*, Oxford 1985, ch.1; and J. Durkan 'Robert Wauchope, Archbishop of Armagh', *Innes Rev.*, 1, 1950, 48–65.

2. *Quadrupertitum in oppositiones conversiones hypotheticas et modales*, Paris, 1510, reprinted 1516.

3. *Tripartitum epithoma doctrinale et compendiosum in totius dyalectices artis principia a Guillelmo Manderston Scoto nuperrime collectum*, Paris, 1517, reprinted 1520, 1523, 1528, 1534.

4. See e.g. N. Kretzmann 'Incipit/desinit' in P. Machamer and R. Turnbull (eds) *Motion and Time, Space and Matter*, Ohio State University Press, 1976; E.J. Ashworth 'The doctrine of exponibles in the Fifteenth and Sixteenth centuries', *Vivarium*, 11, 1973, 137–67; P.T. Geach, 'Comparatives' *Philosophia*, 13, 1983, 235–46.

5. See *George Lokert* ch.3 and *The Circle of John Mair* ch.6.

6. George Lokert, *Scriptum in materia noticiarum*, Paris, 1514, reprinted 1518, 1520, 1524, *c*.1535; Gilbert Crab, *Tractatus noticiarum*, Paris, 1503, reprinted 1505, 1507, 1515; David Cranston, *Tractatus noticiarum*, Paris, 1517.

7. A. Broadie 'Medieval notions and the theory of ideas', *Proc. Aristotelian Soc.*, 87, 1986–7, 153–67.

8. Crab. *ibid. sig.* a ii recto.
9. Mair *Termini*, Paris, 1501, *fol.* 7 recto.
10. Lokert, *ibid. sig.* a ii recto.
11. Mair, *ibid. fol.* 2 recto.
12. Crab, *Tractatus terminorum moralium*, Paris, *c.*1512, reprinted *c.*1513, *c.*1514.
13. *Bipartitum in morali philosophia*, Paris, 1518.
14. C.B. Macpherson (ed.), *John Ireland: The Meroure of Wyssdome*, Edinburgh, 1926, i, 48.
15. Mair, *In secundum sententiarum*, Paris, 1517, *fols.* 120 verso–127 recto.
16. Lokert, *Scriptum in materia noticiarum sig.*, d ii verso.
17. G.G. Smith (ed.), *The Poems of Robert Henryson*, Edinburgh, 1908, iii, 109, lines 17–20.
18. For some preliminary remarks see A. Broadie, 'William Manderston and Patrick Hamilton on freewill and grace', *Innes Rev.* 37, 1986, 25–35.
19. A. Renaudet, *Préréforme et Humanisme à Paris*, Paris, 1953, p.614 fn.
20. *Sequuntur abbreviationes omnium parvorum logicalium collecte a magistro Anthonio Ramirez de Villascusa cum aliquibus divisionibus terminorum eiusdem: necnon cum tractatu terminorum magistri Davidis Cranston ab eodem correcto*, Paris, *c.*1513, *sig.* d ii.
21. For bibliographical and other details see J. Durkan, 'John Rutherford and Montaigne: An early influence?' *Bibliotheque d'Humanisme et Renaissance*, 41, 1979, 115–22.
22. Rutherford, *Commentariorum*, 2nd edition p.45.
23. J. Durkan, 'Alexander Dickson and STC 6823' *Bibliotheck*, 3, 1962, 183.
24. *Gulielmi Davidson Aberdonani Institutiones Luculentae iuxta ac breves in totum Aristotelis organum logicum*, Paris, 1560.
25. For details see Paul Dibon, *L'enseignement philosophique dans les universités Néerlandaises*, Paris, 1954.
26. *Commentarius R. Balforei in Organum Logicum Aristotelis*, Bordeaux, 1616; *R. Balforei Scoti Commentariorum in lib. Arist. de Philosophia Tomus Secundus quo post organum logicum quaecumque in libris Ethicorum occurrunt difficilia dilucide explicantur*, Bordeaux, 1620.
27. *Commentarius*, p.4.
28. *Ibid.* p.461.
29. See A. Broadie, *The Circle of John Mair*, 76–82.
30. *Summa Theologiae*, 1a2ae,6,8,c.
31. Mair, *In Quartum Sententiarum*, Paris, 1519, *fol.* 55.


BIBLIOGRAPHY

Balfour, Robert, *Commentarius R. Balforei in Organum Logicum Aristotelis*, Bordeaux, 1616.
——*R. Balforei Scoti Commentariorum in lib. Arist. de Philosophia Tomus Secundus quo post organum logicum quaecumque in libris Ethicorum occurrunt difficilia dilucide explicantur*, Bordeaux, 1620.

Boece, Hector, *Explicatio quorundam vocabulorum ad cognitionem dialectices conducentium opera Hectoris Boethii philosophi insignis in lucem edita*, Paris, c.1519.

Broadie, Alexander, *George Lokert: Late-Scholastic Logician*, Edinburgh, 1983.
——*The Circle of John Mair: Logic and Logicians in Pre-Reformation Scotland*, Oxford, 1985.
——'William Manderston and Patrick Hamilton on freewill and grace', *Innes Rev.* 39, 1986, 25–35.
——'Medieval notions and the theory of ideas', *Proc. Arist. Soc.*, 87, 1986–7, 153–67.
——*Introduction to Medieval Logic*, Oxford, 1987.
——*Notion and Object*, Oxford, 1989.

Crab, Gilbert, *Tractatus terminorum moralium*, Paris, c.1512.
——*Tractatus lucidus terminorum*, Paris, 1524 reprinted 1527.

Cranston David, *Tractatus insolubilium magistri Davidis Cranston*, Paris, c.1512.
——*Tractatus noticiarum*, Paris, 1517.

Cranston, William, *Dialecticae compendium Gulielmo Cranston Scoto authore*, Paris, 1540, reprinted 1545.

Davidson, William, *Gulielmi Davidson Aberdonani Institutiones Luculentae iuxta ac breves in totum Aristotelis organum logicum*, Paris, 1560.

Dempster, John, (Johannes Themistor) *Dialogus de Argumentatione*, Paris, 1554.

Dibon, Paul, *L'enseignement philosophique dans les universités Néerlandaises*, Paris, 1954.

Durkan, John, 'John Major: after 400 years', *Innes Rev.*, 1, 1950, 131–9.
——'The school of John Major: bibliography', *Innes Rev.*, 1, 1950, 140–57.
——'Alexander Dickson and STC 6823', *Bibliotheck*, 3, 1962, 183.
——'John Rutherford and Montaigne: An early influence?', *Bibliotheque d'Humanisme et Renaissance*, 41, 1979, 115–22.

Galbraith, Robert, *Quadrupertitum in oppositiones conversiones hypotheticas et modales Magistri Roberti Caubraith omnem ferme difficultatem dialecticam enodans*, Paris, 1510, reprinted 1516.

Liddell, James, (Jacobus Ledelh) *Tractatus conceptuum et signorum*, Paris, 1495, reprinted 1497.

Lokert, George, *Liber Posteriorum*, Paris, c.1520.
——*Tractatus exponibilium*, Paris, 1520.
——*Sillogismi Georgii Lokert*, Paris, c.1522.
——*De oppositionibus*, Paris, 1523.
——*Termini Magistri G. Lokert*, Paris, c.1523.
——*Questio subtillissima de futuro contingenti*, Paris, c.1524.

Mair, John, *Inclitarum artium ac sacre pagine doctoris acutissimi magistri Johannis Maioris . . . Libri quos in artibus in collegio Montis Acuti Parisius regentando compilavit*, Paris, 1506, reprinted Lyons 1508.
——*Introductorium in Aristotelis dialecticen totamque logicen Magistri Johannis Maioris*, Paris, 1508, reprinted 1509, 1514.

——*Ethica Aristotelis peripateticorum principis. Cum Io. Maioris theologi Parisiensis commentariis*, Paris, 1530.

Manderston, William, *Tripartitum epithoma doctrinale et compendiosum in totius dyalectices artis principia a Guillelmo Manderston Scoto nuperrime collectum*, Paris, 1517, reprinted 1520.
——*Bipartitum in morali philosophia*, Paris, 1518.
——*Tractatus de futuro contingenti*, Paris, 1523.

Rutherford, John, *Commentariorum de arte disserendi libri quatuor*, Edinburgh, 1557, reprinted 1577.

Tod, Patrick, *Dialecticae methodus Patritio Todaeo Scoto authore*, Paris, 1544.

Wilson, Florence, *Commentatio Quaedam Theologica*, Lyons, 1539.
——*De Animi Tranquillitate Dialogus*, Lyons, 1543.

# The Physical Nature of Man: Science, Medicine, Mathematics
## ALEX KELLER

'Driven by that desire to see foreign parts, which may be detected in outstanding talents, as a young man he sailed to Gdansk', wrote the German scholar Caselius of Duncan Liddel, who had just returned to Scotland after seventeen years teaching at a north German university (Liddel, 1608:f.17v). In very many cases longing for the wider prospects of Continental universities led Scottish students, after graduation at home, to finish their education abroad. But, often, like Liddel, they then took posts on the Continent. That makes the intellectual history of Scotland quite different from that of England in the sixteenth century, and indeed from most European countries beside. When James VI set out from his capital of Edinburgh, to claim his English throne, among his subjects abroad were Alexander Anderson and David Sinclair teaching mathematics in Paris, Robert Balfour teaching at Bordeaux, Liddel teaching mathematics at Helmstedt, then a new university founded by the duke of Braunschweig; the king's physician John Craig had in the past taught (Liddel, among others) at Frankfurt-an-der-Oder. That year would also find Thomas Seget and John Wedderburn studying medicine at Padua. Two other medical men, Peter Lowe and William Barclay, had but recently returned from spending much of their careers in France – Lowe had in 1600 obtained the king's charter for the guild of physicians and surgeons he had founded in Glasgow. Others had preceded them in France, Germany, Italy: like James Bassendyne, or as he called himself in France, Jacques Bassantin, astronomer; others continued the tradition, like Duncan Burnet, who graduated in medicine at Helmstedt the year after Liddel returned to Scotland, and subsequently wrote a textbook of medical chemistry. Virtually all hailed from in or near east coast ports. In Gaelic-speaking areas, medical learning was still being handed down from father to son, and few studied at foreign universities, never mind teach there. Hence many texts were translated into Gaelic, and although many Gaelic physicians knew Latin, and shared one common heritage of Greek and medieval medicine, they were much less affected by the advance of humanism in the sixteenth century, or by the innovations that slowly altered the face of medical science (Bannerman, 1986).

The latter half of the sixteenth century and the opening years of the seventeenth mark the opening moves in that great switch in the perception of the external world which we call the Scientific Revolution. As the schools of medicine were the best places, almost the only places, to pursue the investigation of the natural world, despite what seems to us their conservatism they were the testing grounds for new ideas and practices: in a way the change began as a change in the way medicine was taught. The humanist approach implanted in these institutions the desire to go back to their Greek roots, to recover what the old masters had really taught, and accept them as guides (Wear, 1985; Webster, 1979). But the humanist physician soon realised that Galen and Hippocrates had learnt their medicine from observation, from the accumulation of case histories, from dissection even; and resolved to follow them in their method of acquiring knowledge also. From Hippocrates, they could learn that natural causes constantly produce the same effects, so that the same symptoms indicated the same diseases. More optimistically, they would also assume that a cure which had worked once would always work – but trying to fit these cures into a simple scheme of the hot and the dry, the cold and the moist, and the four humours, blood, yellow bile or choler, black bile, phlegm, they thereby justified a pharmacology which was in fact quite fanciful. If the opinions of Galen, Hippocrates or Aristotle were accepted without reservation, innovation could be stifled, new ideas rejected out of hand. In so far as humanism lived with a sense of awe before the achievements of Antiquity, it acted as a brake on change – yet humanism often had actually inspired those changes, those critical and rationalist attitudes. In Scotland where the northern Renaissance arrived relatively late, the rediscovery of Antiquity was seasoned from the start with a certain relish of experience, and a willingness to adopt Continental novelty.

Students would meet these issues at universities and schools. Since Antiquity, the seven liberal arts, clearly distinct from those merely mechanical, had formed the core of higher education. They prepared the mind for philosophy, and for the studies that led to the three learned professions. Four of the seven were mathematical; arithmetic, geometry, music and astronomy. All were firmly rooted in classic sources, indeed the sixteenth century saw renewed interest in Ancient mathematicians like Archimedes and Apollonius: both were discussed and defended by Alexander Anderson and David Sinclair at Paris. When James Melvill first studied at St Andrews where some books of mathematics, at least 'the treatise on the Sphere, likewise Perspective and the beginning of geometry' had been on the syllabus since its foundation (St Andrews Univ. 1964:15), he learnt no more than that. But at Glasgow, he found that after his uncle Andrew Melvill's reforms, 'the Elements of Euclid, the Arithmetik and Geometrie of Ramus, the Tables of Hunter, the Geographie of Dionysius, the Astrologie of Aratus' were all studied (Melvill, 1829:38–39). At Marischal College, Aberdeen, the original regulations of 1593 called for the third regent to expound, 'geography, chronology and the principles of astronomy' (Henderson, 1947:18). Medicine too was usually treated as part of the general education provided by the universities. King's College, Aberdeen had a 'medicinar' on its books for many years, indeed. But only one distinguished himself as teacher or writer. In practice, the system of regenting meant that nearly all students acquired a smattering of mathematics and physiology. For those who wanted to steep themselves in these sciences, even to obtain a medical degree pure and simple, the great medical schools of the Continent beckoned. That absence of specialisation had its advantages, too; the same man, John Craig, might make a discovery in trigonometry, experiment with magnets, debate new ideas in cosmology – and explore which were the most suitable drugs for particular diseases. Robert Balfour, who published a number of Ancient Greek literary and philosophical texts, could also edit an astronomical work, the *Meteora* of Cleomedes.

At Padua, at Paris, at Montpellier and elsewhere, however, the profession of medicine was coming to demand a long and intensive study. Only those who had devoted themselves to learning all that had ever been known on the subject were truly entitled to practice. At first their learning was primarily taken from the ancient texts, although the teachers' own successes, derived from their erudition, of course, both complemented the knowledge of the texts, and reinforced their reverence for the Prince of Physicians – a title awarded both to Galen, and to Hippocrates. This was the 'Lumbard leid' of the older Continental medical schools, which enabled a Damian to impress James IV; and persuaded the Archibishop of St Andrews to call upon the famous Milanese physician Cardano for a consultation. The Renaissance marks the definitive arrival on the European scene of the graduate physician, who employed the arguments of humanism to establish his status. Medieval authorities were not, it is true, rejected altogether, although often criticised for corrupting the pure stream of the original doctrine. But medical scholars did stress that their predecessors in past centuries had after all acknowledged that they built on Ancient foundations – so why not go back wherever possible to what the founders had written? Many of their texts had been ignored, or even unknown: now, rediscovered, let them be studied, edited, translated into Latin. Over the years, the Italian humanist physicians gave the precedent for the organisation into colleges, which insisted that only those who had thus gone to drink at the first source could know how to diagnose, prognose, and cure. As physicians began to band together to protect their qualifications, they urged that only those who shared their learning should be allowed to treat the sick. Those who lacked such a training could not cure, and should be permitted to practise only under the supervision of physicians, as surgeons, midwives, and apothecaries. Previously health care had been in the hands of diverse practitioners – not least the unlearned 'wise women' of the countryside, with their extensive unwritten traditions of herbal cures and spells (Wear, 1985; Webster, 1979).

To the modern eye, humanist medicine looks no less like sympathetic magic, and was equally dependent on traditions, hallowed only by their long usage, about the curative virtues of plants. However, to the university graduate of that time, he alone had founded his knowledge in study and theory; all others were, as an Aberdeen physician put it, 'barbarous apothecaries, high-land leeches, impostors and mountebankes' (Barclay, 1615). The surgeons in particular resented this and sought to establish their own credentials as educated practitioners, distancing themselves from mere barbers. In 1505, when there were still few physicians trained on the Continent in Scotland, the barbers and surgeons of Edinburgh in fact tried to impose standards of entry that would pre-empt their critics, demanding that those who would practise their art should know the 'anatomell, nature and complexioun of every member of humanis bodie,' specially 'all the vaynis of the samyn' requisite for phlebotomy. As part of their training in anatomy, the guild would receive the cadaver of one condemned man each year, for dissection, 'quhairthorow we may haif experience, ilk ane to instrict utheris' (Comrie, 1927:59–60).

The regular study of anatomy was eventually to challenge the authority of the Ancients. More intense study of the Ancient herbal materia medica also revealed that many plants used by the Greeks were not to be found in northern Europe, while many employed locally in the north had been unknown to Galen and other Greek writers, familiar only with the Mediterranean flora. Realising this, Renaissance doctors did seek to identify and expand the resources of materia medica, looking ever further afield. Thus an Aberdeen doctor could provide Alpine botanists like Bauhin and De L'Obel with specimens from the Scottish Highlands.

The revival of Hippocratic doctrines might also promote interest in environmental medicine. In *Airs, Waters, Places*, Hippocrates had portrayed the effects of climate and situation in the preservation of health, and the relative prevalence of diseases in particular areas. However, even when they were right in their conviction that certain environments were unhealthy, humanist doctors were ignorant of the causal factors involved, and perhaps their assumption that major outbreaks of disease were due to disruption of the balance of climate, and the generation of miasmas, may have hampered them in their attempts to cope. But anyway, no amount of academic restoration, or even anatomic and botanical progress, really affected their inability to cure the terrible epidemics that still afflicted Europe.

Bubonic plague still ravaged the population. Even if the devastation was seldom as terrible as in the original attack of the Black Death, yet few towns could hope to survive quite unscathed for much more than a decade. Pandemics which killed more than a tenth of a town's inhabitants in a few months were not uncommon – 1427 are said to have died of the plague at Perth in 1584/5 – perhaps a sixth of the population (Shrewsbury, 1970:256). It is true that evidence suggests that these plagues were restricted to Edinburgh and other east coast ports, and a few places in the south. However, that evidence is often taken from the regulations which burgh councils drew up to confront the danger, so the apparent immunity of remoter parts of the countryside may be an illusion created by want of information, rather than a genuine freedom from plagues. Pestilence was not necessarily bubonic; winter outbreaks might really be typhus, spread by body lice in the overcrowded quarters of the urban poor.

The Renaissance had inherited from the past one idea that was of some merit in controlling such plagues, perhaps not very effectively, but better than nothing; the idea of infection, which implies that the spread of disease can be prevented if the infected are stopped from infecting further. Ideas of contamination are no doubt very old, and so too are methods of purification by washing or heating. But medical rationalism gradually replaced concepts of pollution by the concept of infection through the transmission of material agents of disease, which might be through touch, or through food and clothes handled by those who bore the infection. In the Italy of the Renaissance, medical schools began to persuade governments that plagues might be held at bay if the traffic in goods which passed on the disease could be blocked. They inspired the institution of quarantine legislation and the setting aside of isolation centres where those who were suspected of coming from a plague stricken area could be detained until they either developed plague, or did not. Those who had plague, if it did break out, despite these precautions, were to be confined to plague hospitals or lazarettos, more to keep them from contact with the healthy than in any hopes of curing them. Health certificates, signed by a town official for travellers to present to the officials of the next town on their road, assured them that no cases of plague were notified there.

In Scotland, the quarantine concept was introduced before the end of the fifteenth century, when the islands of Inchkeith and Inchcolm in the Firth of Forth were designated as holding stations for suspect ships, their crews and merchandise. A pretty unpleasant haven that was sometimes, where sick and hungry crews lay for weeks, while the goods they had brought rotted in the hold. When plague broke out in Edinburgh, both sufferers and those who had been in recent contact with them were despatched to the Burgh Muirs, living wretchedly in huts until they recovered, or perished. To discourage further contact between those banished and the unaffected, a gallows was set up. Various *ad hoc* measures were codified in Edinburgh by the Statute of Pestilence of 1568. These regulations impose isolation by draconian penalties, hanging, branding, drowning, for any who infringed them. When plague struck the south, Aberdeen erected a gallows at the Bridge of Dee, and threatened to hang anyone who tried to trade with the town, when it was forbidden. Once, in Edinburgh, a man was hanged for concealing a case within his family; fortunately for him, the rope broke, and as he was a poor man with a large family, his life was then spared (Comrie, 1927:79–91; Shrewsbury, 1970).

This is the background to the first medical tract to be printed in Scotland, Gilbert Skene's *Ane Breve Description of the Peste*, printed in Edinburgh in 1568 (Skene, 1568). Skene (1522–99), a native of Aberdeen, was at the time medicinar of King's College, but some years afterwards he moved to Edinburgh, where his book had been printed. He explains how the plague had 'laitly enterit in this realme', and that he had sought to put at the disposal of ordinary people the best of 'the sentence and judgement of the maist ancient writaars in medicine'. In view of the decisions taken by the Edinburgh council that year, it is interesting that he says little about the need to prevent infection. The plague, he declares, is in the first instance, God's will, a divine punishment for sin. Then, it was an astrological phenomenon, 'as quhan the maist nocent sterres to mankynd convenis . . . or quhan cometis with other wikit impressionis ar generit'. But then there were terrestrial factors, which explain why particular towns, countries, or even families are hit, when neighbours escape. That enables him to offer good Hippocratic doctrine; that plagues are caused by 'standand Vatter sicas Stanke Pule or Loche most corrupte and filthie: Erd, Dung, stinkand Closettis, deid Carionnis unbureit in special of man kynde', all made worse by continuous rain, south winds, vegetables decaying in the street. All these things produce 'corruptible humoris'. Wet springs and long, warm, humid summers are therefore the signs that plague threatens. He paints indeed a grim picture of the nastier and smellier side of Renaissance life.

Nor was he too far off the mark in pointing to filth as the enemy's stronghold. In 1530 Edinburgh had ordered citizens to clean out their drains; and later decreed that all dogs and swine were to be kept off the streets (Comrie, 1927:83). Nobody however thought directly about the rats which so prospered in the muck. Perhaps Aberdeen's relative immunity was, all the same, due less to declarations of the fate which would meet unwelcome visitors, than to the stone houses, and the absence of comfortable thatch, because, so an old belief went, 'in this cuntry na Rattoune is bred, or brocht in . . . their may lyve' (Comrie, 1927:91). In a pre-microscopic era, microbial agents of disease were unknown, as were their vectors. As rats did not brush up against people in the street, as stray dogs and pigs might do, they were not realised to be a crucial link in the chain of transmission. As for the humanist Skene, he could recommend various complex drugs; one is attributed to a 'well learnit medicinar (the flour of Italie in his time)', which suggests Skene had studied there himself. He also prescribes an aromatic fumigation, relying on the story that Hippocrates had held off the influence of pestiferous winds with the smoke of fires.

As if longstanding terrors like the bubonic plague, that 'evell miserable tiran and manslayar', as Skene calls it, were not enough, the Renaissance was attacked by a new, highly infectious disease – syphilis (Comrie, 1927:45–49). Aberdeen was one of the first town councils in Europe to devise measures, in 1497, to fend off an ailment which was perceived almost immediately to depend on sexual contact. Perhaps more recent panics allow us to see why they decided that 'all licht women be chargit and ordanit to desist fra thar vicis and syne of venerie', under pain of branding (Aberdeen, 1844:425, 437). Then the council thought the disease came from France. A few years later they believed it a 'strange seikness of Nappillis'. Nevertheless, the grandgore, or French, or Neapolitan, or Spanish evil – every nation in Europe blamed it on their neighbours – did still get a foothold, and King James IV dispensed largesse to a number of victims. In 1600, there was sufficient concern over an outbreak in Glasgow, for the burgh council to call a meeting, at which all 'chirurgeons and professors of medicine' in the town were to attend to give their advice. Their leading member, Peter Lowe, had four years before published a tract on *An Easie Certaine and Perfect Method, to Cure and Prevent the Spanish Sicknes*, in London. Lowe calls himself there Arellian, perhaps from Errol (Lowe, 1596). He had been practising in France and Flanders for many years, and the book makes several references to his French, specially Parisian, experience: he had served the Spanish troops helping the Catholic League at the siege of Paris (1590–1). Lowe remarks that 'Nature by reason of appetite and inclination to carnall copulation doth argue (the more is the pitty) the universal raigne and common infection of this contagious disease throughout all Nations'. And he sees little hope of control that way. Indeed he claims that prostitutes are less likely to transmit the disease than others, because not being emotionally involved, they are less 'hot and do not pass the venom'. He acknowledges that the disease is divine punishment, but will not 'intermeddle holy things with prophane', and no more need be said on that account. His mention of astrological theories is even more perfunctory. So he can concentrate on what he regards as the direct causes, because once they were removed the disease could be cured. These are external: infection by sexual contact, since these parts of the body are 'of rare flesh and spongious . . . by frication they are easily heated and rarefied, and the sooner infected'; but also by kissing, suckling from an infected nurse, sitting on a privy used by an infected person, or even inspiring their breath (here Galen's views on infection could be adduced in support), or treading barefoot where an infected person has spat on the ground . . . An 'internal' cause might be 'corrupted meates that doe engender a putred phlegmaticke nurature'. In an interesting comment on the relative susceptibility of different persons to the same disease, he observed that out of 35 clients of a certain Parisian prostitute, only 7 actually took the 'Spanish sicknes', all 'cold and weake men of complexion'.

His book includes nine supposedly successful treatments, all by then established, but here given as part of elaborate successive administrations. The following year, 1597, he produced his *The Whole Course of Chirurgery*, describing himself as a fellow in the college of surgeons at Paris, and in the service of King Henri IV (Lowe, 1597). This is an extensive survey: what surgery is, what it treats – everything from cancer (of which he admitted that most forms were incurable) to false teeth (then 'seldom used'). With this book he published his translation of the Presages, usually called the Prognosticon, of Hippocrates, together with the Hippocratic Oath. This is the first English translation of any of the Hippocratic books, which Lowe made from a contemporary French version. He dedicated his book to king James, and was back in Scotland within the year. In 1599 he was condemned to 'stand at the pillar' apparently for something he said, and then fined for his disrespectful and, no doubt, irreverent and impenitent posture there. A certain rationalist temper breathes through his 'Chirurgerye', like the 'Spanish Sicknes': for instance, speaking of a formula, almost a prayer, which the famous Italian physician Cardano had prescribed, he remarks, 'This forme of cure by words I do not alledge here so much for any effect I look shall ensue thereupon as to content a number of ignorant, arrogant people', who feel there must be a cure for every ailment, and so will have recourse to these (Lowe, 1612:183). A man who had healed the wounded of both sides in the French Wars of Religion was perhaps unlikely to accept easily any party's ecclesiastical discipline. At all events in March 1599 he was appointed municipal physician at Glasgow, and was one moving spirit behind the burgh council's decision that too many 'medicinars and chyrurgianes quha dayele resortis and remanis within this towne' are not really fit, so that a proper organisation should limit the practice to those who were. In the upshot, a guild was duly chartered by the king in 1600, to be administered by Lowe, now the king's chirurgiane 'and chief chirurgiane to our dearest son the Prince'. He and the university of Glasgow's professor of medicine, Hamilton, were to examine all who wished to operate as doctors in the Glasgow region, who must produce a 'testimonialle of ane famous universitie quhair medicine be taught', or at least a recommendation from the king's principal physician. The guild was also to supervise all drugs sold by the apothecaries of the area. This charter is the definitive triumph of academic, learned medicine. But Lowe himself had dealt with much that elsewhere was medical rather than surgical in his books, and he succeeded in avoiding the bitter and somewhat absurd conflicts between physicians and surgeons that soured the practice of the healing arts at Paris and London (Finlayson, 1889).

While at Glasgow Lowe brought out a second edition of his surgery book toward the end of 1612, including a few case histories from his Scottish practice: he died soon after. During the next decade another French-trained physician, William Barclay, published in Scotland three medical pamphlets. Like Lowe, he had spent 'thirty years' peregrination' and like Lowe believed the methods taught in France and Italy were superior to anything in Britain, and should be introduced there. 'Happy the land that has no need of physicians', he exclaims, but since we must have them, let us have the best, 'who can show publicke testimonie of his lawfull calling'. He too had been in England for he refers to the execution 'in Queen Elizabeth's time' of an impostor, who claimed to be the Son of God. But he also had a literary career as a humanist: having studied at Louvain with Justus Lipsius, the most eminent classical scholar of his generation. Barclay's notes on Tacitus' Agricola were printed as an appendix to one of Lipsius' editions of all the works of Tacitus (Irving, 1839:230–3).

This literary training gives Barclay's writing a charmingly baroque flavour. His earliest pamphlet after his return to Scotland was devoted to a new drug, tobacco, which he wished to fit into the accepted framework of Hippocratic therapeutics, by then somewhat modified by new chemical theories. His *Nepenthes, or the Virtues of Tobacco* was printed by Andrew Hart in 1614, prefaced by a 'Merie Epistle' to Hart. Barclay claims that the work was written at the instance of a lady, 'the very Juno of our Ile', presumably the L.E.L.L.F., to whom he dedicated one of a number of brief Latin poems at the end of the book. Barclay was aware that his theme was 'so odious to princes': the king had composed his Counterblast to Tobacco but ten years before. But after all, 'one man's meat is another man's poyson'. If the king might find it disgusting, it could still be good for others in moderation. Tobacco, he decides, is 'the Mercure of vegetals': it can be taken in infusion, decoction, as smoke, as a salt; or the whole leaf, which could be folded into a ball and taken in the open mouth, the patient laying face down. That will encourage salivation, which he holds is a good way to rid the body of unwanted humours, and an excellent treatment for epilepsy. Apart from smoking tobacco in a pipe, however, his favoured technique was 'suffumigation' – the inhalation of the smoke. If Hippocrates had cured hysteria with the fumes of burning feathers or cobblers' waste, and later medieval medics had used other, more aromatic fumigation, why not the smoke of tobacco – which could help cases of phthisis or asthma . . . However the tobacco in this treatment was to be mixed with ambergris, pleony, stirax, musk, aloe-wood and 'magisterium cranii humani' – a heady mixture!

His other two pamphlets were devoted to medicinal springs in the east of Scotland. Baths and wells like these had been popular with the Romans, but the discovery and exploitation of new wells became an enthusiasm of the Renaissance, when sizeable books assessed them, discussing the particular ills they could alleviate, and trying to put them in the context of Classical science. Those who wanted a naturalistic explanation of these healing powers tended to argue that such properties are transferred to the water from minerals in the surrounding rock. Hippocrates' *Airs, Waters, Places* supplied the foundation, which later authors developed. As the sixteenth century drew on, this interpretation took up some of the ideas of Paracelsian chemistry. Even those many medical men, whose humanist sympathies would not let them accept Paracelsus' rejection of the heritage of Antiquity, could agree on the utility of chemical and mineral resources for pharmacology. Then the waters' mysterious virtues could be explained in terms of admixtures of the seven metals, or the presence of the old alchemists' principles, mercury, sulphur and salt. Vague as these concepts might nowadays appear, in comparison with their precise modern signification, they seemed then coherent and useful and within the general Hippocratic view of nature.

One of the first wells to be publicised in Britain was 'The Well of the Woman Hill Besyde Abirdene' as it is called in *Ane Brief Descriptioun*, possibly written by Gilbert Skene, and printed in Edinburgh in 1580 (Well of the Woman Hill, 1580). The well had only been in use for a few years, but the author declares that 'Medicinall and philosophicall doctrine' shows how valuable 'bathis and mineral wateris' can be. This particular well has a laxative effect, and is therefore also 'womative' (i.e. vomitive, emetic). A local brewer 'quha laitly causit brew Aill of this watter' found that no beast would touch it. That hardly seems much of a recommendation, but the author takes this as confirming his view of its laxative character. And then, an unpleasant taste has ever been held desirable in medicines. Comparison is made with a Belgian spa, whose water likewise tastes, as if 'brint with irin'. The association is demonstrated by a kind of chemical analysis: the water leaves deposits, 'the ane in colour sad blew, which promises irin, the other red declining to yellow', which suggests brass. Boiling gives another, darker colour, which he takes as more evidence of iron, but the laxative property implies brimstone. *Airs, Waters, Places* is cited to show that water which passes easily through the system must be laxative, and diuretic, generally dissolving obstructions, so that it will be good for sore eyes too, for catarrh, 'dolour of the Tonsillis', ailments of nerves, stomach, bladder, 'sterilities contractit be suffocation of the barne bed' – Hippocrates' *De Sterilibus* can be cited in support – paralysis, scabs . . . Dosage should be adjusted for age and degree of ill health, and under supervision. Taking the water should not be a substitute for medical advice: indeed, he ends with the hope some 'leirnit physician' will be able to add to the list of diseases cured.

Sure enough, thirty five years later, in 1615, Barclay published his new account of the same well, picturesquely entitled *Callirhoe or the Nymph of Aberdene resuscitat* (Barclay, 1618). He recounts how Hippocrates in *Airs, Waters, Places* enjoins the doctor to explore his area for the qualities of its waters. Between Pentland Firth and the Firth of Tay he has found the best of waters to be at Aberdeen. And very fortunate that it is there and not at some 'beggerly village' (like the original Spa – or Forges, in Normandy, which he thought this well resembled). The Highlanders are 'strong, rude, cruel, longliving laborious and leacherous' which he attributes to their climate, and to their diet of 'milk, cheese, butter, fleshes, oate breade (I will remit the matter of aqua vitae to another place)', and so suffer only from colds and catarrh. The Lowland area, on the other hand, open to north and east, would be cold and moist and by Hippocratic criteria very unhealthy. Yet men can overcome these disadvantages. 'In spight of Aeolus and all his winds', the people of Aberdeen 'do so civilize their burgh with the continual practise of Vertue and learning that, if their soyle were not more barren and barbarous than their soules, even a Frenchman might judge Aberdene to be the Lutetiola of this Septentrionall corner of north Britaine'. His exposition of the qualities of the well owes something to his predecessor, but reveals a stronger tincture of Paracelsian chemistry. Thus he uses a test for vitriol which Paracelsus had popularised, throwing a nutgall into the water, for that alone will 'draw a scarlet colour out of a nutgall like clared wine' and will leave a red residue after distillation, another technique brought into medicine by the Paracelsian school. Although he is convinced of the presence of iron too, it is the vitriol which makes the water a powerful solvent of all obstructions, and so it 'revives weake spirits, weak stomach and languishing appetite', as it dissolves, even if he fears it would not work against serious gallstones or arthritis.

Three years later he published an account of *The Nature and Effects of the New-found Well at Kinghorne*, in the form of a letter to the Chancellor, the Earl of Dunfermline (Barclay, 1618). The booklet explains that all such wells derive their 'spirituall energie and a certain subtile Mercuriall substance' from some metal, which in this case must be tin. For 'the whole fornace of the Paracelsians keep it as a great secret in their Philosophical exhalations' that salt of tin is good for the kidneys: and this water, being highly diuretic, is good for the kidneys: it is aperitive and detersive (cleansing). All these he claims to be virtues of 'Saturn', specifically of *Saccharum Saturni* – unfortunately Saturn was the symbol of lead, not tin, and 'sugar of Saturn' is lead acetate. But the very rock looks to him clear evidence of tin, being 'as it were, embrodered and pessimented with white laces of clear and chrystalline stones'. Then – the definitive touch – when distilled the water leaves a 'salt unsalt, white like Chymic salt which is unsavorie'. Once satisfied as to the metallic content, he can pronounce the effective component 'a Mercurie quintessenced from Tinne' and so also sudorific, good like that of Aberdeen for a wide variety of ailments, small kidney stones and other nephritic problems, it 'bindeth' the belly of most drinkers', but 'louseth the belly of some', helps internal ulcers, poor sight, and used as a cosmetic for the female complexion, 'it polisheth their faces, removeth all blots and furrows, leaveth no frumples in the skinne'.

When the barbers and surgeons of Edinburgh in 1505 were also expected to know 'in quhilk members the signe hes domination for the tyme' (Comrie, 1927:59), and classical explanations for the plague had to seek at least a partial answer in the skies, astrology was evidently a key to much of medical practice. All the principal organs of the body, all the senses were ruled by their planets and houses, all disequilibria of humours might have origins in some occult influence of the stars. In the writings of Lowe and others toward the very end of the century a sceptical note is to be heard, but even they did not reject astrology root and branch. Personal difficulties and political destinies were governed by these factors no less than health and sickness. When challenged that his prophecy of the fall and captivity of Queen Mary was 'false and ungodly' the astrologer James Bassendyne insisted that his art is one of 'the naturell sciences that ar lawful and daily red in Christian universities'. His own *Astronomique Discours* (1557) was written as he pointed out, to assist in astrological predictions, although it was a straightforward account of *astronomy* as then understood. Any scholar knew that the same Claudius Ptolemy who in the 2nd century AD had compiled the masterwork of Ancient astronomy, had also established the foundations of astrology in his 'Tetrabiblos'.

The seven planets – Moon, Sun, Mercury and Venus nearer, and Mars, Jupiter and Saturn beyond – circled around the Earth, which

Ptolemy could prove must be in the centre of the universe. Each was carried on a rotating sphere; beyond Saturn, furthest and most sluggish, lay the sphere of all the fixed stars, also turning around the earth every day. No change of any kind could take place in this celestial world; planets and stars were 'impassive', and suffered none of the growth and decay, birth and death, that prevail in our inferior earth, at the bottom of the universe. As this system implies that planets in their spheres are always at the same distance from us, and always turn at the same speed and in the same direction, Ptolemy had to posit secondary circles, epicycles, to account for the fact that the planets do vary in apparent magnitude, appear to halt in their tracks and even loop the loop, moving backwards and changing in latitude. This was the accepted procedure which enabled astronomers in fact to account for the observed positions and predict future ones, as Bassendyne sets it forth. And this was the cosmos which has become so familiar to us from the literature: so Gavin Douglas pictures it in his 'Palice of Honour':

> The air, the fire, all the four elementis,
> The spheiris sevin, and primum mobile,
> The signes twelf perfitelie everie gre,
> The Zodiak haill as buikis representis,
> The Pole Antartick that ever himself absentis,
> The Pole Artick and eik the Ursis twane,
> The sevin starnis, Phaton, and the Charlewane,
> . . . . . .
> Of planeitis all the conjunctiounis,
> Thair episciclis and oppositiounis,
> War portrait their, and how thair coursis swagis,
> Thair naturall and dylie motiounis,
> Eclipsis, aspectis and digressiounis,
> Thair saw I . . . . . .

Looking for a system of the world that would be physically simpler and mathematically accurate, Nicolaus Copernicus proposed in his *De Revolutionibus Orbium Coelestium* (1543) that all these difficulties could be avoided if the sun rather than the earth was conceived to be the centre of planetary motion, and the earth was itself a planet. Few could then be found to accept this revolutionary idea. A second edition in 1566 however, if it did not convince many, did put Copernicus' hypothesis more firmly on the agenda. Significantly, copies of this edition now in the four university libraries of Scotland were in the hands of Scots by about 1600. Edinburgh University's copy belonged to John Craig, James VI's physician, and passed from him to James Douglas, the king's secretary. It contains a number of notes, which do not originate with Craig, who never became a Copernican, but were copied by him from those of his teacher Paul Wittich (Gingerich and Westman, 12:53–4).[1] Craig had gone to study at Koenigsberg in 1564, then moved to the new Lutheran university at Wittenberg, moved again to Frankfurt-an-der-Oder in 1573. After studying with Wittich there he himself taught logic and mathematics from 1580, in which year he also took his medical degree at Basel. His only published work is his doctoral thesis on the nature of the liver (Craig, 1580).

Wittich had become interested in the need for a reformed cosmology through his work with the Danish astronomer Tycho Brahe. Although convinced that Copernicus' theory was a physical impossibility, Brahe was in his own way a scientific revolutionary too. When a new – quite unknown – star appeared in 1572, he realised that Aristotle and Ptolemy had been wrong to suppose that no change could take place in the heavens. A star had appeared from nothing, had grown, diminished, finally vanished. Its failure to reveal any parallax showed it must be among the fixed stars; throughout its existence it had always kept the same angular distance from its neighbours. The only bodies in the sky that were previously recognised as coming and going were comets, which were for that reason assumed to be meteorological phenomena, at the least nearer to us than is the Moon. Brahe resolved to check up on the next comet to appear. He persuaded the king of Denmark to grant him the island of Hveen, with income enough to construct the finest observatory that had been seen in Europe until then, so that he could carry out a precise survey of planetary movements, that should enable him to re-found the whole of astronomy. His Star Palace of Uraniborg became the first research centre, admired throughout Europe. When Craig returned to his native land in about 1583, he had hoped to visit Brahe, but bad weather prevented him (Brahe, 7:175). In 1587, however, Brahe did receive another young Scot, Duncan Liddel. Born in Aberdeen in 1561, Liddel went to Gdansk in search of learning in 1579, travelled on to Frankfurt where he studied with Craig; from there he moved on to Breslau, to study mathematics and physics with Wittich, as we are informed in a letter from Caselius, which prefaces Liddel's medical textbook (Liddel, 1608). The Aberdeen University Library's copy of the 1566 Copernicus was his, and also has notes copied from Wittich. He also acquired a copy of the first edition, to which he added notes and diagrams of his own. Returned to Frankfurt he began to teach 'out of Euclid Ptolemy and Copernicus'. When the town was visited by plague Liddel moved to Rostock, where he met some of the leading astronomers of Germany, but it seems they were 'less knowledgeable in those hypotheses' of Copernicus, which Liddel expounded to them. While at Rostock, he made a personal copy of Copernicus' first essay of his hypothesis (Dobrzycki, 1973:124). That was the year of his visit to Brahe, who discussed with Liddel his own new hypothesis, a compromise whereby the Sun went round the Earth, but all the planets, the Moon excepted, travelled round the Sun, which thus carried them around a central and immobile Earth. Brahe pointed out that when in opposition to the Sun, parallax argument shows that Mars must then be closer to the Earth than the Sun is, so that its 'sphere' must intersect that of the Sun.

In Rostock Liddel had been 'the first in Germany to teach the theory of celestial motions according to both Ptolemaic and Copernican hypotheses'. Now Brahe wrote to Liddel congratulating him on having picked up his theory so well, and thereafter Liddel taught this third theory too. From his annotations, it is clear that he continued with his own astronomical observations.

Meanwhile Scotland and Denmark had been drawn together by the negotiations for the marriage of James VI. On his journey to fetch his bride in 1590, the king himself visited Brahe, and left a Latin eulogy, which the Danish scholar could use to preface his next book. In an English poem, James praised what he saw at Uraniborg:

> Looke Tichoe's tooles; there finelie shall be founde
> Each planet dansing in his propre spheare.

Earlier, one of the king's envoys about this marriage had gone to see Tycho and on his recommendation, Brahe sent to Craig a copy of his new book *De Mundi Aetherei Recentioribus Phaenomenis*, in 1588 (Brahe, 4:515–8). Here he maintained that comets too are above the Moon, and cut through at least one planetary sphere, so 'spheres' must be fictitious. Craig's reply is full of thanks but disagreed with Brahe's conclusions. For him the impassivity of the heavens was a fundamental assumption of natural philosophy, which could not be abandoned just because Brahe had been unable to perceive any adequate parallax in the movements of comets. For all his flowery compliments, he did regard Brahe's doctrine as quite ridiculous, and Tycho felt he was being ticked off sarcastically like a naughty schoolboy. He replied in kind, and several letters passed between them, in which courtesy and sharp comment alternate (Brahe, 7:passim). Really, Craig was out of his depth; his mathematics was quite good, but his astronomy was not. Clearly, specialisation was beginning to replace the belief that one could know all the arts equally well.

As he acknowledged, 'more is spent here on rhubarb and senna than on all the revolutions of the planets' (Brahe, 7:176): there was no Uraniborg at Edinburgh. He always asked Brahe about his chemical investigations, and sought to exchange views on various recent medical experiments in that field. But he could not see what to Brahe was the main issue. In 1592, while apologising that the distractions of his medical practice kept him from astronomy, he could still write, 'yield therefore and embrace the truth, and do not try further to add new stars to the sky; why should you disturb the tranquil Aether?' (Brahe, 7:335).

Meanwhile Liddel had his troubles with Tycho Brahe as well. In 1591 duke Julius of Braunschweig offered him a post at his new university of Helmstedt; at first to teach medicine and later mathematics. Seven years later Brahe was informed through his kinsman Holger Rosenkrantz that whereas at Rostock Liddel had always attributed this 'third system of the world' to Brahe, now at Helmstedt he was giving out that he had thought of it independently himself. In fact it seems from a letter of Craig that both Liddel and he had toyed with their own hypotheses, but had never elaborated or published them (Brahe, 7:193). But Brahe readily believed what he was told and complained bitterly to his friends and correspondents. He felt that Liddel had only pretended to acknowledge the Dane's priority; now that he had a secure post, he let it be known the idea was really his. Brahe even found evidence of Liddel's supposed duplicity in the official lecture programme, which refers to the rival systems as Ptolemaic, Copernican, and 'that which Tycho describes in his book' on comets – as if Tycho had merely discussed the theory, not invented it. Actually, Tycho never did work out his thesis in detail in a book specifically devoted to it. At all events Tycho saw here only craftiness: *O! astutule et nasutule Scotule* (Brahe, 8:185), he exclaims, to imply what you dare not assert outright. Liddel, when he heard of Tycho's complaints, wrote to him in 1600, to deny any such intention: Brahe passed the letter on to Johannes Kepler, the most brilliant of his associates, but it has not been published. Liddel continued a successful career at Helmstedt, rising to be pro-rector. Then, after visits to Scotland, 'either at the request of Craig or other friends, or motivated by natural love for his country' he resolved to return to Scotland in 1607. First he made arrangements for the publication of his *Ars Medica*. This introduction to the study of medicine was apparently based, as his opening remarks indicate, on lectures at Helmstedt. Indeed, the text evolved out of theses defended by his students, which then normally reflected closely their tuition. The book is introduced by a letter to Craig from Caselius, a German scholar, which outlined Liddel's life, and is dedicated by Liddel to King James, observing that wise kings 'preserve letters in splendour and erect Schools and Academies at great expense'. King James, he is sure, will thus 'revive that glory for piety and erudition, extinct in some parts of your kingdoms for many centuries'. That sounds almost like a plea to the king to found chairs for such as Liddel. Liddel may have planned to develop a school of medicine and mathematics at home, and gave Marischal College money for scholarships, and for a chair in mathematics, which would be one of the first in Britain; the incumbent was to be 'well versed in Euclid, Ptolemy and Copernicus, Archimedes and other mathematicians' (Russel, 1974:154–6). However he died in 1613, and the university was unable to establish his chair until 1623.

After Brahe died in 1601, leadership in astronomy passed to Kepler, who devoted the next decade to solving the problems set by Brahe's observations, in order to construct a cosmology that would match the data. The result was his *Astronomia Nova* of 1609, in which he put forth (amid much else) the first laws of planetary motion. The next year he was shaken, and excited, by a little book handed to him by his friend Thomas Seget, of Seton near Edinburgh. This book, *Sidereus Nuncius*, was the work of a Paduan mathematician, Galileo Galilei, who there published the discoveries he had made with a new instrument, the telescope. He had seen, for instance, that the Moon's surface was pitted with hollows, which he took to be seas, and studded with mountain ranges, whose height he could estimate. He had seen a vast number of stars, previously invisible: most important, four of them accompanied the planet Jupiter in its orbit round the sky, revolving round Jupiter as they did so – just like the Moon in the Copernican system. Seget, the intermediary between Galileo and Kepler, studied first at Edinburgh, then at Leiden with Justus Lipsius, was at Louvain in 1597, and moved on to Padua the next year. His *Liber Amicorum*, or collection of autographed inscriptions (quite a common practice then among young men on an intellectual grand tour of Europe) contains several well known names. Unfortunately, Seget was involved in some serious trouble at Padua. Details are obscure, but seem to be linked to secret visits to a nunnery. He spent some two years imprisoned before the British ambassador could get him released, on condition that he left the city (Favaro, 1911:xxv). He went to Prague, where he became friendly with Kepler. Having known Galileo too, he was a natural choice to present Galileo's book, for which he composed a poem of praise. Kepler records that Seget observed the skies with him that autumn of 1610, as they searched for Jupiter's satellites. Once Seget asked him whether he saw the divine hand in this welter of new discoveries. The next year, however, Seget went to Poland; he may have been back in Prague for a while, but he reappears in 1627 when he registered at Leiden University to study law. Perhaps to support himself, he translated into Latin a book on contemporary Italy, but died just before its publication at the end of 1628 (Rosen, 1949).

Meanwhile Galileo had another Scottish admirer, who was to take the same road from Padua to Prague; John Wedderburn of Dundee (Favaro, 1911:xxvi). Wedderburn also registered as a student at Padua in 1598, and remained there. In 1610 he took part in the storm of controversy that broke over the *Sidereus Nuncius*, by answering a persistent critic and foe of Galileo, Martin Horky. For his *Quatuor Problematum quae Martinus Horky contra Sidereum Nuntium de Quatuor Planetis Novis Disputanda Proposuit, Confutatio* (Wedderburn, 1610;

Galileo, 3:147–178) tells us something of the ferment excited at
Padua by the telescope's new worlds, and serves as a philosophic
defence of what Galileo had revealed. In reply to Horky's sneer that
Galileo presumed to see what no-one else – not even Tycho Brahe
– had ever seen, Wedderburn explains the power of the telescope,
which had produced an entirely new situation. Now 'time will teach
us, and the daily discovery of new things . . . for therein lies the
whole beauty of every instrument' (Galileo, 3:163). That the purpose
of instruments was to find out new things, was itself a startling new
idea. So Wedderburn could use his book to make known Galileo's
continued progress: how he had modified his device to look at
objects close by, but too small for normal vision – what the next
generation would call a microscope. Through it Galileo had found
that a certain insect has 'an eye clothed in a membrane . . . pierced
by seven holes like a knight's visor'. Wedderburn explains too how
Galileo could measure subdivisions of a degree, using brass strips
across his lens, taking the Moon's diameter as his gauge. In answer
to Horky's second problem, Wedderburn shows that these four little
stars with Jupiter must be truly moons, not just fixed stars lit up by
Jupiter as it passes them. And when in his fourth problem Horky
demanded what use these satellites could be, Wedderburn replies
sarcastically that they are good for 'exercising, tormenting and
troubling those who, like you, superstitiously try to apply every
least twinkle in the sky to particular effects, and would like to rule
the free will of men' (Galileo, 3:178). Thus the faint light of Praesepe
had been imagined to presage poor eyesight, but now Galileo
showed it was really a congeries of very bright but tiny stars. With
Wedderburn then the march of science begins to overthrow astrology
and old error. Still a humanist by training, he saw that the
fundamental beliefs of Antiquity might have to be cast aside. The
future, no longer the glorious past, was to be arbiter now.

After Galileo moved to Florence, Wedderburn transferred to Prague,
where he too made friends with Kepler; one of Kepler's correspondents, writing in December 1613, asks to be remembered to Seget
and 'Waterborn'. In the dedication of his *Nova Stereometria* of that
year, Kepler refers to Wedderburn as 'my very close friend' (*mihi
amicissimus*), as well as an excellent mathematician (Kepler, 9:10)
By this time he was personal physician to Prince von Lichtenstein.
He retained property in Dundee and donated money for the Sang-
schule there, but stayed on in Moravia, where he is last heard of,
still practising medicine, in 1628. Perhaps it was through his
influence that his cousin Sir John Wedderburn acquired the 1566
Copernicus now in St Andrew's University Library. Even by the end
of the sixteenth century Copernicus had won another Scottish
adherent in David Sinclair, who was then teaching at the Collège
Royale, at Paris. He owned the 1566 Copernicus now in Glasgow

University Library, and in a different manuscript he calls Copernicus 'venerable', speaks of him as establishing 'the admirable structure of the universal world machine' and succeeding 'in a most faithful demonstration of phenomena . . . supported by his hypothesis as a sure foundation'. However, some might view these changes in our world picture with concern. William Drummond of Hawthornden is witness to the scepticism such discoveries inspired. What had been known for sure for thousands of years was now in doubt. '. . . the Earth is found to move, and is no more the Center of the universe, is turned into a Magnes; Starres are not fixed, but swimme in the etheriall Spaces, Cometes are mounted above the Planetes; some affirme there is another world of men and sensitive Creatures, with Cities and Palaces, in the Moone; the Sunne is lost, for it is but a Light made of the conjunction of manie shining bodies together . . . is observed to have Spots . . .'

Probably it was astronomy that prompted the most striking innovation to emerge from the seedbed of Scottish humanism, the invention of logarithms. At all events, the inventor, John Napier of Merchiston (1550–1617) singles out 'both kinds of trigonometry' as likely to benefit, and that was – as Bassandyne and all other astronomical writers make clear – primarily studied as the foundation for celestial observation. Many of the examples which Napier uses to show the applications of logarithms are taken from spherical trigonometry. His English translator stresses their employment in navigation, but Napier himself, although interested in technological improvements, seems to have pursued mathematics for pure pleasure.

Indeed, he stands apart from all that has been said of medical and mathematical scholarship. He never held an academic position: sent to St Salvator's College, St Andrews, he declares that there 'in my tender years and barneage' he acquired that passionate conviction in matters of religion which he always retained. But he did not graduate. His uncle Adam Bothwell urged his father to 'send your sone Jhone to the schuyllis: over to France or to Flanderis, for he can leyr na guid at home . . .' That was three years before John went to St Andrews in 1563 (Napier, Mark:67). But if he went on to some Continental study, we have no positive evidence for it, and he was back in Scotland, which he apparently never left again, by 1571. All the correspondence that survives relates to family business, as he was heir to substantial estates, often at loggerheads with neighbours – and occasionally within the family too . . . He married twice, and had in all twelve children, and for some twenty years after his first marriage lived in quiet obscurity on his estate at Gartness.

Suddenly, in the 1590s, he figures prominently in political and religious conflicts. He was a representative of Edinburgh in Assemblies of the Kirk, and in 1593 a member of the delegation to urge the king to act more rigorously against the Catholic nobles. That year he published his first book, *A Plaine Discovery of the whole Revelation of Saint John*. In his dedication to the king he takes up the theme of the delegation, urging him to purge his Court of all 'Papists Atheists and Neutrals'. Napier felt the Reformation in danger, and was concerned that the two Protestant peoples of Britain were still threatened by Spain, and by the foes of the Reformation at home. So the *Plaine Discovery* concludes, at least to the author's satisfaction, that the Antichrist of Revelation is none other than the Pope. Many others must have been satisfied too, for there were translations into French, Dutch and German. However politically biased, the book does show that Napier was a man of immense erudition, well read in Classical sources, not just biblical exegesis, and aware of such local antiquities as a Roman inscription lately unearthed at Mussel-burgh. His political fervour, and fears aroused by dangers that apparently threatened Reformed Christianity, provided a motive too for an attempt to turn his learning to military account. In June 1596 he sent on to the English government a list of 'Secrett Inventions' intended 'for the defence of this Iland'. The first was a 'burning mirrour', for which he asserted he could provide 'proof and perfect demonstration, geometricall and algebricall', to focus the sun's rays 'in one mathematicall point', to set light to the rigging of enemy ships. If need be, 'some materiall fier or flame' could substitute for the Sun. Although he does not mention it, this idea had for centuries been used to explain the destruction which Archimedes wreaked upon the besieging Roman fleet at Syracuse. Then, he had thought of a piece of artillery which 'shott, passeth not linallie . . . destroying only those that stand in the randon thereof, and fra them forth lying idely . . . but passeth superficially, ranging abroade within the appointed place' (Napier, Mark, 2478). Sir Thomas Urquhart's reference to Napier's secret weapon, which was worked by 'vertue of some secret springs and inward resorts' suggests this might have been a mine, carried on a vehicle or boat, and timed to explode at the right moment. The fireship with which the citizens of Antwerp blew a hole in the bridge of boats which the besieging Spaniards had thrown across the Scheldt, could be described in similar terms; it too was fired by 'secret springs and inward resorts', and Napier would have known of it. Despite Urquhart's less plausible tale of a test in which sheep and cattle were killed, 'whereof some were distant from other half a mile on all sides, some a whole mile' however, Napier talks of 'a piece of artillery', which suggests rather a cluster of guns rotating on a turntable, with some reloading mechanism, such as appears in manuscripts of fifteenth century inventions of war machines. The same might be said of the 'round chariott of mettle' which could move forward, driven by the soldiers within, to break up the enemy's ranks, or if stationary, wear down attacks 'by continuall charge and shott of harquebush through small holes': that sounds very like a well known Leonardo da Vinci drawing, as do the 'devises of sayling under water' to which Napier also refers. Whether Napier had really tried out, or constructed his inventions, is doubtful – he does say he will not only need God's help, but 'the worke of expert craftsmen'. Napier's inventions may have inspired those which Drummond proposed, to help another Protestant 'crusade', the relief of La Rochelle. As with Napier's these too have a whiff of the library about them, in their classical Greek names: they may have been deadly in conception, but there was a long step between thought and action.

More surely Archimedean in inspiration is a peaceful invention, of a 'hydraulic screw and ingenious turning axle, which would at each revolution raise water more copiously and easily than pails or pumps or any instruments hitherto used in Scotland'. With this, Napier hoped to drain flooded mines; he was to receive 10 marks for each screw pump employed. This is evidently an Archimedean screw, so where the novelty lay is not clear – probably in the *axis versatilis artificiosus*, for even if these screw pumps had not been used in Scotland, there was much enthusiasm for them in sixteenth-century Europe, as a piece of Ancient cleverness, associated with the name of the greatest mathematician of Ancient Greece. (*Register of the Great Seal*, 6:172). But little evidence as to their acceptance by miners or mineowners survives. Nor do we know how widely another Napier innovation was practised, for which his son Archibald received a patent in the same year, 1598. This was a programme of salting fields of grain or pasture, as a fertiliser. The idea is worked out in detail, the quantities specified, as are the hours of the day which cattle are to spend in a succession of grazing 'parks', and subsequently in the common-fold from which their presumably salt-rich dung is to be collected. Did the average herdsmen of the day really note what o'clock it was? Perhaps Napier's concern for precision in time was somewhat too exacting? (Napier, Mark, 1834:284–7).

He remained active in public affairs, at least on a municipal level, well into the next century, presumably until failing health prevented him. In 1608, he inherited the estate. It may be that he now resolved to publish the work on logarithms which had been on his mind for so many years. Anxious about the reaction of mathematicians to the ideas of this amateur, he may like Copernicus have hesitated before he dared expose to criticism what for him was love, not business. He had his own professional friends: one of the poems printed in honour of his *Description of Logarithms* was by Andrew Young, an Edinburgh university teacher, who carried out some astronomical observations (Russell, 1974:125–5). Napier also knew John Craig. Craig had been working on tables of sines at least since the late 1580s. Tycho Brahe, in one of his first letters to Craig, thanks him

for 'certain compendia of Triangles' although, 'where the first
number is a whole sine', he was familiar with the material. But he
asks for further information, when properly worked up, specially
on 'that invention which by you is called the Geometrical Helix'
(Brahe, 7:196). In a reply, Craig enquires about errors in the tables
of sines, because 'something singular I have to hand ("*notis singulare
quiddam prae manibus est*") in perfecting of which this table (or rather
"*Canon*") proffers vast riches'. Evidently these questions were already
under discussion at Edinburgh. What was the 'something singular'?
Some procedure on which Craig was working, or do we have
evidence for an early stage in Napier's calculations? There can be
less doubt over a later comment of Craig, however. In a letter of
March 27th, 1592, he writes, 'A wonderful Canon is being constructed
here by a certain noble kinsman of ours, who has enough leisure and
talent for such a great task; when it is perfected, it will be communicated to you'. (*Canon mirificus a generoso quodam consanguineo nostro
hic construitur, cui otii et ingenii ad tantum opus satis est: cum perfectus
fuerit, tibi communicabitur.*) Now leisure was just what Napier did not
have for the years that followed. The year 1592 is worthy of mark:
Kepler's remark, often cited, in a much later letter, says Brahe had
a hint of what Napier was doing in 1594; Kepler knew of this only
from hearsay. But this must be the hint to which he refers, and
Napier was already hard at work on the *Canon Mirificus*, as he called
his logarithmic tables, by 1592. But in 1593, he began his political,
religious and technological involvements.

Arithmetical and geometrical progressions had been studied since
Antiquity, and methods of handling ratios, and the use of powers
to deal with very large numbers, go back at least to Archimedes. So
the principle on which logarithms are calculated could also be said
to be rooted in the Greek inheritance of Renaissance mathematics.
But it had not been realised that that offered a way to escape
exhausting calculations of multiplication and division and extraction
of square or cube roots, and reduce all to simple addition and
subtraction. What may have enabled Napier to advance so far
beyond his sixteenth-century predecessors was the translation of
ratios into proportionate movements and velocities.

When at last he published his *Mirifici Logarithmorum Canonis
Descriptio*, in 1614, printed by Andrew Hart, he begins with the
definition: 'A line is said to increase equally when a point describing
it advances through equal intervals in equal moments', giving as
example

```
1  2  3  4  5  6  7  8  9  10 11 12
C  D  E  F  G  H  I  K  L  M  N  O
```

A ————————————————————————————————————— Z

```
   B  B  B  B  B  B  B  B  B  B  B  B
```

Let A be a point from which a line is to be drawn by the flow of another point B, 'so that in the first moment B flows from A to C, in the second from C to D', and so on (Napier 1614:1). Hence, as a corollary, in times equally differing, quantities equally differing must necessarily be produced. In the Second definition he speaks of a point 'passing through' (*transcurrens*) a line, in equal moments, and so cutting off segments of the same ratio continually to the line from which they are cut. The Fourth definition speaks of synchronous motions, i.e. those made 'at one and the same time' (*simul et eodem tempore*). There could therefore obviously be motions faster or slower than any given motion. The logarithm, then, of any number – or rather, as he writes, any sine – is 'the number as closely as possible defining the line which increases equally in the meantime, while the line of the whole sine decreases proportionally to that sine, both motions being synchronous, and at their beginning of equal velocity' (Napier 1614:3). So, in a comparable figure, B moves with the same speed with which b began to move, from a. Then in the first movement B moves AC, and b proportionally ac; the number expressing AC shall be the logarithm of the line, or sine cz. And so on: when B moves CD, and b proportionately cd, the number expressing AD shall be the logarithm of sine dz. (Napier 1614 uses Greek letters: these minuscules are from the English translations.)

Napier's use of the term 'fluxus' has drawn comparisons with Newton's fluxions (Napier, Mark: 445–7). But a more striking, and more natural parallel may be drawn with Galileo, for those definitions of time, velocity, and moments of time and speed which form the basis of his kinematics are remarkably similar. And Galileo was working on them at Padua in the very years when Napier was pursuing his calculations. It does not seem necessary that logarithmic relationships should be perceived in terms of points moving at velocities in constant ratio to other moving points; but that is how Napier thought of them, evidently. Is there not here a novel conception of time as a geometrical dimension, which could be represented by lines and line segments, which makes it possible for both Galileo and Napier to move from the static world of Classical geometry, and occupy new territories? Since a moving point is always somewhere, its motions can be treated as continuous flow; and this enables the mathematician to proceed also toward other mathematical successes of the later seventeenth century.

The *Description* was as well received as Napier hoped: over not much more than a decade, his technique was generally welcomed: in particular, it was adopted by Kepler, who rejoiced that a way had at last been found to cut through the lengthy calculations which had always slowed his progress. Almost as soon as the *Description* was published, an English translation was made, which led to a friendship and collaboration between Napier and Henry Briggs, professor of geometry at Gresham College, London, who became in effect Napier's intellectual heir. Perhaps it was his visits which encouraged Napier to publish, early in 1617, his *Rabdologia*, an account of 'Napier's bones', as they came to be called, a simple aid to difficult multiplications by use of inscribed parallel rods. This little booklet (dedicated to the Chancellor, who had his own set of 'bones' engraved in silver) includes alternative instruments of ready reckoning. One, the Promptuary of Multiplication, with its sliding ebony strips in a box-like frame, recalls the sketches of the oldest attempt at a calculating machine, built by Wilhelm Schickard, a friend of Kepler, only a few years later (Napier 1617:92–101, fig.32). However, within a few weeks of publication of this later book of his, Napier was dead. Urquhart has a tale, that when he was already suffering from his terminal illness, someone asked him for the secret of his devastating artillery. But he refused: 'For the ruin and overthrow of man, there were too many devices already framed which if he could make to be fewer, he would with all his might endeavour to do; and that therefore seeing the malice and rancour, rooted in the heart of mankind, will not suffer them to diminish, by any new conceit of his the number of them should never be increased.'

## NOTE

1. Professor Owen Gingerich, of Harvard University, kindly allowed me to consult his forthcoming *An Annotated Census of Copernicus De Revolutionibus* (Nuremberg 1543 and Basel 1566) from which information about the history of copies now in Scottish university libraries is derived: I should like to express herewith my gratitude to him for that, and for his guidance through the controversies, reflected in these annotations.

## BIBLIOGRAPHY

Aberdeen
    1844 *Extracts from the Council Register of the Burgh of Aberdeen, 1396–1570*, published by Spalding Club, Aberdeen
Anderson, Alexander
    1616 *Vindiciae Archimedis*, Paris, 1616
Balfour, Robert
    1605 *Cleomedis Meteora Graece et Latine a Roberto Balforeo . . . repurgata*, Bordeaux
Bannerman, John
    1986 *The Beatons: a Medical Kindred in the Classical Gaelic Tradition*, Edinburgh
Barclay, William
    1614 *Nepenthes, or the Virtues of Tobacco*, Edinburgh
    1615 *Callirhoe, or the Nymph of Aberdene Resuscitat*, Edinburgh

1618 *The Nature and Effects of the New-Found Well at Kinghorne*, Edinburgh

Bassantin, Jacques
1557 *Astronomique Discourse*, Lyons

Brahe, Tycho
1913–29 *Tychonis Brahe Dani Opera Omnia*, Ed. J.L.E. Dreyer, Copenhagen

Comrie, John D.
1927 *History of Scottish Medicine to 1860*, London

Craig, John
1580 *Diexodus Medica De Hepatis Dispositionibus*, Basel

Dobrzycki, Jerzy
1973 'The Aberdeen Copy of Copernicus' *Commentariolus'*, *Journal for the History of Astronomy* 4:124–7

Drake, Stillman
1978 *Galileo at Work*, Chicago

Eade, J.C.
1984 *The Forgotten Sky. A Guide to Astrology in English Literature*, Oxford

Favaro, Antonio
1911 *Amici e Corrispondenti di Galileo Galilei*, (XXV Tommaso Segeth, Venice; XXVI Giovanni Wedderburn) 2:935–74, 979–85

Finlayson, James
1889 *An Account of the Life and Works of Maister Peter Lowe*, Glasgow

Forbes, Eric
1983 'Philosophy and Science Teaching in the Seventeenth Century', in *Four Centuries* Ed. G. Donaldson, Edinburgh

Galilei, Galileo
1930 *Le Opere*, (Edizione Nazionale, A. Favaro ed.) vol. 3, Florence

Gingerich, Owen & Westman, Robert S.
1981 'A Reattribution of the Tychonic Annotations in Copies of Copernicus' "De Revolutionibus"', *Journal for the History of Astronomy* 12:53–4

Gordon, D.
1625 *Pharmaco-Pinax*, Aberdeen

Henderson, George David
1947 *The Founding of Marischal College, Aberdeen*

Irving, David
1850 *Lives of Scottish Writers*, Edinburgh

Kepler, Johannes
1937–75 *Gesammelte Werke*, Munich

Knott, Cargill Gilston
1915 *Napier Tercentenary Memorial Volume*, London

Liddel, Duncan
1608 *Ars Medica*, Hamburg. The first edition of 1607 does not include the letter from Caselius, to Craig, which is the main source for Liddel's life.

Lowe, Peter
1596 *An Easie Certaine and Perfect Method to Cure and Prevent the Spanish Sicknes*, London
1597 *The Whole Course of Chirurgerye . . . with The Presages of Hyppocrates*, London

1612 *The Whole Course of Chirurgerye . . . with The Presages of Hyppocrates*, London

MacQueen, John
1982 *The Enlightenment and Scottish Literature*, Vol. One: *Progress and Poetry*, Edinburgh

Melvill, James
1829 *Mr. James Melvill's Diary*, Edinburgh

Napier, John
1614 *Mirifici Logarithmorum Canonis Descriptio, Ejusque Usus, in Utraque Trigonometria; ut etiam in Omni Logistica Mathematica . . . Explicatio*, Edinburgh
1617 *Rabdologiae, seu Numerationis per Virgulas*, Edinburgh
1619 *Mirifici Logarithmorum Canonis Constructio*, Edinburgh

Napier, Mark
1834 *Memoirs of Lord Napier of Merchiston, his Lineage Life and Times, with a History of the Invention of Logarithms*, Edinburgh

Register of the Great Seal
1886–1907 *The Register of the Great Seal of Scotland*, Ed. J.M. Thomson

Rosen, Edward
1949 'Thomas Seget of Seton', *Scottish Historical Review* 28:91–5

Russell, John L.
1974 'Cosmological Teaching in the Scottish Universities', *Journal for the History of Astronomy* 5:122–132, 145–154

St Andrews University
1964 *Acta Facultatis Artium Sanctiandree*, Ed. A.I. Dunlop, St Andrews

Shrewsbury, J.F.D.
1970 *A History of Bubonic Plague in the British Isles*, Cambridge

Sinclair, David
1622 *Davidis Sanclari Pro Archimedis et Euclide*, Paris

Skene, Gilbert
1568 *Ane Breve Descriptioun of the Peste quhair in the Causis Signis and sum Speciall Preservatioun and Cure thairof ar Contenit*, Edinburgh (1971 *The English Experience* No. 415, New York & Amsterdam)

Wear, A. (Ed.)
1985 *The Medical Renaissance of the Sixteenth Century*, Eds. A. Wear, R.K. French, I.M. Lonie, Cambridge

Webster, Charles (Ed.)
1979 *Health, Medicine and Mortality in the Sixteenth Century*, Cambridge

Wedderburn, John
1610 *Quatuor Problematum quae Martinus Horky contra Nuntium Sidereum de Quatuor Planetis Novis Disputanda Proposuit Confutanda, Confutatio*, Padua
(also in Galileo Galilei, *Le Opere*, q.v.)

Well of the Woman Hill
1580 *Ane Brief Descriptioun of the Well of the Woman Hill Besyde Abirdene*
(1969 *The English Experience* No. 104, New York & Amsterdam)

Wightman, W.P.D.
1962 *Science and the Renaissance*, Edinburgh

## Education: The Laying of Fresh Foundations
### JOHN DURKAN

The period is so critical for the future and the Renaissance such a protean term that boundaries are not easily set. It has been argued that the existence of several universities is in itself evidence of an elite emerging from larger foundations underneath in pre-university education. More recently a bleaker if not a blacker picture is presented of an elite with no popular base. Since the texts of grammar have never been looked at more than cursorily in recent times, it seemed worthwhile to look properly now. The outcome has necessarily been the curtailing of the long perspective in Scots humanist education in order to compensate for these areas of neglect.

I.

Our information about pre-Reformation schooling in Scotland is rudimentary. But the pattern observed elsewhere can be discerned when scattered bits of information are reassembled. From the twelfth century, the Church was involved, as the master was usually a secular chaplain or occasionally parish clerk, even though the patrons, as with Edinburgh and Haddington, might be canons regular, or, as with Perth, Stirling and Dundee, Benedictine monks. The schools were 'general' or 'common', open to all who could afford the fees, endowed institutions being few: some Celtic schools probably survived intermittently, in altered form, though the continued existence of any school is impossible to document. There was private education too in the internal schools of religious houses, not only for novices or selected brethren, and not confined to theology, as grammar was the necessary doorway giving access to any learning and music a requisite for lay choristers in the Lady chapels of cathedrals and great monasteries: but even here secular priests and not monks were generally the schoolmasters and this in the cloisters and not only in the small almonry schools at the abbey gates where boys were boarded. Scholars also occasionally were lodged in hospitals, as in Gorbals near Glasgow where in 1494 the leperhouse chaplain was also grammar master for the city. Lacking the English evidence of chantry certificates even if incomplete (as evidence was suppressed at times from Henry VIII's acquisitive eyes), it is impossible to say how many chantries like Carmyllie afforded a musical training or how many parishes, like Kettins, as the Maules of Panmure testify, afforded schooling or occasional tutoring by a chaplain 'curate'. Friars too had their internal 'lector' in theology, as the Dominicans had at Perth and Edinburgh, or in arts as at Glasgow in 1476, or even in grammar as at Ayr around 1420. But as with the schools of grammar and song in collegiate churches the numbers in attendance could be small. Other small schools, largely sewing schools for girls, were conducted by women or even by nuns, though these seldom emerge into record. The essential distinctions are between song and reading schools and full grammar schools, distinctions to bear in mind coupled with some flexibility of inter-pretation, for song and reading often overlapped. The term 'grammar school' might conveniently be confined to schools where a fairly complete course (four to seven years) was available as distinct from those Latin schools largely restricted to the rudiments. (For detailed references for this and later sections of pre-university schooling, see my *Early Schools and Schoolmasters in Scotland*, Scottish Record Society, forthcoming.)

When John Mair in his *History* maintained that the Scots gentry failed to educate their children in letters and morals, he spoke in general terms. If, as he also affirmed, even the meanest laird kept a household chaplain, it is likely that in some households the laird's children, boys and girls, and others committed to his care (like the farmer's son Mair also refers to) had the benefit of some tutelage, besides training in physical skills, at least where his chaplain was a man of education. And since, as Mair also noted, in many parishes villages lay at some distance from church and thus the laird's chapel was made available to villagers, the same must occasionally have been true of his educational facilities, at least for the offspring of favoured tenants, and where the laird's patronage extended to several chaplains in a collegiate foundation this probability is increased. As for music lessons, though Mair lamented the ignorance in some ordinands even of plainsong, he could still observe that though Scotland did not produce such polished musicians as England did, yet the English had not so many. But some men preferred to send their children to a school of repute in a sizeable town, hence young Mair, a villager from Gleghornie, like Bishop Robert Cockburn, attended school in the town of Haddington, and there was brought up as a new boy 'in the sweetest milk of the art of grammar'. One such country school existed at Elphinstone in Midlothian where a future Comptroller of finances, George Home of Wedderburn, displayed as an infant prodigy to Mary of Lorraine, was along with his step cousin, taught his rudiments by a certain James Knox in the 1550s.

Monastic schools have had a bad press of late beyond their desserts. The Augustinian canon of Cambuskenneth, Robert Richardinus or Richardson, published in Paris in 1530 his criticisms of contemporary religion, in his commentary on the rule of St Augustine. Among causes of breakdown in religious life among canons regular he cited the concentration on music, especially choral polyphony, and consequent neglect of bible study and 'undue neglect of the initial education of the novices and the boys' (their associates in school and choir). Musically the Scots were over-educated, he complained, and he oddly compared part-singing to the sophisms and logical tricks which even good men, like his own old 'preceptor', John Mair, had formerly got up to. Significantly only the juniors at Cambuskenneth and Scone abbeys were Richardson's correspondents, and it is notable that on coming back from Paris in 1531, he and his friend, Robert Logie, were in dispute with the community, only making their peace on the night of the Assumption. The 'boys' in Richardson's account are like the 'boys and youths' that the subprior of St Andrews found in 1554 as night-boarders in the priory at Pittenweem, or the 'master of the boys' who survived the Reformation for a time in Dunfermline, presumably indication of a choir school. Further consideration of monastic schools at Paisley, Culross and elsewhere must await another occasion except to note that the Cistercian house at Deer, in its 1537 regulation, enjoined daily grammar lessons for juniors and selected seniors, an arrangement soon signalled by the purchase in Paris of the 1537 edition of the grammar of Despauterius.

The Italian tutor at Kinloss, Giovanni Ferrerio, was brought in to update its educational programme. In the early 1530s, he opened a series of discourses in the abbey's chapter-house to the whole community, and in his own room to selected monks. There was no instruction in Greek, but at least he could take for granted a general grasp of rudimentary Latin. His task was to revive its lost eloquence. The community addresses would aim at capturing the sense of the text as a whole and less at attempting a minute textual analysis. The religious poem on St Paul by Pierre Rosset gave his hearers a snippet of Latin verse in heroic metre. Popular in the 1520s when Ferrerio studied there, Paris booksellers sold in one handy volume a philosophical amalgam of Cicero at his less complicated: his *Offices* (or duties) on morals, and practical problems arising from clashes between virtue and expediency; the moralising dialogues on *Old Age* and *Friendship*; the *Paradoxes of the Stoics*, no inept choice for Cistercians with its black and white portrayal of vice and virtue; and *Scipio's dream* with its other-worldly and contemplative slant. To this moral diet was added Ferrerio's own *Arithmetic Practice*, almost certainly based on a similar title by Jacques Lefèvre of Etaples. This course was an appetiser for private teaching elaborating on these foundations. Terence's *Andria*, the Latin drama chosen, was a sure favourite and the selected poet was Virgil in his pastoral *Eclogues* and two books of the *Aeneid*. Cicero's *Offices* was reverted to, perhaps with a closer eye to the techniques of rhetoric, the exploration of its theme ('invention'), the arrangement of its material ('disposition') and finally its clear and attractive presentation ('elocution'). With this turning to oratory, there was Quintilian's *Training of an Orator*, the Rhetoric 'ad Herennium' often ascribed to Cicero, whose varied skills as a masterly pleader were brilliantly exemplified in the judicial speech *On behalf of Milo*. The *Precepts of Elegant Speech* of Agostino Dati followed the pathway outlined by Valla, and there was Erasmus, of course, in his twofold treatise on *Copia* (amplification), illustrated from many sources other than Cicero. The *Syntax* of Melanchthon was repeated from the general course, along with his elementary rhetoric introducing the figures and the more advanced *Rhetorical Institutions*. For those humanist teachers who followed Cicero and Valla in affirming the need for an intimate bond between philosophy and eloquence, Melanchthon indeed was an understandable choice. Educators would find his grammar book religiously neutral, but in the *Rhetoric* his definition of faith, with its presupposition of imputed justice, is squarely Lutheran. It is thus hardly surprising that we find two Dundee schoolmasters, John Fethy and Walter Spalding, being moved to embrace Luther's ideas and to flee Catholic Scotland for Melanchthon's own Wittenberg.

When the Reformation came, the damage to kirks, altered programmes and the search for personnel to man the schools must have caused chaos for some time. In his little work *Against Sacrilege*, Robert Pont, minister of St Cuthberts, Edinburgh and ageing eyewitness of those events, claimed that while the first Reformed noblemen could be excused sacrilegious destruction for various reasons, others, a great many, 'not only of the raskall sort', could not, pulling down not only 'idols' but places, not distinguishing parish kirks from others. As far as the towns were concerned it could be said that education merely faltered, but the rural situation, as the General Assembly itself averred as late as 1597, was more desperate. The authors of the *First Book of Discipline* seem to have looked for a massive movement towards them so that those already teaching could carry on after investigation and trial. They hoped for a school in every parish, not an unfamiliar notion in Protestant and Catholic circles: Jean Gerson had a similar project in the previous century, Martin Bucer in the sixteenth. Yet it was not an idea canvassed in so many words in the educational programme of the Scottish Catholic councils of reform 1549–59, though they do legislate for schools even in parishes with a slight endowment. It is true that most of the *First Book of Discipline* envisaged towns and town parishes, not expecting rural parishes to convene to doctrine more than once weekly. But even so there was ahead an immense work of re-education, to which the new appointees were expected to give over their Sunday afternoons, not the one-way sacramental exhortations that the Catholic provincial councils proposed, but question-and-answer sessions on the catechism, preferably of Calvin, learned from repeating what the young had memorised rather than from reading. Familiarity with the bible was not to be with snippets but with whole chapters read by the minister or his reader, yet not usually by personal possession of an expensive English bible: pocket bibles were still some distance away. In the 1560s the youthful James Melville did not start off with bible-reading at school, but with Calvin's catechism and suitably edited and selected texts. When Musselburgh grammar school had its kirk visitation in June 1592, George Nisbet, its master, 'wes found to be cairfull not onlie in training wp the youth in letteres of humanitie, but also in catechising thame according to Caluyne and teaching of Buchanane psalms'. Too much is sometimes made of the duties of reader. Some had to be replaced soon after 1560: Ninian Winzet made the point that many were youths with little educational equipment. The *First Book of Discipline* was well aware of schoolmasters as a separate category. It is clear from the duties of the reader of Gogar in 1598 that what was expected of him was not the rudiments of grammar, but the rudiments of piety. However, readers as well as some ministers undoubtedly taught school. If it is argued that few schoolmasters appear in the official registers of deeds before 1600, and therefore most schools belong to the next century, it needs to be pointed out that few readers appear either, even though we know from the Books of Assignation that they existed country-wide. Although it was hoped to support schoolmasters from the teinds, the *First Book of Discipline* saw that the teinds would not supply for all needs, so chaplainries and related offices were to be tapped as well: indeed some chaplains continued as readers or schoolmasters. The schoolmaster chaplain at Deer, Sir Alexander Pittendreich was still active at his death circa 1570. Some schoolmasters were obstinately 'papist' and proved difficult to remove.

The first priority was patently to restore schools where schools had been before. Cathedral cities or superintendents' towns were obvious candidates. At different dates in the period 1560–1633 the schools of collegiate kirks at places like Kilmaurs, Bothans (now Yester), Lochwinnoch and Crichton functioned under new management, though now without music. Monastic sites like Jedburgh and Melrose soon had schools. Others had never stopped, it seems. The parish of Ednam in 1627 claimed that it 'ever had a school'. Logie near Stirling in the same year stated it had once a grammar school that then was no more. But there is reason to doubt the negative statements of other parishes in the 1627 reports to the commissioners

(Lasswade is one example) for they contradict the known facts. The kirk had a part in the development, as is apparent from the General Assembly records in particular, but at kirk session level it was often uninterested or, more accurately, impotent in the face of unsympathetic heritors. Visitations by presbyteries were supposed to look into schoolmasters and their provision, but unless they misbehaved by performing plays in the traditional way or were otherwise malefactors, the visitors seem to have ignored them. It is possible that Presbytery records abbreviated visitors' reports from more wordy originals, but, even where an original survives, as at Dunblane, it is silent except about the school at Dunblane itself. When a crisis comes for the kirk, as in the 1590s, more information emerges, and one learns then of a chain of schools round Edinburgh, at Liberton, Wester Hailes, Ratho and Cramond. But as late as then, Irish (i.e. highland) scholars were found in Glasgow who were ignorant of the grounds of religion.

The highland area both before and after the Reformation is uncharted territory. We know there were schools of harping and piping, bardic schools and medical schools, but these did not have the readily recognisable institutionalised form characteristic of the lowlands. It is likely that in both periods Latin could be learnt from a scholarly priest or a scholarly minister. In 1622 Martin McLachlan was a student at Kilmeny in Islay, probably under the person who signs himself as minister there, Duncan McEwan (though Scott's *Fasti* of ministers placed him at Kildalton). However there was a school at Rothesay by at least 1619, at Kilberry on Loch Fyne by 1617 and at Inveraray by 1628. In the highland part of Moray the late seventeenth century recollections of Lachlan Shaw suggest that no school ever was in this area, though a school existed at Cromdale at 1628 and probably earlier and later too.

The original Book of Discipline programme for schooling conforms to a basic pattern. The first two years were within the grasp of every parish, however remote and poor, where a minister, reader or schoolmaster was envisaged as confining himself to the rudiments of religion along with 'some entry' into the rudiments of grammar, teaching, as we saw, that might be a 'Sunday only' affair in remoter places. Latin, though, is envisaged if the town is 'of any reputation' and that might call for a schoolmaster since readers were chosen for their ability to read the Geneva bible in English. Of eight readers chosen for Kyle in 1560, most vanished shortly thereafter, though two were ex-chaplains and one an ex-chorister. Towns which were 'notable' were expected to provide more, that is a college where the arts were taught, 'arts' here meaning the humanities, that is rhetoric, logic (perhaps surprisingly) together with the 'tongues', generally, however, expected to include Latin and Greek alone. There is no evidence that logic was ever attempted at this stage, but the Book's complete grammar course ran for the seven years expected in the bigger towns and accounted for in the State bursaries that began to be provided: yet the problems set for even the richer burghs were formidable.

However, a 'school in every parish' did not necessarily mean a 'parish school in every parish'. Rural 'adventure' schools could be found at busy crossroads, at any gathering place, a mill (e.g. Primside Mill), an ancient chapel or a big house: a laird could provide accommodation at least, if he provided nothing else, and occasionally a schoolmaster can be identified as classed as his 'servitor' like the former household chaplain. The picture painted in most shire histories of education has, for this period, apart from Fife, been uniformly bleak, more or less suggesting that little happened before the first post-Reformation Act of Parliament of 1633. The royal intervention in favour of music in 1579 was a watershed in the way these Acts were not. The sad fact was that no music was printed, though manuscript keyboard, lute and songbooks fortunately have chanced to survive as well as books of sacred music (printed psalms were not for part-singing). A treatise ascribed to John Black, survivor from the pre-Reformation tradition who adapted himself to new ways, seems to be a musical programme for the new era. There was probably some fairly simple singing going on in schools that is totally unrecorded. How many of the vernacular schools taught 'Inglis' in any recognised sense of 'received pronunciation' is speculative, even when taught from grammars that were themselves anglicising: the evidence of national records suggests that clerks translated local linguistic forms into their own established usages. One imagines that some taught simple types of Scots verse-writing, roundels (triolets), for example, occurring in common-place books. Some bilingual discomfort with current anglicising trends might account for the disproportionate Latin verse production that occurs, only partially reflected in the famous *Delitiae* of 1637. A very few schools attempted Hebrew, John Davidson's at Prestonpans being a notable instance. Writing was not always an accompaniment to reading in 'lecture' schools though in 1607 Aberdeen had a school confined to writing and arithmetic. James Melville learnt French in the 1560s, and no doubt it was often an additional item. In 1617 the burgh of Edinburgh even thought of bringing out its own French textbook.

In all 600 or so schools have been excavated from the manuscript registers, mostly civil records, and of these a fifth are 'adventure' schools under, often, 'baronial' patronage. It is probable that as many as a hundred more can be added, though the sources suffer from the law of diminishing returns. Even so, it would be a mere half of the *c.*1150 medieval parishes at a time when reading ability was a more urgent need and the population of most parishes

growing. The critical days when it was thought desirable to cut
down Scotland's parishes to 600 were over, and the existence of
university colleges is some index to increased provision lower down:
and even where little or no provision existed locally, remedial
grammar classes or 'sieges' were available in university colleges. The
credit must go largely to the kirk, though, from these figures one
must subtract at the very least 100 medieval schools.

Yet it would be unwise to ignore the evidence of State collaboration
and encouragement in all this, something that made up for the lack
of endowment that Winzet complained of in the 1560s and that on
the whole continued. But endowment must not be confused with
existent schooling: Moffat school was not endowed till 1639, it
existed long before. Yet while heritors, or many of them, contributed
grudgingly to schooling, and the aim of making all schools a charge
on the teinds remained remote, heritors too made their contribution,
for whatever motive, to this development if not of a national, at least
of a nation-wide, system of popular education, for schools existed
everywhere in Scotland by 1633, from Scalloway in Shetland to
Stranraer in Wigtownshire and, in some favoured areas, were even
fairly thick on the ground.

## II.

However we define the Renaissance or assess its relative importance,
there is little doubt that the men of this time saw themselves as
embarking on a whole new cultural programme. They had a more
comprehensive interest in ancient writings than their medieval
predecessors, having been made aware of more sources worth
quarrying (like Tacitus or newly exhumed lost works like Cicero's
De Oratore), assigning an even more central place to classical studies
than in the medieval curriculum and forging stronger links between
such pivotal studies and every other scientific pursuit. This availability
of more ancient literature magnified the sense of discontinuity
between medieval and ancient learning despite the fact that they
were both products of ages forming a single historical continuum.
Humane studies now stood for an encyclopedia of learning, the core
of which involved, besides grammar and rhetoric, history (to which
three Scots academics would make notable contributions), poetry
and morals. To write and speak well was to write and speak as the
old Romans wrote and spoke, avoiding the 'vices' of medieval Latin.
Since Latin was the language not only of the schools but of Church
and State and of much of everyday business, others, royal secretaries,
for instance, like Archibald Whitelaw and James Foulis, had a
professional interest in these new developments. To put a precise
date on Renaissance beginnings in Scotland is, however, far from
easy and thus to encapsulate everything in a necessarily brief
account an impossible task.

Concentrating on schools means concentrating on grammar as then understood, comprehending literature besides linguistics, except that all reading schools understood a solid foundation in grammar as the vital requisite for further studies. Basically there were three groups: those tackling a little only, the bare rudiments; those attempting a more detailed course in 'etymology' (vocabulary, accidence) and syntax; and those high schools where a distinctively literary and rhetorical crown was placed on the whole edifice. Some still stressed the role of dialectic while throwing out the so-called 'sophisms' of late medieval days: Sturm following Melanchthon, and, in his eccentric way, Ramus, who, though part of the general movement to harmonise philosophy and eloquence without any great departure from the traditional order of study, ruthlessly simplified rhetoric and rhetoricised logic. Others, like Erasmus, also looked to removing logic from its excessive dominance and had the visionary ideal of combining the learning of Latin and Greek from the outset. Vives was passionately suspicious of dialectic in literary studies and typified the group that sought to keep its corrupting influence at bay. The outcome was considerable disorder, especially for the many pupils forced to break their education, thus finding themselves coerced into re-learning under new schoolmasters attached to different traditions: the young James Melville was first exposed to William Lily and Thomas Linacre, then to Sebastian Novimola's simplification of the Louvain grammar of Johannes Despauterius ('Despaultre' in Louvain records) and finally, under his uncle, to Ramus.

Of the two leading grammarians in medieval use, Donatus and Priscian, Donatus continued to dominate. By the early sixteenth century, the medieval grammar course of Alexandre de Villedieu, his rhyming *Doctrinale*, was still the staple in Paris, and, by way of Paris, throughout Europe. The powerful intervention of Lorenzo Valla's *Elegantiae* had already disturbed this scholastic peace, bringing a revolutionary move away from a medieval Latin characterised by a loose Latin word-order on the pattern of popular speech and the emerging vernacular languages but remote from the distinctive elegance of the Latin of antiquity: William Elphinstone, founder of Aberdeen university, owned Valla's treatise in manuscript, while his first principal, Hector Boece, was the friend at Paris of Erasmus, one of Valla's earliest propagandists in a Northern European setting. Giovanni Ferrerio, continuator of Boece's *History*, praised the Italian innovator, Niccolo Perotti, for abolishing old ways so that henceforth 'adolescents might be properly taught to use elegance of diction' in their arts studies.

The first known Scots convert to this grammatical revolution was David Lowis (Lauxius), an Edinburgh man and graduate of Paris. In December 1503, as schoolmaster in Arras, Lowis was addressed by the Paris humanist printer, Josse Bade, in Bade's edition of the grammar of Giovanni Sulpizio of Veroli, one often reprinted with its dedication to the Scot. The new trends in letter-writing also engaged the attention of Lowis, to whom Bade in the previous September similarly dedicated his edition of Giovanni Filelfo's book of epistle-models. Lowis never left France, becoming a canon of Arras, but there is no reason to doubt some influence on future literary training at home. (See my notes in *Edinburgh Bibliographical Society Transactions*, iii, pt.1 (1952), 78–80, pt.2 (1954), 156–7; *Essays on Scottish Reformation*, ed. D. McRoberts (Glasgow 1962), 325–6; *Bibliotheck*, IV, 200–201.)

At King's College, Aberdeen, John Vaus was an early owner of the Caen edition of Sulpizio dedicated to Lowis. Vaus too had a Paris degree and probably was known to Bade about this time, graduating as he did in 1506, for later Bade referred to their intimate acquaintance of long standing. On going back home, Vaus probably became responsible for an early Scots version of Donatus, of which a mere fragment remains, close enough to Vaus's own known version. Vaus became 'humanist' at Aberdeen under Elphinstone's foundation, and in a letter of 1523 addressed to Aberdeen students, Bade described how on a voyage back to Paris Vaus lost his belongings. The commentary Bade published restricted itself to part only of the massive medieval grammar of Alexander de Villedieu, the first part or 'etymology', dealing with verbs, nouns and their inflexions. Bade was persuaded all the more readily as the founding fathers of King's were Parisian students, and moreover, with the fervour of a new institution would be uninhibited by the old-fashioned trifles under such an excellent teacher as Vaus. Vaus for his part declared that for years Scotland was without suitable texts and university 'dictates' had been negligently put together, thus forcing him to brave highway robbers and pirates to deliver commentaries whose ease and brevity matched those of Bade. His words suggest the mutual devotion of teacher and pupils. A former student was Robert Gray, who, citing Aulus Gellius in his account of the sea trip to Dieppe, aired also some criticisms, echoing the view that Vaus should have broken more definitively with the past and followed Sulpizio, Perotti, Aldus and Torrentinus rather than deferring to the school-boy's traditional preference for traditional texts. Many of their elders, he granted, would be supercilious about Vaus's industry, men who damned good literature being themselves sunk in barbarism from earliest youth. Such men performed 'like glorious knights', made a lot of noise, rattled their words like swords, suffering from tongue disease yet were too flabby to face reality: an elaborate indication that the grammatical revolution had many enemies, as More's and Lily's had in England. The 1543 edition of Villedieu had more help from Bade, due to the loss of Vaus's manuscript forwarded to Paris in advance, but, though his Donatus was reprinted, this was to be the last of Villedieu. Indeed Vaus's own library was a reflection largely of newer tastes, and these must have been further fortified when his assistance and successor, Theophilus Stewart, arrived from Paris. The obvious replacement was another versified grammar of humanist persuasion, the equally prolix Johannes Despauterius, who, along with Melanchthon, was recommended by an undoubted former student of Vaus, Florence Wilson, in his Lyons *Epitome of Latin grammar* issued in 1544. Another disciple of Vaus or at least of Stewart was the key figure of Andrew Simson, whose name dominated the scene for two centuries. Meantime the importation of some English grammars, or of George Buchanan's Latinisation of the Englishman Thomas Linacre's *Rudiments*, seems highly likely.

On 26 August 1559, a remedy to the existing situation was proposed. A royal privilege was granted to the experienced school-master, William Niddrie (Nudrye), for a sequence of booklets 'for the better instructions of young chylderin' who were expected to write as well as read not in Latin but in Scots with the use of a 'Short Introductioun Elementar' in seven concise tabulations. The title of his compendious 'Trilingual orthopoeia' raises questions about what he meant by 'Trilingual'; it certainly included parts of speech in Greek and Latin treated together, but whether Hebrew was the third language is unclear. 'Meditations on the Grammar of Despauterius' was a more advanced commentary; 'meditations' is a usage remi-niscent of another Flemish grammarian, Nicholas Clenardus (Cley-naerts). It was traditional also to pass on wise saws in nutshell form, hence the projected 'Meditations on Publilius Mimus' and the 'Sayings of the Sages'. So far 'etymology' was being covered. A 'Syntax of Letters in Three Tongues' broke fresh ground followed by an overview, 'Questions on trilingual Grammar', to check pro-gress on ground already covered. General behaviour rules, similar to those in Vaus's grammar, were to be mastered from 'An Instruc-tioun for Bairnes to be lernit in Scotis and Latene'. The later ideal of virtuous discourse was foreshadowed in 'Ane Regiment for Education of young Gentillmen in literature and virtuous exercitioun'. Less intrinsic to the course was 'An ABC for Scottis Men to reid the Frenche toung, with an exhortatioun to the nobles of Scotland to favour thair old freindis', implying that the inclusion of some French in the curriculum was not too unusual. That oral Latin was a first aim as well as written is gathered from Niddrie's final proposal for 'Formulae for everyday Speech, taken from the comedies of Terence' (*Registrum Secreti Sigilli*, v, 658). The Reformation crisis blocked this publication and, doubtless, others as when early in 1568 the royal printer, Robert Lekpreuik, was licensed to print Donatus 'for boys' and, simplified from Despauterius, the rudiments of Jean Pellisson; there was also the first hint of a monopoly, a single personal grammar.

In desperation authors turned to Antwerp, where George Buchanan's friendly relations with the printer, Christophe Plantin, helped a young schoolmaster to make his debut with Alexander Hepburn's rudiments, *Grammaticae Artis Rudimenta Breviter et Dilucide Explicata* of 1568. All we have of this is a single sheet of thirty-two pages preserved in the Moretus-Plantin museum. This work has no commentary, no vernacular exposition, the rules alone. The final page was sixteen lines of Latin verse addressed to the reader by 'H.R.', that is Hercules Rollock of Dundee, presumably Hepburn's pupil, for the author as 'preceptor' of its school was honoured by the town in 1565. This Hepburn is likely to be the man mentioned by Aldo Manuzio as teacher of the Admirable Crichton, since Hepburn had certainly moved to Dunkeld before 1571. Before Dundee, Hepburn had taught in Elgin, not too far from Ferrerio-influenced Kinloss, inheriting from Ferrerio a copy of a work of Angelo Poliziano. (*Eminent Burgesses of Dundee*, ed. A.H. Millar (Dundee 1887), p.40; *Protocol Books of Dominus Thomas Johnsoun*, Scottish Record Society, 1920 no.957). The work is more an introduction to Despauterius than to Buchanan's Linacre, though echoes of Linacre are inserted into the definition of pronoun and adverb. A very rudimentary syntax is included.

In a hitherto unknown communication, Buchanan distils some experience in introducing the book: 'Two things are quite harmful to boys on the very threshold of grammar, obscurity and prolixity. For, either it happens that because of their inexperience in teaching boys, writers on the arts think they must not overlook anything relevant to the complete art, or else they strive out of some unworthy ambition to outdo their betters whom they cannot surpass in teaching by inculcating pointless facts. Thus they will have obscured with confusion any pointers towards a method in the material they are charged with transmitting. Better in my view is he who considers as a virtue in a Grammarian that he thinks some things ought to be passed over. This is the opinion of Alexander Hepburn. Hepburn has expounded these first rudiments of the art in such a way that obscurity does not put the reader off nor a mass of rules deter him from learning; and he has so presented this short cut to learning that he leaves nothing out that, seemingly, boys need to know. Those facts he has considered ought to be passed on to you, Reader (and that not with a zeal for the glory he acquires but rather with an eye to public utility) should appeal to you by virtue of the clear advantages they offer'.

Buchanan's proposed 'college of humanity' (*c*.1563) at St Andrews was an abbreviated course as envisaged by earlier reformers, including the whole gamut of grammar in a full six-year course on the lines of the French collège 'de plein exercice'. Yet to the casual eye it inspires the question, can these bones live? The purpose was to relate language rules to basic ancient texts. The first three years took the child up to the verge of adolescence, drawing heavily on the memory, when church attendance was exacted on Sundays only, as befitted small children. The sixth (really the first) class began to memorise Latin verbs and nouns with their inflexions. Immediately after this, it turned to the colloquial Latin and animated dialogue of Terence, as Erasmus advised: Buchanan believed in dialogue and drama, as his career showed, a necessity anyway if Latin conversation was routine. Two or three lines were to be written (in their 'paper books'), the regent drawing attention to every word and its component letters, indicating where the accent fell: alongside the Latin the children were to copy out his dictated Scots version. They were required to specify each part of speech and write down the nouns and verbs, grouped separately, for correction next day. The monitors or 'nomenclators' in charge of each class-section or 'decurio' collected the scripts for the regent's inspection: a hazardous business for himself as well as the offender if he overlooked his errors. Spoken Latin was already compulsory and the beginnings of composition (necessitating a rudimentary syntax to complement the 'etymology'). The fifth/second class moved on to more drama in Terence, alternating with some of the less demanding letters of Cicero, both authors to be copied out, plus more rules, still minus commentary. The fourth/third class passed the next six months with yet more Terence and Cicero and on syntactical exercises in elegant expression (based perhaps on the *De constructione* of Erasmus) before turning to the verse epistles and elegies of Ovid (entailing presumably the rudiments of prosody) with the composition of longer themes. The third/fourth class marked a turning point. Greek grammar was introduced. More taxing letters of Cicero were now attacked and some of his less formidable orations, in connection with which an introduction to rhetoric was mastered. Verse took more prominence. An unspecified work of Ovid was to be studied along with prosody. Part of Linacre, obviously his far from elementary textbook on Latin construction, and with the acquisition of a wider prose vocabulary, more proficiency in composition. Elegance now required more stringent attention. The top classes (second/fifth and first/sixth) turned to the theory of rhetoric in Cicero and its practice in his orations, consonant with Jean Sturm's ideal of periodic eloquence. More advanced Latin verse study in Virgil and Horace, with in Greek a modicum of Homer and Hesiod, rounded off the course. Each of the upper school classes took monthly turns at public exercises in verse-writing, oration and declamation. Saturday afternoons were reserved to disputations, class ranged against class, composing themes on ideas thought up often by other regents or other masters. Notable absentees from the reading list are two Buchanan favourites, Livy and Euripides. Obviously he was composing a national model, though other schools lacked the anticipated resources of St Andrews and would prune down the six years. The end product of the system was ideally expected to pen verses and elaborate speeches and turn out a general or religious pamphlet with flair and elegance.

Comparison with the scheme of 1576, based on a committee of urban grammarians presided over by Buchanan and the royal preceptor, Peter Young, is illuminating. Greek printing was apparently out of the question, but Terence, Cicero, Virgil and Ovid still figure on the proposed list, this time with some history, Livy and Caesar thrown in, and the Latin dialogues of contemporaries like Mathurin Cordier, Juan Luis Vives or Erasmus at choice. (*RSS*, vii, 828.) The committee also added 'ane onomastik' (list of classical names), 'certane select sentences' and 'the catechisme for young bairnis'. Its main purpose, as set up by Regent Morton, was to father a national grammar, which two at least of its members, Andrew Simson and James Carmichael, would now set about furnishing. However, Despauterius had already conquered the field as Thomas Bassandyne the printer's pre-1577 stock clarifies beyond doubt. He held 620 Rudiments of Despauterius alongside only four Linacre grammars, plus 407 of his Syntax, not to mention odd volumes of adaptations, e.g. the Mechelen synod's Despauterius, Jean Pellisson's and Sebastian Novimola's. (R. Dickson and J.P. Edmond, *Annals of Scottish Printing* (Cambridge 1890) pp.292–304.) This was before John Ross's printing of Despauterius's long general grammar and his syntax in 1579. He chose as 'certane select sentences', the popular 'Sayings of the Sages' (the edition associated with Erasmus and Lily) and the 'Moral distichs' ascribed to Cato, both established favourites, issued in 1580 along with a brief syntactical compendium on grammatical 'agreements' and 'governance' and an undated John Spangenberg 'On the making of epistles' with the various types of letter illustrated from ancient and recent models. The 1580 printing of Andrew Simson's 'Rudiments' seems, however, to have been the work of Plantin in Antwerp, not a copy of which edition survives. (*The Library*, series 5, XIV, 44.) No Scots words are found in these Ross publications except in the Despauterius. There is one more text, 'ane Grammatica Cheperini', in Bassandyne's inventory as registered in the commissary record. This must be a scribal error, as it corresponds to no known text, for 'Hepburnii', that is the rudiments of Hepburn.

Andrew Simson, born about 1526, had links with the Aberdeen school of grammarians. His name occurs among a class list of students in Vaus's grammar of 1511 (King's College copy), and can be assigned to the class of Vaus or his successor, Theophilus Stewart. On the same list is William Pendrech, found as a monk of Deer in 1544, Deer being a house where the grammar of Despauterius was in use: it is likely therefore that Aberdeen had abandoned Villedieu by Simson's time. By the end of May 1550 he was schoolmaster of Perth when admitted burgess and guild-brother, his wife, Violet Constyne, being the daughter of a guild-brother (MS Guildry Book of Perth, item communicated by Dr M. Lynch). The 'Constynes' are better known as Adamsons and in July 1544 there is a feu-charter by the chaplain of the Jesus altar in the parish kirk to the schoolmaster and his wife, Violet Adamson (Perth, King James Hospital Charters, SRO GD79/4/18). Their eldest son, Patrick, was born in 1556. According to Ross's history, the schoolmaster was at first a 'zealous papist' but was influenced in favour of the Reformation by a work of Sir David Lindsay. Simson and his wife took the impoverished youth, James Lawson, later subprincipal at King's College, into their house and yet did not follow Lawson and his own son-in-law, James Carmichael, into outright opposition to King James, which brought Carmichael to remind him of his warlike purpose in his younger days when 'did use yow to go before uthers in the beginning of the Reformation with the reade knapska.' (Woodrow Society Miscellany, i, 442.) Simson could strike terror in his pupils, as David Hume of Godscroft recalls, with his black looks and readiness with the tawse; but also in milder moments the yoke of the Muses would be shaken off and games allow innocent fun. As a member of Buchanan's 1575–6 committee he was assigned the first and second rudiments. The 'First Rudiments' appeared in 1580 before he moved from Dunbar parish to Dalkeith, and he presumably worked on the second about the same time, though they were not printed as late as 1593 by which date he was dead. Indeed the first licence to print is only recorded in 1599, though Edinburgh was using it as a text book two years earlier; yet not a single leaf of the 'Secund rudiments of Dunbar' of the 538 copies held by Robert Smyth in 1602 has come down to us. The *First Rudiments* in dialogue form are readily identified by the master's opening words, 'Quum literarum consideratio.' The *Second Rudiments* by 'M.A.S.' exist in a damaged copy of 1607 edition, a text not, as is regularly assumed, identical with that which continued to be printed thereafter with Simson's first section. Instead we have the second rudiments taken from Andrew Duncan's 'Key to the Studies of Boys', which became available in 1597. According to another pupil of Simson's, Alexander Hume, his master followed Despauterius. There are, however, echoes of Linacre, including the admission of a 'potential mood' in the verb. Duncan's examples are more pious than Simson's; the latter even has the odd humorous fling: 'How old is your father? A hundred!'

A more significant figure was Alexander Hume whose epitaph summarised his career: 'He produced the seeds at Dunbar, the flowers at St Andrews and the fruit at Oxford.' (Cited in Glasgow Univ. Library, MS Gen.362). Born in April 1550, he went to school at Dunbar, learning his Despauterius under Andrew Simson. Thence he went to St Andrews where his regent in St Mary's College was John Hamilton, later a convert to Catholicism. Afterward he accompanied c.1580 a young Scots nobleman to Oxford, where he spent two years in residence. He was next found as schoolmaster in Bath (1582–92), but there was compelled to use the royal grammar based on William Lily. While there he got caught up in a theological dispute with a canon of Salisbury, Adam Hill. He paid a brief visit home in the summer of 1590, but returned to find Hill had circulated a paper attacking him in his absence. His rejoinder was published in 1594 by which time Hume was back home in Dunbar. The presbytery of Edinburgh readily authorised publication after a 'sycht' of it by sympathetic censors, John Davidson of Prestonpans and Robert Rollock. Hume was skilful in deploying Greek philology and showed an acquaintance with Hebrew. For the Church Fathers he had no excessive reverence: like Beza and Calvin they too were new once.

On the removal from office of Hercules Rollock in 1596, it was decided to approach Hume in Dunbar to succeed to the headship of Edinburgh high school. In his self-composed epitaph he says he found no method, but chaos in grammar, logic and rhetoric and when he tried to remedy this, he aroused nothing but envy. A new school order was laid down in 1597 for which he felt prepared by studies in Valla, Sulpizio, Aldo Manuzio, Melanchthon and above all Linacre. There were to be four regents teaching in separately partitioned classes. The first taught the first and second rudiments 'of Dumbar' (i.e. Simson), the colloquies of Mathurin Cordier and on Sundays the Palatine Catechism. Drama is no longer envisaged at this stage. The second regent advanced to 'etymology' in the more difficult first part of Jean Pellisson, a French adaptor of Despauterius. For a letter-writing model there were Cicero's *Familiar Epistles* and there was exercise in prose translation. Sundays were given over to the Palatine Catechism (Latin version this time) and Ovid's *Tristia* with their nostalgic sadness, an earlier introduction to verse than Buchanan had proposed. The third regent proceeded to part two of Pellisson, the syntax supplemented by Erasmus's *Syntax*. Terence at last entered the curriculum briefly, followed by Ovid's *Metamorphoses* with their rich mythological content and on Sundays Buchanan's *Psalm paraphrases*, of which no Scottish edition was as yet available. The fourth class turned to Pellisson's third part (versification) along with the recently printed *Prosody* of Buchanan, the 'figures' and the rest of Omer Talon's *Rhetoric* (a Ramist-inspired text), the 'figures of construction' from Linacre's syntax, some undefined Virgil, the histories of Sallust, Caesar and the epitome of Roman history by Florus (mostly epitomised from Livy), a feature absent from Buchanan's programme but liable to interest young noblemen attracted to military history. The final crown on this course was available not in the school but in the university and it was possible now to leave school having no Greek whatever. It was the university's regent in humanity who introduced it with some unspecified Greek texts. His text in rhetoric was what was in use in St Leonard's thirty years earlier, namely Georg Cassander. Unspecified orations of Cicero exemplified the rhetoric and brief weekly declamations provided the practical use. Verse study progressed to Horace and Juvenal and drama to Plautus. An oration of Cicero was to be rhymed off in public audience by each pupil. 'Lecture scholes' for readers elsewhere in the burgh were forbidden to use any Latin text even of the rudiments and nobody lacking perfect mastery of the vernacular and some writing ability was qualified for admission to the high school. One can envisage the potential for conflict between Hume and the humanity regent in the university, especially as Hume found Despauterius both opaque and barbarous and found himself turning to Ramus whose method, he averred, had in several matters penetrated Scotland. In 1614, John Ray, former humanity regent and now Hume's successor, broke away from points in the 1597 order he found objectionable. Simson's first and second rudiments were both reaffirmed as necessary prologues to the later use of Despauterius. The vocabulary of Stanbridge, totally anglicised and introduced to Scotland by the Englishman, Waldegrave, was laid down for declension practice, and the time-honoured *Sayings of the Sages* and Cato's *Distichs* for syntactical exercises. The second class proceeded to Despauterius himself not to Pellisson. Cordier was no longer a first year text, the *Minor Colloquies* of Erasmus and Johann Sturm's selections from the epistles of Cicero. As soon as the pupils embarked on book three of the first part (deviant forms and exceptions to the rules), they were to attempt alternately Latin prose and prose translation. Ray's third class continued with the second part (syntax) of Despauterius along with Cicero's epistles and easier treatises of Cicero like that on *Old Age* or on *Friendship*. Terence began this year as a compulsory text. Some were obviously dubious about a too precipitous initiation into verse-reading as distinct from verse-writing, but if these doubts could be dispelled, Ovid's *Epistles*, presumably the *Heroides* rather than the *Pontic* Epistles, or his *Tristia* were counselled as texts. There was to be practice in prose themes and letter-writing only. The fourth class turned to versification, with the third and fourth parts of Despauterius accompanied by some 'fables of Ovid', that is the *Metamorphoses*, or Virgil, with historical material in Quintus Curtius and Caesar, and for the brighter youths, Suetonius. Practice continued in translations, proses, scanning of verse and verse-writing for those with the aptitude. The fifth or high class was for rhetoric with some of Cicero's orations or his *De oratore* or *De claris oratoribus*. Sallust for history, Plautus (suitably expurgated, no doubt) for drama, Horace, Juvenal and Persius for more advanced verse. Cicero and Ovid dominated the curriculum. In the last class students finally approached Greek grammar and its literature through simpler texts like Hesiod's *Works and Days* and Theognis. The stress on Despauterius was a far cry from Hume.

When, however, one turns to Hume's *New Grammar* of 1612 one finds the fashionable Ramism has been drastically remodelled by an original mind. In many of Hume's definitions extra-grammatical preoccupations predominate. Theological or metaphysical presuppositions led him to abandon the Ramist definition of the noun as 'a word of number'; with Hume it becomes a 'personal/impersonal word', 'person' being itself defined as 'the subsistence of a thing indicated by a word', a definition worlds away from the purely structural Ramist one in which 'person' is a 'special termination of the word.' He is close to the Ramist definition of gender as 'according to sex', but more precise in explicating, 'according to an indication of sex'. Unlike Ramus in his rejection of mood in the verb, while sympathising with the reason adduced, Hume retains mood because of its evident utility, and in details such as in the wide application of the notion of 'person' he clearly was in Linacre's debt. Otherwise Ramist dichotomies emerged in the various subdivisions of declension and Ramist also is his division of grammar into two parts only, 'etymology' and syntax, according to Hume's *First Elements of Grammar* (1612). His *New Grammar* is claimed as a recall to method and in his dedication to the Chancellor of Scotland, Alexander Seton, earl of Dunfermline, written in October 1608, he asserted that he first considered a revised grammar in 1598. After sixteen years in England he was forced by the Edinburgh climate of opinion to adhere to Despauterius, whose method he disliked. Ramus remained the one alternative; he had some hearing in Scotland, a land, Hume claimed, where there were many great, but few learned, men. In his prefix to an appendix of notes he listed the commissioners appointed to examine his grammar, a task they took a year to fulfil: Thomas Henryson of Chesters; Adam King, church representative; James Sandilands and William Seton, advocates; and Patrick Sandys, who besides years teaching at Edinburgh university had the experience of literary study in France, Italy and Germany. On their advice two parliaments decided that Despauterius be excluded and one national grammar prescribed. In all this Seton, the chancellor, had proved Hume's trusted patron whose aid he compared to that of Henry VIII's chancellor, Thomas More, given to William Lily, forced to abandon Oxford for John Colet's school at St Paul's in London. More, he claimed, used his authority to overcome the envy of the vulgar such as Hume himself was experiencing, seeing to its reception in every school to the exclusion of the older books. The devotion of such men of affairs to the republic of letters deserved, he went on, every thanks both now and in time to come.

Among those thanked was Andrew Melville, and Hume sent a revealing letter to him in exile at Sedan, subscribed on 8 November 1612 from 'Pannis' (Prestonpans, wrongly dated by McCrie). It referred to an earlier letter five months previously, so it is obvious they were close friends, and that it was this, and not Hume's Ramism, that excited the enmity of the Scottish bishops. Seton had often tried to reconcile Hume to Gledstanes, archbishop of St Andrews, but Hume was prepared to make no personal overtures: he also risked the displeasure of Edinburgh ministers, Patrick Galloway and John Hall, by not sending them customary gift copies of his book. In any event John Ray at Edinburgh grammar school was hostile and the town authorities followed suit. Through Archbishop Spottiswoode, despite his previous approval, the King was persuaded to revoke Hume's monopoly, a revocation publicly proclaimed at the cross in Edinburgh. When his attention was drawn to this, Seton pointed out that the decision in Hume's favour was not reached in a hurry; that, though ready to obey a royal order, he did not think it right that a decision come to after such serious thought should be overturned by letters impetrated for reasons clouded by uncertainty. Seton's view carried the day, but Hume's opponents refused to let the matter rest. There was hope that Seton would become governor (*prorex*) in Scotland and Spottiswoode replace him in the chancellorship. But the root of episcopal grudge was Hume's addiction to Melville. While at dinner, Hume had heard John Johnston, Melville's associate, accused of inhibiting Robert Wilkie, principal of St Leonard's, from collecting Melville's university revenues while absent in the Tower of London. This he did with the concurrence of Melville's relative at St Mary's College in St Andrews, Patrick. Hume protested in a letter, unwilling to credit that Johnston would side with Gledstanes and the new head of St Mary's, Robert Howie. On Johnston's death that letter was found among his effects. Gledstanes retained it, boasting that he could if he liked have Hume held for treason to His Majesty, King James. Hume wrote that he had never hurt His Majesty by look, word or gesture, but was not averse from harming the bishop's majesty. He just wished that James would be more wise and hate the malice of the bishops, for he believed all reasonable men already saw through them. (Edinburgh U.L., MS Dc.6.5, Melvini Epistolae, p.309.)

Reasons far from consideration of scholarship motivated the episcopal intervention; John Ray was regent in humanity by 1598, having graduated in Edinburgh in 1597. Born in Angus in 1567, he had evidently been brought up on Despauterius. On the noun substantive, Hume maintained that it had one gender. Ray's reaction was instantaneous and exaggerated, Hume claimed, for he shouted, 'This is an utter disgrace'. But other Scots schoolmasters found Hume's terminology misleading, as when he persistently favoured the Ramist expression 'affections' of the verb for the generally received term 'accidents'.

It is hardly surprising that Hume's grammar was never reprinted and that the 1633 revision still remains in manuscript. But he did not abandon his lost monopoly after Melville's death. Parliament had returned often to the question, notably in 1607. The 1610 commission excluded Ray. The exclusive use of Hume was authorised in November 1612. In 1623 Hume alleged that 'some discontented personis possesst his Majesties royal earis' complaining of obscurities that put it out of the reach of youth. Ray again intervened when a revision was effected and other schoolmasters with some representative schoolboys brought together to test its teachability gave it the thumbs down. Yet, once again in 1630 the question of Hume's 'new grammar' raised its head, again without success. Meantime, some-time after 1617, he had ventured into orthography with a treatise 'Of the Orthographie and Congruitie of the Britan Tongue', which was dedicated to King James. In writing, three things had to be observed: the symbol or written letter as it appeared to the eye; the thing symbolised as the letter sounded in the ear; and the congruity between the language as spoken with the language as read. Unlike Buchanan, he made a 23 letter alphabet and spoke of the problems Robin Hood would have with southern vowels if asked to 'bow' (bend) the bow of his bow and arrow. The Scots, Hume averred, were more correct in their articulation of words of Latin pronunciation, citing the evidence of Giles Laurence, regius professor of Greek at Oxford. While apparently arguing for the received pronunciation, he clearly expected the English to adopt some Scots usages. The second part dealt with agreement in person, number, gender and case and other grammatical agreements, the book being intended for schools. Hume adverts to the King's long-term interest in such matters, 'commanding at your first entrie to your Roial sceptre' a project for grammar reform and the teaching of Aristotle 'in his aun tongue, quhilk has maed the greek almaest as common in Scotland as the latin.'

For a further proof of potential opposition to Hume, the Glasgow grammar school curriculum may be cited. It is usually dated 1573, but must be much later, possibly about 1600. (Grant, *Burgh Schools of Scotland*, pp.336–7.) The pattern of this very much anticipates or follows Ray's Edinburgh order of 1614. Simson's name was omitted, but Despauterius was the basic text and Terence was postponed to the middle school. Cassander figures as rhetorical authority, but Buchanan's *Prosody* as a versification text: as this did not appear in print till *c*.1595, that fact alone excludes an earlier date.

Like so many other schoolmasters, Andrew Duncan was a product of St Leonard's college where he was both scholar and regent after graduating in 1575. Some time after Melville's arrival as a 'graet student' of theology he was won over to his side.

In 1591 he was appointed to Dundee grammar school and from there issued his *First part of Latin grammar* (1595), dealing with 'etymology' alone. He dedicated it to John Kennedy, earl of Cassillis, a dedication in the Buchanan tradition. Duncan, however, was too young when the commission of 1596 was chosen, and there were complaints during his tenure of office, which he resigned in 1597 to become minister of Crail. This first work was fortified by Latin lines from Robert Wilkie, new principal of St Leonard's; by Duncan's predecessor (1567–91) as schoolmaster, Thomas Ramsay; and his successor, David Lindsay, former schoolmaster at Montrose. John Johnston's verse referred to the common concern shared by great men like Joseph Scaliger and Justus Lipsius for words and letters: one, it may be added, of their few shared concerns. The book strives less for originality than for simplicity. His definitions of parts of speech have a deceptive modernity, but their formal, structural appearance resulted from brevity more than from forethought. Echoing Ramus, he divided grammar into two, not the four parts found in 'the vast and fearful ocean of Despauterius', yet claimed to follow Despauterius nonetheless. If he departed from strict logical procedure, he explained, it was for the better service of youth. Thus he excised the verse mnemonics which he did not think helpful and the crowded marginal glosses as over-prolix and not self-explanatory. Even less friendly to Despauterius was John Echlin, one of Duncan's sponsors, and professor of eloquence and philosophy at St Leonard's, scathing about the prospect of growing aged in the gloomy school of Despauterius or wasting time with Villedieu so as to be unable to appreciate the fruits of scholarship after years of hunting the husks. Like Simson, he followed Linacre in including a potential mood, and his adverb, 'an invariable word adding the circumstance to the thing', is reminiscent of Melanchthon. In the same year he issued a separate *Appendix to the Etymology* where fuller details and vocabularies were provided for those who wanted them, though he did not think at the rudiments stage schoolboys should be weighed down with a farrago of words.

Two years later Duncan issued a *Key for the Studies of Boys*, a handy summary of what are now the three parts of grammar, 'etymology', syntax and prosody. The second part of this was later anonymously reprinted as the second part of Simson, possibly because, when it first appeared, Simson's own second part, the syntax, had not seen the light, though it soon did. The first part, however, was less lucky. A prosody section to this is defended on the grounds that from the very start students might practise on 'Buchanan's psalms and suchlike', typical of Duncan's religious concern; hence his postponement of scansion to the 'last act of the play'. Indeed, he admitted that the teacher might want to skip prosody at this stage. His whole attitude was practical and pupil-centred. The quarrels among grammarians had no point to one, who, apart from a few sons of the nobility, found the bulk of his pupils among future merchants, sailors, farmers and artisans like tailors and cobblers. Anglicisation was prominent in Duncan's vocabulary, the article 'ane' before consonants being in retreat, with forceful Scots phrases balanced by standard English: *edax* means a 'great eater' but also 'a greedie gutte'. In his will, a movingly written document, drawn up in April 1626 when he felt himself persecuted by the episcopal party, he prayed Christ to send his holy angels to transport his soul to Abraham's bosom and classed his possessions as no more than 'baggadge and clathrie'. To John Spottiswoode, archbishop of St Andrews, he wrote, citing the proverb, that 'Hall-Binks are slidderie . . . and earthly courts are kittle'.

Duncan was also responsible for *Rudiments of piety*, the forerunner to which, he claimed was the 'torch' of I.N., that is John Craig's vernacular catechism which he had 'transfused' into Latin for the benefit of his Dundonians. There followed a statement on the threefold nature of man's condition, before the fall, in the state of sin after the fall, and last in the state of grace, accompanied by a simple catechism to which a brief guide was attached. The creed and decalogue were added for memorisation, but no manual of civility such as Giovanni Sulpizio's versified booklet or the hygienic instructions common subsequently. This work, dedicated to Andrew, earl of Rothes, was constantly reprinted: it was intended as a companion work for the 1595 grammar and even be studied in advance of it. In fact, Duncan's main concern was piety since indulgence led to the gallows. Even so, he was anxious that pupils should be motivated by love, not terror, and that schooldays should be enjoyable.

The grammar of the Frenchman, Petrus Ramus, has figured less in modern discussion than has his logic. Scots were indeed early Ramist enthusiasts, due to the patronage of the Guise relatives of Mary of Lorraine. Ramus considered that language and thought were two areas that should have as little to do with each other as possible. Ramus's innovative ideas in grammar were paralleled by the *Rhetoric* of Omer Talon, his disciple, with one edition of which, in 1559, a Scot abroad, Duncan MacGruder, was involved. But neither was recommended in Buchanan's programme for St Andrews, nor is there any evidence for their introduction into a university course till Andrew Melville came to Glasgow in 1574, by which time Ramus had become a Protestant martyr. Yet, though these grammatical works are found in printers' inventories in the 1580s, they scarcely challenge the dominant Despauterius. Indeed nothing by Ramus or Talon was published in Scotland in the sixteenth century, and though the *Rudiments* of Ramus were taught in Stirling (possibly also in Glasgow) in 1602 it was along with the 'common rudimentis professit in all uther scoles' (i.e. Andrew Simson) and the first part of Pellisson, based on Despauterius. Yet a Scot, Roland McIlmaine, translated and published Ramus's logic in 1574, hoping for Scots as well as English sales, though writing in the London dialect. He made a plea, however, for the mother tongue to be used in learned works, extending its vocabulary to do so, just as Cicero employed Latin rather than Greek in addressing his own Romans.

James Carmichael had certainly read Ramus, but not, it seems to any great purpose. Born about 1546, he is first met with as a student in St Leonard's in 1561, his graduation not being recorded. By July 1570, he was schoolmaster in St Andrews when he criticised Robert Hamilton, provost of the rival of St Mary's college and local minister for failing to denounce the murderers of the Regent Moray. In August his patrons appointed him minister of Haddington and he soon had three more parishes in charge. Schoolmasters were scarce when in April 1572 the council got the commendator of Holyrood to accept him as their schoolmaster too. About the same time he married Violet, named after her mother, wife of Andrew Simson. His activities away from Haddington helped his schoolmastering so little that in May 1576 the council determined that in future never again would their minister be schoolmaster as well. But Carmichael found an ally in the commendator and did not at once surrender the post. He was, of course, one of the convention of grammarians. Exiled along with others suspected of involvement in plots against King James, he had contacts with English politicians like Walsingham and the earl of Leicester, whose schoolmaster, John Leech, he possibly knew. He read King James's *Essayes of a Prentise in the Divine Art of Poesie* (1584) and reported that some political features of that work were unpopular in the south. He also took the opportunity afforded by absence from his charge to fulfil his promise to compile a *Second Part of Latin Grammar* (Cambridge 1587).

This is really an extended 'etymology', part revision of Simson's first rudiments, part breaking fresh ground. By 1586 Carmichael had a library of over 400 books and this is reflected in a book too learned for schoolboys. Though he cited the Latin dramas of Buchanan he avoided the dialogue method and campaigned against 'prophane plays' (A.J. Mill, *Medieval Plays in Scotland*, 1924, repr. 1969, pp.254–5). He seemed unaware of Hepburn's grammar, but named Vaus. He cited Buchanan frequently, occasionally also Beza and Ramus, but notable absences from his bibliography are Erasmus, Sturm and Talon. In a verse-letter to James Wilkie, the aged principal of his old college, he confessed that his grammar contained nothing except what he learnt in St Leonard's: yet for him the current provost of St Mary's, recently his fellow-exile, Andrew Melville, was the 'arch-poet' whose criticism he most feared. Unlike the old 'Greeks' in the 'Greek versus Trojan' grammatical war of Sir Thomas More's time, Carmichael was a convert to early memorisation, but retained their devotion to Greek. The Greek alphabet was included along with the transliterated Hebrew in what, in one respect, is really a dictionary as well as a guide to genders and to all sorts of grammatical 'exceptions': obviously that was in line with Buchanan's ideas. There are even references to Hebrew and Syriac, Angelo Caninio being one authority cited. Among more recent names are those of Robert Estienne and his son Henri, with the two Scaligers and Lipsius. While plainly at ease in southern English in this work his Scots seems less anglicised than Duncan's. Like Buchanan in his *Prosody* he cited Catullus as well as Ovid.

Besides a wider choice of ancient grammarians (Varro seems an especial favourite) he had consulted Lily and Linacre and his introduction to James VI was influential in the 1593 national regulations, for he too dealt with the problems raised by children passing from school to school and thus from one theory to another. Schoolmasters, he explained, were creatures of habit and preferred what they themselves had first learnt or were accustomed to teach, and otherwise were at the mercy of whatever booksellers were prepared to sell. In general this work, though Hume would attempt to follow it, must have fitted uncomfortably into the curriculum and was never reprinted. This may have discouraged a man whom Melville called a 'profound dreamer', though he went on collecting literary materials. With his belief in the transmission of proverbial wisdom, he assembled a number of Scots proverbs in manuscript, and in class may have produced his own 'sentences' just as the Englishman Leech did his own dialogues. Some of these proverbs, incidentally, are not what are conventionally expected to be treasured by a Puritan minister. Even so, Carmichael was a gifted man lured by the spell of words. His Melvillian friend, James Lawson, drew up his will in Scots after a brief English exile, though Calderwood's version of it is anglicised. Carmichael's stay was short enough for him to remember his Scots tongue, but long enough to anglicise his regular speech if his correspondence is any indication.

Another Haddington assistant teacher or 'doctor' was George Lightbody, who after graduating at St Leonard's in 1610 taught in Oldhamstocks before turning up in Haddington while Carmichael was resident there, though his *Grammatical Questions digested into a Compendium* (Edinburgh, 1628) were issued in the year of Carmichael's death. The work was dedicated to a Berwickshire worthy, Sir William Cockburn, laird of Langton, to whose son he was tutor prior to young Cockburn's philosophical studies. The work had a ten-year privilege from Charles I, but was not reprinted till the Restoration. Lightbody may have heard of the English grammarian John Leech, who certainly listed Nicodemus Frischlin's similar grammar among his sources in 1587. His general orientation is towards Despauterius whose versified rules for syntax he expected his pupils to memorise. Grammar for Lightbody is essentially a prelude to logic in the spirit of Julius Caesar Scaliger whose work he cited. Disputation is clearly envisaged, for pastors and divines must be able to test their students' ability to respond rapidly, promptly and fearlessly: hence the very thorough question-and-answer method adopted between master and pupil and constant insistence on clarity in definitions. Occasionally Lightbody can be vague. Following the teacher's dictum that the circumflex accent is out of use among Latin speakers, the student naturally asked when this happened, to which Lightbody responded merely: Once upon a time! There are vestiges of Linacre in the distinction between 'just' and 'figured speech' and the acceptance of the 'potential mood'. Like Carmichael Lightbody likes to refer to his literary sources: approved authors including besides the usual Cicero, Terence, Ovid, Virgil and Horace others like Persius and Tacitus. His calendar starts oddly in March rather than January. Conjunctions interested him as a Puritan author with a bent towards syllogistic reasoning, borrowing extensively from the ancient grammarians for subtle distinctions. Like Carmichael in his proverb collection he can be near the bone as in, 'The urinator lasts marvellously well under the water.' In 1638 he published in Holland a Puritan pamphlet against the King's service book entitled, *Against the apple of the left eye of Antichrist*.

Of Robert Williamson's early career nothing is known, unless he is identical with the applicant for the schoolmastership of that name occurring in Aberdeen in 1580 and the St Leonard's graduate of two years previous: if so, he lived like Hume to a very great age. His *Elements of Latin prior to Despauterius' grammar* (1624) was first published in 1609, but of that edition no copy survives. By 1624 he held the post in Cupar. His dedication to the son of Sir John Preston of Airdrie (Fife) claimed that basic grammar could be learnt by more mature boys (over ten) in a year. He provided the Ariadne's thread through the learning labyrinth: three months for declensions and conjugations with repetition of his 'etymology' compendium for a further six; syntax would take three more, with readings and exercises in Cordier, Cato, Cicero and Erasmus; then the two first parts of Despauterius would be run through by sticking to commentary alone. Essentially Williamson followed Donatus and Priscian but in the syntax section obviously borrowed from Linacre. After listing a few figures of speech, he broke off with the observation that something had to be left to teachers on the spot if they were real teachers, otherwise, if they went on at excessive length, art would grow old and grammar teaching fall away. In 1632 he elaborated on his earlier scheme. The boys under age ten were to spend their days on the bare conjugations and declensions with some vocabulary and scripture. 'Etymology' and syntax should take one year more. The third year should encompass verse study and verse-writing (its method at least). The fourth and possible fifth year should cover 'ornament' (rhetoric). On prosody and rhetoric he hoped to follow up with a separate text-book, but his programme has nothing new. Some sentence models have a pious ring to them, while ample use was made of Despauterius's mnemonics. Williamson was in 1630 trying to win royal favour for 'ane Grammer to be universallie teached' as the 1597 act phrased it, and armed himself with commendations from Ben Jonson's friend, Thomas Farnaby, who approved of Williamson's approach but doubted if his vote counted for anything, though the book's brevity and perspicuity made it preferable to other text-books he had seen. Two other London schoolmasters, John Turing and Henry Bonner, the former certainly a Scot, praised it unreservedly as did several masters in Edinburgh, Perth, Linlithgow, with three Fife teachers including Williamson's own assistant at Cupar. On a copy being forwarded to the king, Charles I addressed the Scots Privy Council, noting its claims for speed and accuracy, that Williamson had borne the printing costs and adding his willingness, subject to their approval, to grant it a 21 year patent.

Williamson also compiled a *Moral Pedagogy* (1635) of which two earlier editions are lost, dedicated to the sons of Preston of Airdrie and Arnot of Fernie. These he aimed, he said, to teach in addition to grammar (inclusive of the rules of poetry and rhetoric in Latin, Greek and Hebrew) the commandments of God and rules of civil conduct, for he who was proficient in letters and deficient in morals was more deficient than proficient. The work included prayers, one a version of Buchanan's 'Morning Hymn to Christ', plus versified prayers and a question-and-answer catechism, in which one is reminded that any man's election by God should not be the subject to over-anxious scrutiny. Bible texts apt for memorisation completed this section. Part two touched on civilised behaviour, elementary precautions like shading one's mouth while belching; clothes; behaviour in kirk and school or at games, in company, at meals and in privacy. Some lines of the earl of Essex on earthly instability were translated into Latin from the 'angelical English tongue', which shows how far southern Britain was now a cultural exemplar. For a time he demitted his post and on reinstatement was required to promise to teach Wedderburn's grammar and not his own. His will, registered in 1649, is uninformative.

David Wedderburn is the best known of these grammarians. He was an Aberdonian, born probably in December 1579, and was a co-disciple at Aberdeen grammar school of Thomas Dempster. In February 1602, on the death of their former teacher and after a four-day test in 'oratorie and poesie' with prose and verse composition, he and the future Latin secretary of King James in England, Thomas Reid, were given a year's joint appointment in the Aberdeen school. Arthur Johnston, poet and royal physician, described how he encouraged Wedderburn's first slow steps in learning, only to find him surpassing him to the summit, a pardonable exaggeration. His early hesitations were perhaps dissipated when Reid moved on and he was honoured by additional duties as humanity regent in Marischal and King's Colleges. An ardent royalist, he saluted Prince Henry, James VI and Charles I in turn with his verses. He first considered a publication of his own when summoned to Edinburgh in 1630 to give his views on Hume's monopoly. He was granted a subvention by Aberdeen and allowed leave of absence to prosecute his own claim to supersede Hume's *New Grammar*, and in this won the support of the Convention of Royal Burghs. He had still to forestall Williamson's objections, but Williamson himself found Aberdeen and Dundee critical of him in turn. In 1638 the burghs were finally compelled to adhere to Wedderburn's monopoly and objecting masters were threatened with deposition. Meantime Hume was bought off, on condition that he and his son, John, were free to teach from their own textbook in Dunbar.

Wedderburn's *Short Introduction to Grammar* for facilitating the use of Despauterius appeared in 1632, and was eventually approved on condition of accepting the Privy Council committee's amendments. It deals exclusively with 'etymology', and is in the Vaus-Simson tradition. An echo of Linacre is the inclusion of the potential mood, by now an accepted feature; ordinal and cardinal numbers in common use gave a nod in the direction of arithmetic. He made no effort to restrict himself to Latin, with the defence that those who taught Greek taught it in Latin not in Greek, but the English Wedderburn used was remote from the speech of ordinary Aberdonians. A second edition appeared in 1637, though it never displaced the Simson/Duncan rudiments in national favour. Lorenzo Valla was the one Renaissance writer cited. Wedderburn's *Grammatical Institutions* (dated 1633 for 1635?) dealt only with 'etymology' and syntax, omitting prosody, while the 1634 edition added orthography and prosody (the latter dealing with both accent and quantity). The 1634 edition also gave Greek and Hebrew forms for declension without the use of the print types of either; it cited classical authors (with Martial and Tibullus) and, among the post-classical, J.C. Scaliger and Melanchthon. The latter's influence can be seen in the definition of noun as an 'inflected diction by which is signified either the thing itself or an accident of the thing.' Great use was made of the mnemonics of Despauterius; Valla was echoed in the phrase 'formulas of elegances'; and in the prosody section Buchanan appeared in a single citation. The history of Despauterius in Scotland continued for a century more, but must be left here. The key text for pedagogical method was still Erasmus's *De Ratione Studii* printed regularly with Despauterius by Scottish printers from 1579 on. More popular, however, nationally than Wedderburn's grammars was his

*Vocables* (1636 etc.) which replaced Stanbridge as a vocabulary aid, becoming an accepted annexe even to reprints of Simson/Duncan.

### III.

It is not necessarily the beginning of the story to start with the 1496 donation to the Pedagogy in his university by Alexander Inglis, archdeacon of St Andrews, a Pedagogy derelict and badly in need of re-animation. (Modern transcript of lost original, St Andrews University archives.) The gift included not only standard classics like Virgil, the poetic epistles of Ovid, the letters of Cicero, Seneca's tragedies, and, it seems, Horace, but also encouraged the new approach to literature at university level by making Italian Latinists available in the common library: the Ciceronian epistolary models of Gasparino Barzizza, the even more celebrated models of his pupil, Francesco Filelfo, as well as the *Vocabulary* of the Neapolitan, Gianiano Maio, a vast classical compendium compiled from the works of his friends at the court of Naples, Valla and Pontano, besides the ancient philologists. Another gift was the 'poetic pearl', *Margarita Poetica* of Jacob van Eyb, a store-house of classical source-material with not only abundant citation from Virgil and Catullus, but also from Petrarch himself and with constant acknowledgement made to Barzizza. Formed on works like these a generation of readers would acquire quite novel literary standards.

The re-entry of grammar into the university curriculum was to face a stiff battle if logic was to be dislodged from its key role in engaging so much of the students' energies. Even so, Cuthbert Simson was hired to lecture daily at Glasgow in 1501, and in 1506 a Frenchman, Jacques Charpentier, lectured in poetry and oratory at St Andrews. Meantime at Aberdeen John Vaus was already grafted on to the university establishment. What propagandists like Valla and Juan Luis Vives wanted, however, was to slim down the time assigned to Logic to the slenderest proportions, and remove the linguistic schizophrenia of the academics of the John Mair school, then enjoying an Indian summer in Paris: of a man like Robert Galbraith, the prefaces to whose *Quadripartite logic* were classically composed and cited Angelo Poliziano, while the body of the work employed the 'abject' Latin that the invective of Valla and Vives had set out to banish.

Aberdeen was the latest foundation of the medieval universities. Its founder, Bishop William Elphinstone, owned Valla's *Elegances* while a contemporary chronicler styled him another Nicholas of Cusa. Moreover he chose as principal Hector Boece, colleague and friend of the young Erasmus in Paris and in touch with Florence Wilson, former alumnus and humanist abroad. Boece was part also of the Mair school's Indian summer but that combined with an interest in 'eloquent history' with, however, the minimum of attention to rigour of documentation, suffused throughout with a blind national passion. Though a visitation of 1549 points up a subsequent decline in its initial ardour, a fragment of a surviving King's College library borrowing register shows that the curriculum had a strong input of Lefèvre consequent on friendly relations between its regents and Ferrerio at Kinloss. At the Reformation, under the protecting hand of the Catholic earl of Huntly, King's remained stubbornly attached to the old faith. Not till 1569 did the Regent Moray and his councillors, with Kirk support, duly set out to suppress this anomaly. A Protestant spokesman chosen by Moray, George Hay, was aware that his audience of college members might censure his 'effrontery', yet he elected to assail their attachment to the 'stinking pools' of Tartaret, a Parisian Scotist still used in the classes and lectures 'hammered out by their own efforts', as indeed Boece's own textbook might be described: Hay's own preferred text-book seems to have been George of Trebizond. Significantly the replacement staff were to be recruited from St Mary's college graduates, Alexander Arbuthnot, James Lawson and Hercules Rollock. The decisive argument employed to repel the deposed Catholic regents was their opposition to the new establishment, composed of those, as Hay averred, 'whom in view of the position which they occupy in the state, I neither can nor should oppose.' How far these new leaders of 1569 really won the collaboration of the Aberdonians is questionable, for when a new foundation was proposed by State and Kirk in 1583, apart from a complaisant principal, there was such resistance that King's College persisted as the solitary Scottish foundation unreconciled to bearing the stamp of Melville's image. (J. Durkan and W.S. Watt, 'George Hay's *Oration*', in '*Northern Scotland*', vi. 97–112.) Though these 1569 depositions did not affect the post of professor of medicine, an original creation by Elphinstone, since the 'mediciner' conformed, yet these plans of 1583 still envisaged its discontinuance.

The challenge of Aberdeen to which even students from Glasgow diocese (like the poet, Adam Mure) were being drawn, inspired a new foundation at St Andrews, again clerically endowed. In it the classical tastes of the king's son, Alexander Stewart, the young archbishop, pupil of Erasmus in Italy, were married to Prior John Hepburn's expectations of recruitment for his priory and the Church generally of university-trained clergy. The College of St Leonard (1513) was to be a 'college of the poor', based on a relaxed form of the austere College of Montaigu in Paris. Its first head, John Annand, was a regent from Montaigu, and it, like Montaigu, prided itself on being a 'holy society' and a 'congregation'. It was an annexe outside the priory proper, attended by some novices certainly but also by others like them (*aequales*), developed apparently from a house part hospital, part almonry school. Though poor students are found elsewhere, St Leonard's was the first Scots college to flaunt its poverty as a college of 'poor clerks'. Annand was a Scotist interested in 'signs of origin', 'formalities' and 'common natures' as Duns Scotus was. (Major, *History*, p.440). Yet, though a theologian, he was distrustful of the fashionable canon lawyers around him, who knew the Decretals but scarcely understood them, so there would be no law taught at St Leonard's. Alexander Stewart's charter provided for a principal master who would be a chapter canon and twenty scholars sufficiently instructed in grammar (at least half way through their syntax) to begin arts and six students in theology. The student bursars were known as 'Hoods', reminiscent of the 'Capettes' at Montaigu, and as a nursery for worthy clerics the college was unlikely to succumb to the vices associated with wealth. In the original statutes there was a daily lecture in grammar, poetry or oratory modified in the revised version to thrice weekly, for subsequently the original laws were supplemented, against the will of some leading members, to make room for rich pupils. A climate of reform was certainly nurtured there, Knox referring to Reformers who had drunk of its well. Alexander Alesius (Alane), early Scottish Lutheran, and Gilbert Winram, known to young Martin Bucer, were students. Though few in fact did join the Reformers, all St Leonard's members were imbued, both before and after the Reformation, with a powerful Augustinian piety, oddly linked with both Mair and Erasmus as Gilbert Winram's library shows.

If the College was a well of religiosity, it was likewise a well of good grammar. John Law, its mid-sixteenth century principal had formerly been schoolmaster at Ayr (1515). His manuscript chronicle in Edinburgh University library reveals a special interest in the deaths of humanists, not apparently merely copied from foreign chronicles: the 'elegant writer', Francisco Petrarch; the poet-philosopher, Giovanni Boccaccio; the grammarian-rhetorician, John of Ravenna; Gasparino Barzizza; Leonardo Bruni, elegant poet and historian; Bracciolini Poggio, powerful orator; Giovanni Tortelli, learned in Latin and Greek; Valla himself, noted philosopher, theologian, rhetorician and grammarian; Matteo Palmieri, historian and philosopher; Guarino of Verona, learned grammarian and orator; Francesco Filelfo, poet laureate; Niccolo Perotti, who wrote the *Cornucopia*; and, finally, Fausto Andrelini, poet laureate. It is a plausible surmise that many of these names were to be found in the canons' library at St Andrews though Perotti alone figures in the late sixteenth century college inventory. Law's list may be compared with that of Friar John Grierson, alumnus of Aberdeen. (*Innes Review*, xxviii, 39–49.)

Turning to another religious house and a university course given outside a university, to the monks of Kinloss abbey, one finds Ferrerio, at the abbot's request, opening his lessons in 1531 with commentary on Jerome's letter to Paulinus, 'Frater Ambrosius', in commendation of scripture, proceeding through the bible book by book, on the ground that the example of the genuinely wise urged one to do so, and in so doing, wish to know nothing else. This introduction scarcely seems to match what follows, in large part a parallel arts course. Thereafter Ferrerio plunged into the logic of George of Trebizond, one freed from the subtle preoccupations of the Mair circle, but did not follow Valla in making logic a department of rhetoric. Rudolph Agricola's work on 'invention' was not part of Ferrerio's general course but one for a more restricted group of monks, yet it annexed the rhetorical notion of 'invention' to logic, thereby anticipating Ramus in reducing rhetoric to style. It was Lefèvre's edition of Trebizond that heralded this approach among Northern humanists, but where Agricola tended to ignore the place of judgement in logic, Trebizond's manual repaired this omission. (John Monfasani, *George of Trebizond*, Leiden, 1976.) Of the logic typified by Mair, it retained only the theory of 'obligation', that is the method of avoiding logical traps in one's discourse: a logic for preachers. The rest of the course follows the usually Aristotelean pattern as far as metaphysics, all based on textbooks edited by Lefèvre. Ferrerio discoursed where the scholastics questioned. For him, as for Lefèvre, Aristotle's works if uncorrupted by medieval translation, were beautifully eloquent, pathways to the happiness he wrote of at Kinloss. The summit of such felicity was the works of Dionysius the Areopagite, as presented by Lefèvre again in his strong mystical vein, for he was believed to be a disciple of St Paul, and on him the Italian discoursed to a single selected monk. He may have felt that thus the declared aim of the course as enunciated by Jerome had not been frustrated.

The name of Mair was so potent that it was possibly only with the arrival of William Cranston at St Andrews that a changed philosophy took over, for he not only produced a thin *Dialectic* but showed signs of the influence of Agricola. He became provost of St Salvator's, and on his departure to France with his fellow regents at the Reformation, John Rutherford's less insubstantial compendium, compiled while a tutor to the family of Michel de Montaigne, took over, as Rutherford moved from St Mary's to take over the headship of St Salvator's. Rutherford was an anti-Ramist. From the books he left behind, it is clear that he favoured the reform whereby the modern commentators were to be abandoned for the ancient ones like Simplicius and Themistius. The text was to be studied in Greek, hence the 'classical preceptor' who is found in the 1562 philosophy course. A wider choice of text was available in Cicero, Plato and Xenophon besides Aristotle. One Italian philosopher he used was Agostino Nifo who had criticised Valla on lines similar to his own criticisms of contemporaries. Rutherford and Patrick Buchanan had both been influenced

by Nicolas de Grouchy while teaching with George Buchanan at
Coimbra: Grouchy revised the obscure Ciceronianism of Joachim
Périon's translation, and Rutherford followed suit. If the Buchanans
had not left the Vives camp, the Vives who had seemed to be
following Valla whole-heartedly, it was because latterly Vives had
seen danger in too much addiction to philology, in that words lost
their definition and that only bred the kind of scepticism which
Calvin branded in his treatise 'On Scandals'. Whether many of the
young bloods persuaded by their fathers to study at St Andrews
altogether grasped the drift of conflicting philosophical schools is a
moot question: we hear of one young nobleman called Montgomery
who found himself caught out by the argument of an opponent and
answered by slapping him on the face, a response later dignified
with the title of 'Montgomery's proof'. (David Hume, *De familia
Humii Wedderburnensi*, Abbotsford Club, 1839, p.43.) Later St Salvator's
men, like Robert Balfour, anti-Ramist philosopher at Bordeaux, and
John Napier, who could not credit even Valla's exposure of the so-
called Donation of Constantine, were reflecting long-standing tradition there.

In the 1520s Archbishop James Beaton I decided that a fresh start
had to be made. Mair's ideal was still the old type of scholastic
curriculum. A boy should learn grammar, rhetoric, logic and music;
if he was apt for learning he could add arithmetic and geometry, as
they did not demand experience of life or transcend the imagination,
in the latter of which natural philosophy resembles it; morals should
follow to obviate harmful effects on character; then at twenty when
the human mind is at its finest, metaphysics, as a foretaste of the
happiness of heaven. The programme advised by the archbishop's
nephew, Archibald Hay was rather different. Hay's book was
published in 1538 and was in the form of a panegyric of Beaton. It
attacked Henry Cornelius Agrippa for his scepticism regarding all
learning apart from the bible, not only the peripatetic Aristotelians,
but the mutual invective of philologists like Valla and those admirers
of oratory who would risk turning pagan so as not to cease being
Ciceronians. Hay commended all the traditional studies but added
that theology was blind if studied with no background of the biblical
languages. He omitted logic till the second edition, but this may be
included under the blanket term 'philosophy': yet he made quite
plain his opposition to the Mair school's approach to logic which
had everywhere felt the force of the big humanist guns. Arabic and
Chaldee (Aramaic) ought rather to be studied instead, along, of
course, with Greek and Hebrew. The main strength of Aristotle was
said to be his philosophy of nature and the 'divine Plato' was a
necessary supplement. The university needed a well-endowed
library and a printer who had Greek types. Hay had also edited the
*Hecuba* of Euripides in the translation of Erasmus, and his was a full-

blooded Erasmian programme. The second edition of the oration was dedicated to Cardinal David Beaton who replaced Archbishop Beaton I and under him Hay came to St Andrews in 1545 from Paris. Subsequent events, including the cardinal's murder, scarcely improved the new St Mary's college prospects. However, he was eventually inducted as principal in July 1546, proferring a highly ornate oration to mark the occasion. If he delivered any public lectures on the model of the Paris royal lecturers it is conceivable that two St Leonard's students, Robert Pont and John Row, had then their first taste of Hebrew; but if so, it could only have been a taste, since Hay fell in battle after fourteen months in office, at Pinkie in September 1547. (J.K. Cameron, 'A Trilingual College for Scotland', *St Mary's College Bulletin*, no.31, Christmas 1988.) In his place at St Mary's, John Douglas was appointed, and his influence combined with that of John Rutherford, a teacher whom Douglas (abetted by the cardinal's successor, Archbishop Hamilton) invited over from France, would be decisive (in the fact of their joint patronage of the preachers in the future Reformation crisis) for determining the course of future events. The impact of some learned refugees from Protestant England must also have helped to shape the course of things as well as the attraction of moderate Catholic reform inspired by Cologne and the duchy of Cleves with Georg Cassander and his friends. (J.K. Cameron, '"Catholic Reform" in Germany and in the pre-1560 Church in Scotland,' *Scottish Church History Society Records*, xx, 105–117.)

Shortly after the Reformation a commission was appointed, inclusive of Buchanan, for the reform of St Andrews. This involved three specialised colleges: a college of humanity, a college of philosophy and a college of theology. It is instructive to see how Buchanan proposed to assign duties. The three acting ministers, David Guild at St Salvator's, James Wilkie at St Leonard's and Robert Hamilton at St Mary's were really excluded from the scheme. Buchanan himself was to have the public lectureship in the college of humanity, the principal of which could be either Douglas or Rutherford. The college of philosophy's principal was either of these. Most interesting of all, the principal and reader in Hebrew would be William Ramsay in the college of theology and William Skene as reader in law. Ramsay, therefore, must have known some Hebrew, as a former regent in Bordeaux and student in Wittenberg. He had conformed briefly to Catholicism and lectured in Greek in Glasgow and also as royal lecturer in Edinburgh under Mary of Lorraine. (J. Durkan, 'The Royal Lectureships under Mary of Lorraine', *Scottish Historical Review*, lxii, 73–8.) This manuscript of Buchanan's proposals also added a footnote that might have reconciled Ramsay to the elementary teaching involved, 'The lector in hebrew sall reid the grammer of hebrew in the begynnyng and in tyme to cum to the

effect that he be traualit in gretar materis the eldest bursar sall reid
the grammair thair tyme about and ane of thame als the common
places of theologie of caluin or ather as salbe moist common and
proper'. (Scottish Record Office, Parliamentary Papers 10/1, fo.6.)
Buchanan's original suggestion left the Calvin commentary out and
involved Hebrew and biblical exegesis solely. How far, moreover,
law would succeed tailed on to divinity in the new situation was
questionable. Part of the Queen Dowager's Edinburgh initiative was
to create a public lecturer in law. Part inspiration in all this was the
pre-Reformation bishop, Robert Reid, who saw that most of the
lawyers were in Edinburgh anyway and, evidently under the
inspiration of Ferrerio who knew the Paris royal lectureships at first
hand, left in his 1558 testament eight thousand merks for an
Edinburgh college made up of three schools: one for grammar; the
second for poetry and oratory, and the third for canon and civil law.
The Reformation put paid to that project, though part of the money
was salvaged for the new foundation of Edinburgh university in
1583. Other reforms at St Andrews have already been touched on.
John Douglas and John Winram were signatories to the Book of
Discipline plan for education yet not only does the 1570 reform avoid
mention of Hebrew or Greek, though the *Sentences* of Peter Lombard
have been abandoned, but the exegesis is left open, not tied down to
anybody's school of theology which certainly was not acceptable at
Geneva: even Buchanan is ambiguous here. Yet otherwise old
terminology was preserved, even in the naming of biblical books: the
name Paralipomenon even suggests the Vulgate and where doubts
remained they could have been doubts raised by Thomas de Vio
called Cajetan or even Erasmus. The potential students of divinity
were possibly themselves unsure.

The 1574 intervention by the Regent Morton's commissioners
completed the work of 1563. Each college principal had duties set
down, to give a public lecture in Latin once weekly in divinity. The
third master in St Salvator's was to lecture daily on rhetoric; the third
master of New College had four lessons on the mathematical
sciences; the second master in St Salvator's had four on Greek; but
the second in St Mary's (Mr Robert Hamilton), four in Hebrew. Since
the provost of New College was on the point of death during
Morton's visitation, Archibald Hamilton may already have been envisaged as continuing the Hebrew lectures when Robert was advanced
to the provostship. He certainly was qualified to do so, possibly
learning it from Patrick Buchanan, the poet's brother (J. Durkan,
'James, Third Earl of Arran: The Hidden Years', *S.H.R.*, lxv, 157).

The real watershed in the Scottish university situation was,
however, the appointment of Andrew Melville to Glasgow as
principal in 1574. First of all he brought Petrus Ramus into the
philosophical and literary curriculum, though there had been some

interest in his work in Scotland before Melville. Ramus's appeal, apart from his concern with method in education, seems mainly to have lain in his endeavour, by reducing the scope of rhetoric, to bring some thought content back into a literature now replete with extravagant stylistic mannerisms. To do this he attacked Aristotle's traditional definitions and his assistant, Omer Talon, compiled a new rhetoric to fit the bill. Melville had been at St Andrews, Paris and Poitier before arriving at Geneva where the professor of philosophy, Simone Simoni, and Theodore Beza were both militantly anti-Ramist, which did not prevent Melville visiting Ramus's personal lecturers on Cicero's *Catiline* oration at Lausanne. Obviously, therefore, his Ramism was not imported from Geneva. In Geneva also Melville had proved an apt student of the Hebrew scholar, Bonaventura Cornelius Bertram, and this was a potent influence on him. Moreover, his uncle Henry Scrimgeour lived in the town and professed law at the academy, though Melville himself only taught in the preparatory college. His friends at the Scottish court included a relative, Peter Young, tutor to the young King James along with George Buchanan. Thus it was in the very year of Morton's university visitation of St Andrews that Andrew Melville received his State appointment to Glasgow. With him was his nephew, James, a student from St Leonard's, who had, however, missed Buchanan's recent principal-ship there. It was not till 1570 that James Wilkie replaced him officially in the post, Buchanan having deserted long since to the college's 'grit hurt and skaith' (St Andrews Univ. Archives, SL110). Only a profound moral passion could have carried Andrew Melville through the programme he attacked in Glasgow, a passion that, as in Mair's day, had attracted so many matriculations that the small college building overflowed, precisely by how many is not known due to Melville's habit of neglect in record-keeping, though it is likely that numbers dropped steeply before graduation. Setting the regent in residence, Peter Blackburn, some administrative chores, he fell immediately to his scholastic task, giving special regard, however, to an elite few among the students. The 1574–5 session was devoted to Greek grammar (his nephew had complained of not reaching beyond the alphabet at St Leonard's), after which he struck out on entirely fresh lines for Scotland by importing into university teaching the *Dialectic* of Ramus and his collaborator Talon's *Rhetoric*, the latter replacing the *Rhetoric* of Cassander that his nephew had learnt at St Leonard's and which Talon failed ultimately to displace in the curriculum. These master texts were then applied to a variety of ancient classics, in Latin (Virgil and Horace) and Greek (Homer and Hesiod) with five more besides: verse predominated and the tone was uniformly serious, no Aristophanes or even Euripides. In 1576 he approached mathematics in a Ramist framework along with Euclid, the geography of Dionysius Periegetes useful only in a

classical context, the *Tables* of Johann Honter (whose early editions
excluded America from the maps) and ancient astronomy in Aratus.
However, Melville constantly updated his texts for in 1577 he
purchased a new edition of Dionysius. That year was totally absorbed
by morals of a traditional, if eclectic nature: besides Aristotle,
Cicero's *Offices, Stoic Paradoxes* and *Tusculan Disputations*, Aristotle's
*Politics* and selected Platonic dialogues, presumably the *Phaedo* and
the pseudo-Platonic *Axiochus*. By 1578 he had turned to natural
philosophy with the traditional *Physics* of Aristotle and his related
treatises, yet eked out (it is hard to see how) by Plato and Jean Fernel.

History had been envisaged in Archibald Hay's planned curriculum;
but Melville struck a more contemporary note, utilising J. Sleidan's
*Four Monarchies* alongside Melanchthon's edition of the apocalyptic
chronicle of Johann Carion. This ended the course in arts. Behind
him Blackburn had charge now of the first class and no doubt taught
as he had himself been taught under John Rutherford in St Andrews.
In 1575 James Melville had preceded him in the first year's literary
course (he uses the St Leonard's word 'seage' for a class) with a more
manageable booklist, Greek language practice in Isocrates, the first
book only of Homer's *Iliad*, the verse of Phocylides, Hesiod's *Works
and Days* and, of course, the techniques of Ramus and Talon brought
to bear this time on the Latin prose of Cicero's *Catiline* oration and
the *Stoic Paradoxes*. James went forward next year to the abbreviated
mathematics of Psellus that James Wilkie had taught at St Leonard's
plus a slimmed down course of Aristotle's logic, but most of the time
he spent on moral matters in the high seriousness of Aristotle's
*Ethics*, the *Phaedo* of Plato (Wilkie was attached to Plato also) and the
*Axiochus*. When the royal re-foundation of 1577 was established, the
nephew ascended to being a specialist professor in charge of a
second year, repeating his threefold course on mathematics, logic
and morals.

Theology ran concurrently with the arts teaching, and the unusual
presence of a charismatic educator from Geneva attracted some post-
graduates from St Andrews. Andrew opened with a brief overview
of Hebrew grammar later to be amplified, with thereafter the
Chaldee (Aramaic) and Syriac dialects, inheriting some textbooks on
both from his pre-Reformation predecessor, Principal John Davidson.
The literature studied (often dwelling on figures of speech unfamiliar
nowadays) was mostly from the Old Testament apart from one
Pauline epistle, that to the Galatians, from the New: the Psalms, the
books then still ascribed to David and Solomon and Ezra. A more
general survey of both Testaments accompanied this. But this was
not exegesis freed from external theological preoccupations for, as
he proceeded, dogma went hand in hand in linguistics. This was
taken from the 'common-places', such as sin, grace, justification,

faith and works, Covenants New and Old: this is found in the revised version of Buchanan's university plan as well, though not in the 1570 statutes of Winram. Melville inherited the Genevan view that Paul's epistle to the Romans was the epitome of all Christianity (Wodrow Society, *Miscellany*, i, 407).

This Glasgow programme was allowed to flesh out even more when in 1579 a Scottish Sorbonne, a college restricted to theology alone, got the go-ahead for St Andrews and Melville appointed first principal and a dynasty of Melvilles (for Patrick Melville soon joined James and Andrew) took over from a dynasty of Hamiltons. It seems Melville had trained no divine as yet qualified to work with him and still there remained a scarcity of academics qualified in the three languages. He even considered employing two English Puritans, Thomas Cartwright and Walter Travers, which would have caused a furore in St Andrews among rival colleges greater even than the new principal experienced. One of the many quarrels he was to have with the State authorities may have arisen from initial neglect in filling these vacancies. On the negative side, he seemed to hinder the 1579 foundation by beginning to absent himself from his duties and that not only during his enforced English exile; by appearing more engaged in national politics than in university administration and seemingly either negligent of college accounts or spending funds assigned for education on external propaganda. On the other hand, although other factors had a place in this, his learning attracted the first considerable groups of foreign students; his example was copied, at least in part, in Glasgow, Edinburgh, and Marischal College, Aberdeen; while his attachment to Ramus and Talon infiltrated other St Andrews colleges, even St Salvator's, where in 1588 Homer Blair, its mathematician, taught from the arithmetic of Ramus while the second year took its rhetoric from Talon. Not till that year is there a record of the student body at Melville's college, comprising the names of future ministers and others, though evidently it was a course too demanding for some. It might be a useful task to discover how far the numbers justified the theological monopoly that had drawn these theologians away from the other colleges. Eventually the State that had originally appointed Melville became the State that was to depose him. Even so a notable humanist influence had been exerted: less in the introduction of the pedagogy of Ramus with its diagrams, dichotomies and keys to universal knowledge than in the solid bases laid for investigating the Greek, Hebrew and allied tongues and through them for wider access to the ancient world itself, an access Melville's work had in large part promoted (J.K. Cameron, 'Andrew Melville in St Andrews', *St Mary's College Bulletin*, no.22, Easter 1980, pp.14–25).

SELECT BIBLIOGRAPHY

County histories of pre-university education exist for Aberdeen (I.J. Simpson), Angus (J.C. Jessop), Ayr (W. Boyd), Banffshire (W. Barclay), Kirkcudbright (J.A. Russell), Stirlingshire (A. Bain), Wigtownshire (J.A. Russell). Of these, the most useful for present purposes is J.M. Beale, *History of the Burgh and Parochial Schools of Fife* (Edinburgh, 1983). For Lanarkshire, the Glasgow Ph.D. thesis, M. Mackintosh, 'Education in Lanarkshire: a historical survey to 1872' (1969). Of general works the best is still J. Grant, *History of the Burgh and Parish Schools of Scotland*, i, (London, 1876); surveys for the period by the present writer in D. MacRoberts, *Essays on the Scottish Reformation* (Glasgow, 1962). For the highlands, D. Withrington, 'Education in the 17th century highlands', *The Seventeenth Century in the Highlands* (Inverness Field Club, 1986), pp. 60–69. See also J. Durkan, *Early Scottish Schools and Schoolmasters* (Scottish Record Society, forthcoming).

For early humanist influences, J. MacQueen, 'Some Aspects of the early Renaissance in Scotland', *Forum for Modern Language Studies*, iii, 201–275; For Kinloss, J. Durkan, 'Giovanni Ferrerio and religious humanism in 16th century Scotland', *Studies in Church History: Religion and Humanism*, xvii (ed. K. Robbins, Oxford, 1981), pp.181–194.

For Scottish universities:

**General**: J. Durkan, 'The Scottish Universities in the Middle Ages' (Edinburgh Ph.D. thesis, 1971).

**St Andrews**: J.K. Cameron, articles in *St Mary's College Bulletin* cited in text. R.G. Cant, *The University of St Andrews : a Short History*, 2nd edn. (Edinburgh, 1970); *The New Foundation of 1579 in Historical Perspective* (St John's House Papers, no.2: Edinburgh, 1979). J. Durkan, 'John Rutherford and Montaigne: an early influence?' *Bibliothèque d'Humanisme et Renaissance*, xl, 115–122.

**Glasgow**: J. Durkan and J. Kirk, *The University of Glasgow 1451–1577* (Glasgow, 1977).

**Aberdeen**: L. Macfarlane, *William Elphinstone and the Kingdom of Scotland 1431–1514*, Aberdeen, 1985). J. Durkan, 'Early Humanism and King's College,' *Aberdeen University Review*, xlviii, 259–279; (with W.S. Watt), 'George Hay's *Oration* at the purging of King's College, Aberdeen; a commentary' (with text), *Northern Scotland*, vi, 97–112.

**Edinburgh**: J. Durkan, 'The Royal lectureship under Mary of Lorraine,' *Scottish Historical Review*, lxii, 73–78; *Universities, Society and the Future*, ed. N. Phillipson (Edinburgh, 1983).

**Philosophy teaching**: A. Broadie, *The Circle of John Mair* (Oxford, 1985).

## Humanism and Religious Life
### JAMES K. CAMERON

Humanism bears many faces. Some see it as advocating 'individual-ism, secularism, and moral autonomy against medieval culture'; others as 'an epitome of medieval Christian culture and humanists as true champions of Christian Neoplatonism and Augustinianism'. Others, as Steven Ozment has pointed out, define it as 'the scholarly pursuit of eloquence, viewing it as strictly an educational and cultural program dedicated to rhetoric, scholarship, good language and literature, with only a secondary interest in metaphysics and moral philosophy, whether Christian or pagan'. (Ozment, 1979, 136; Weinstein, *JHI*, 33 (1972), 165–176.) In this chapter our concern is with humanism as the thought and literary culture of the Renaissance as it affected the religious life of Scotland particularly in the sixteenth and early seventeenth centuries. In Scotland, as throughout western Europe, religion touched upon almost every aspect of life in its concern for the spiritual well-being of the individual and the nation. Hence it will be necessary to refer to subjects which have already received specialist treatment in earlier chapters.

A prominent feature of humanism, but by no means exclusive to it, was a deep-rooted desire for reform both moral and educational throughout the life of the Church. This concern expressed itself in Scotland in a variety of ways but particularly in efforts to reform and deepen the spiritual and cultural life of the clergy both secular and regular. Predominant among those efforts was the holding of Provincial Councils in 1549, 1551–2, and 1558–9. David Patrick (*Statutes*, lii) attributed this 'unwonted energy' to the stress of the Reformation. Of those who attended, some, however, had particular humanist interests and not surprisingly all three councils remind us of the moral earnestness of Erasmian and Fabrisian humanism. In the prologue to the 1549 council reference is made to 'the corruption of morals and profane lewdness of life in churchmen of almost all ranks together with the crass ignorance of literature and of all the liberal arts' (*Statutes* 84) as at least partly responsible for the spread of heresy. The Statutes and canons condemn, for example, clergy and monks for engaging in secular pursuits to the neglect of their spiritual exercises and for their self-indulgence to the detriment of the poor (*Statutes*, 92f), and they advocate efforts to uphold high standards in religious life so that piety might flourish and 'the murmurs of the outside world be silenced' (*Statutes*, 95). In the matter of education the council of 1549 in large measure followed the enactments of the Council of Trent. (Winning, *IR*, 10 (1959), 311–37.) There is particular emphasis on the need to have the Scriptures studied and expounded in the monasteries and in the attached churches by theologians, who were to be maintained where possible by the bishops.

The low standards of education and spirituality of those in monastic orders were a common complaint of humanists. It is not therefore surprising to find this criticism strongly presented. The monasteries were to be reformed so that they might become centres of education from which would go forth and 'flourish anew men of letters and preachers eminent in sacred eloquence and the fruitful nurture of souls' (*Statutes*, 106). It is particularly relevant to note the decree, requiring monasteries to send one, perhaps even two of their number 'having a special aptitude for literary studies and good natural abilities, to the nearest universities or to others as it may please them, there to remain for the space at least of four years engaged in the study of theology and holy Scripture' (*Statutes*, 106). It was intended that there be a continuous succession of regulars at the universities. According to the scheme appended to the act there would have been at the universities at any one time at least forty regulars. In fact the practice of sending regulars to the universities had been going on for some time (Durkan, *IR*, 4(1953), 5–24).

There is also in the statutes an emphasis on public preaching in which an exposition of the Epistle or Gospel as well as catechetical instruction were to be the essential components (*Statutes*, 108). In one statute humanist influence is particularly evident both in the language and the content. Reference is made to the study of the scriptures and of theology 'in the public schools (*gymnasiis*) and academies (*academiis*)' where it is also hoped to make provision for 'the profitable teaching of the liberal arts' (*Statutes*, 108). Nevertheless, it must be noted, there is no reference to the original languages of Scripture; it has to be deduced from the references to Peter Lombard's *Sentences* and the commentaries of Aquinas and Bonaventure that there is no rejection of scholasticism. Also the emphasis on Latin grammar and dialectic is thoroughly traditional. Thus the evidence points only at times to humanist influence, one that is not in any way a challenge to the 'Catholic sense' of the Church's teaching (*Statutes*, 124).

It is, perhaps, in the *Catechism* authorised by the Council of 1552 rather than in the statutes themselves that we can discern more clearly elements of humanist thinking. This work exemplifies the humanists' desire to avoid 'contention and stryif in matters of our christin religioun' (Law, 4f.) and 'manifests', according to its editor, T.G. Law, 'an independent and liberal character' (Law, xxxiii). Indeed he went so far as to say of the book, after indicating several places where he detected a tendency to modify the expression of Roman Catholic doctrine, that 'it betrays the influence of the new learning' (Law, xli). A few examples will probably be enough to illustrate what Law may have had in mind.

There is throughout the work constant insistence upon attention to the Scriptures and there is nothing against reading them in the vernacular. No one it is asserted can sufficiently express the benefits to be derived from the diligent hearing and learning of the word of God, the true understanding of which is the second gift of the Holy Spirit (Law, 198). 'Our christian faith is nocht,' it is affirmed, 'groundit apon the natural reason of man, bot apon the trew and infallibil word of God' (Law, 206). As for the interpretation of the Scriptures, the *Catechism* states its position without qualification. They are to be interpreted according to the mind of the Holy Spirit. Their true sense is arrived at by comparing scripture with scripture, that is to say, by using those passages where the meaning is clear to explain those where it is found to be obscure and by paying attention to the context. Thereafter recourse is to be had to the opinions of the doctors of the Church, in fact to those early fathers to whom Erasmus had given so much attention, viz. Jerome, Ambrose, Augustine, Gregory and Chrysostom. The third authority is provided by the decisions of lawful general councils, taken as representing the whole Church. A second and significant emphasis is the practical concern for a life of moral obedience. It is the constant concern of the *Catechism* that those who read and hear it 'learn lessons profitable for their edification' (Cf. Law, 149, 159, 161). Christianity is repeatedly construed as a new life, guided by the spirit of God, ordered by faith, hope, and charity and resulting in good works (Cf. Law, 162).

All who have studied this formulation of the doctrine of the Church have noted that there is no explicit reference to papal authority, and that the doctrine of transubstantiation (naturally without philosophical or theological treatment) is clearly and simply enunciated. It has, however, been pointed out that there is 'no distinct section on the sacrifice of the Mass' (Law, xxxiv, 203–5). Indeed in the brief statements that are made the memorial element is prominent and this is not out of line with Erasmus' own understanding.

Thus the *Statutes* of the Provincial Councils and the *Catechism*, paralleled by similar events on the continent (Cameron, 1979, 105–17), bear witness to some of the ways in which the new learning was influencing Scottish life, but this can in no way be regarded as having a strong humanist thrust. There was, however, no time to put such admirable legislation into effect before the Reformation, yet evidence is not lacking that some earlier attempts along similar lines had been made. Dr Durkan informs us (*IR*, 10 (1959) 82), that the 'nearest attempt' to provide cathedral cities with theologians was made in Kirkwall by Bishop Robert Reid, and that in 1547 in Aberdeen a licentiate in theology was appointed to lecture in the cathedral, and there is evidence that Cardinal Beaton had indicated that he wished all bishops to provide for theological professors and preachers. The clergy of a council in 1547 wrote to the Pope seeking his backing for their recommendation with a papal mandate. It was certainly intended by some that a programme of educational reform and theological instruction be put into effect.

Several of those churchmen who took part in councils had much earlier come under the influence of humanism and had already made considerable efforts to introduce into Scotland the benefits of the new movement. Outstanding among them was Robert Reid, Bishop of Orkney; while others such as William Elphinstone, Bishop of Aberdeen, and David Beaton, Cardinal and Archbishop of St Andrews, had been patrons of those who had accepted the new learning. Humanism was in fact no middle of the century phenomenon in Scotland.

At the turn of the century Bishop William Elphinstone, who must be regarded as one of the outstanding prelates of the Scottish Church in the late Middle Ages was, along with his many political, legal, and economic concerns, deeply interested in the spiritual quality of life, as can be seen in his involvement in the *Aberdeen Breviary*, one of the earliest of Scottish printed books, and in the reform and education of the clergy. He is today best remembered as founder of the University of Aberdeen and of King's College. His academic training was scholastic, Aristotelian and legal, yet he was, according to his biographer Dr L.J. Macfarlane (1985, 323f;), 'increasingly open to Renaissance and humanist ideas, and had wished to reflect all that was best in this movement, whether French, Italian or English, when initiating his Arts courses at Aberdeen'. Perhaps his most significant act in this area was his invitation in 1497 to Hector Boece to return from Paris to Aberdeen, first to teach in the Arts Faculty and eventually to be principal of his new university. Boece had at Paris been the friend of Erasmus and along with other Scots there such as John Major and Patrick Panter, had been deeply influenced by the new learning (Cf. Durkan, *AUR*. 48 (1979–80) 260). Boece's task with the assistance of John Vaus, the University's first grammarian, was to introduce a number of humanist reforms into the arts course that was basic to all higher studies, and in this way seek to influence the basis for the later higher theological studies. The new approach was 'both Christian and humanist, neo-Platonic and classical' and made King's College 'pre-eminent in this field among the Scottish Universities before the Reformation' (Macfarlane, 1985, 365f.). Dr Durkan (1979–80: *AUR.* 48, 266ff.) tells us that 'Lefèvre was popular reading at King's' and recalls Boece's letter to Erasmus telling him that 'Erasmus's New Testament Paraphrases were constantly in his students' hands'. Elphinstone's humanist plans did not, however, extend to the regular teaching programme of theology. The normal course of the later Middle Ages remained; there appears to have been no attempt to introduce the teaching of Greek or Hebrew which is not mentioned till 1553 (Durkan, 1979–80, *AUR.* 48, 263), or to study the Scriptures in the original languages. Nevertheless the way was being prepared, and the basis being laid for humanist studies that were not only to bring renown to Aberdeen but to enrich the study of theology and the life of the Church in the North, although for a time humanist studies at Aberdeen suffered a mid-century eclipse.

Archbishop James Beaton of St Andrews and his successor Cardinal David Beaton, whose political and ecclesiastical influence looms large in Scotland's history, acted as patrons of several young Scottish scholars attending the University of Paris. Although the Beatons in no way compare favourably with Elphinstone, they were instrumental in assisting humanists in their endeavours to advance studies in Scotland, and in St Andrews University in particular, by seeking to erect on the basis of the ancient Pedagogy what was to become St Mary's College. The original plans for this college clearly owed something to Elphinstone's arrangements at King's College. David Beaton's recent biographer, Dr M.H.B. Sanderson, writes that 'It is generally regretted that the Cardinal did so little to set the new college on its feet, but considering the other calls upon his attention, it is remarkable that he did anything at all' (Sanderson, 1986, 122f.). Nevertheless he did succeed in bringing as principal of the new college, Archibald Hay, a relation whom he probably had encouraged at Paris. Hay had distinguished himself as a teacher and had shown his allegiance to humanism having reissued Erasmus' translation of Euripides' *Hecuba*. In his *Oratio*, published at Paris in 1538 and addressed to Archbishop James Beaton, and also in his *Panegyricus* addressed to the Cardinal, Hay set out his design that the new college should follow the pattern of the Trilingual Colleges of the continent, by providing that teaching in Greek, Hebrew, and other oriental languages, as well as Latin, be part of the curriculum. He also emphasised the need to have a library and a printing press. It was fundamental to his plans that the Church, which he saw in need of radical moral and educational reform, be the prime beneficiary, as had been also stated in the Archbishop's supplication to the Papacy and in the Bull licensing the foundation issued in 1538. At his induction in St Andrews, Hay was enthusiastically welcomed as a herald of the new learning but did not live long enough to execute his plans. He was almost certainly killed at the Battle of Pinkie (Durkan, *IR 4*, 1953, 14f.; Cameron, 1980, 277–301).

Robert Reid, abbot of Kinloss and bishop of Orkney (1558; Watt, 1969, 254), undoubtedly the most learned of the prelates before the Reformation, had met in 1528 in Paris Giovanni Ferreri (Johannes Ferrerius), an Italian scholar, who had much in sympathy with the French humanist Jacques Lefèvre. Reid invited Ferreri to Kinloss. From the information about him and his activities in Scotland, assiduously researched by Dr Durkan, we obtain the picture of a devout humanist who advocated living according to the Gospel (*IR*, 4.15). At Kinloss which would appear to have previously enjoyed high standards of education and spirituality he did much to encourage academic study by, among other things, considerably increasing the number of books in its library. Of Kinloss Abbey in the 1530s writes Dr Durkan 'There can be little doubt that such a monastic house acted as a radiating centre for learning in the whole of the north of Scotland' (*IR*, 4.15). From the details of Ferreri's Scottish contacts it may be concluded that, despite the popular image of Scottish monasticism and spiritual life in general, there were at work in Scotland forces for reform along humanist lines and that there were those who were ready to welcome and benefit from the new learning. Among them none was more active than Bishop Robert Reid, who has also an unassailable claim to be upheld as the proto-founder of the University of Edinburgh.

As has been seen Archibald Hay's plans for trilingual learning in St Andrews did not have an opportunity to be put into effect. It was left to Beaton's successor, John Hamilton, to set about 'refounding' St Mary's College. Hamilton, who became Archbishop in 1547, had returned from Paris in 1542 where he appears to have been associated with a circle of young Scottish scholars all of whom were influenced by humanism.

At this stage, Hamilton was probably like Elphinstone, nearly half a century earlier, also impressed by humanist objectives. It is significant that Knox in his *History* reported, no doubt with exaggeration, a contemporary rumour that both Hamilton and Panter were likely to become protestant preachers (Laing, 1846, 1. 105). It was during Hamilton's primacy that the provincial councils whose reforming statutes we have already discussed, were held. Equally significant were his plans for St Mary's College, which had suffered considerably with other parts of the University as a result of the political disturbances that followed the murder of the Cardinal. John Douglas, a leading member of the contingent of Scottish scholars at Paris in the 1530s and 40s[1], who had been commended by Archibald Hay in the peroration of his *Oratio* as one among the many who 'eagerly prayed' for the success of the new college, not surprisingly now received collation of the principalship on 1st October 1547. (St

Andrews University Muniments SM.110 B15.7; Dunlop, 19 lxv, cliii; Durkan and Kirk, 1977, 206, 219n2.) It was plain from Hamilton's efforts that the college was intended to be an instrument in fulfilling his reform programme. It is of interest to note that in a fresh supplication to Rome he claimed that his aim was to further the study of grammar, rhetoric, poetry, music, arts, medicine, theology and laws and that for this purpose he had searched far and wide for scholars. Among the scholars secured by Douglas were John Macquine, who had been a lecturer in scripture at Paisley Abbey, Richard Smyth, Regius Professor at Oxford and an exile from England and subsequently head of the College of Douai, and the Dominican Richard Marshall, who was almost certainly the main author of the *Catechism* of 1552 (Durkan, *IR*, 9 (1959) 434f. 409). The needs of the Church were uppermost in all that was happening. The emphasis was upon theological and in particular biblical study. The head of the college was to have as his particular academic responsibility lecturing on the Bible and preaching the divine word. No fundamental changes, however, in the arts or divinity curricula were indicated. Education of the clergy had been singled out as one of the principle means of reform and of attacking the spread of heresy. It would be unrealistic not to see in these plans the hand of Douglas. There is, nevertheless, no direct evidence of a decidedly humanist influence, but such influence there must have been, for Douglas was undoubtedly one of those responsible for the section on the reform of the universities in the *First Book of Discipline* which bears the influence of the new learning. Among those who were incorporated in the 1550s were John Rutherford, who represented new trends in philosophical studies (Durkan, 1979, 115ff) and Alexander Arbuthnot, subsequently Principal at King's College, Aberdeen whose humanism is well attested. For many years he was to be a close friend of George Buchanan and of Andrew Melville. (Durkan and Kirk, 1977, 266ff., 288f.; McCrie 1856, 366f.) Among the students were others who subsequently made names for themselves in both Catholicism and Protestantism, such as Robert Abercromby, a noted member of the Society of Jesus, and Patrick Adamson, who became Archbishop of St Andrews in 1574.

How extensive the impact of humanism was as a positive force upon the Church of Scotland in the pre-Reformation period can probably never be precisely estimated. That it was a potent force cannot now be denied. The tide of events was, nevertheless, running too fast for it to make significant headway. Radical change could not be long delayed. Humanism as represented by men such as Hector Boece, Robert Reid, Archibald Hay, and John Douglas and many others was not a detached academic concern. They all advocated moral reform and a life lived according to the precepts of the Gospel. And that too was the burden of the Provincial Councils. That the

Reformation came about with comparatively little dislocation was no doubt in part due to the extent to which humanist reforming ideas had impressed leading academics and clergy.

Humanism, however much its advocates proclaimed their loyalty to the Church and its faith, had, as Erasmus's critics on the continent were quick to point out, a detracting aspect. The papal legate Aleandro reporting to Rome on the religious troubles that had followed upon Luther's emergence, stated that Erasmus was 'the source of all this evil' (Rupp and Drewery, 1970, 55). Aleandro may have been biased for his initial friendship with Erasmus developed into a prolonged and bitter hostility, but his opinions were shared by others (Oberman and Brady, 1975, 65–70). In Scotland, as on the continent, the Church suffered attack not just from those who questioned, indeed rejected her teaching but from those who deeply resented her inability to raise the moral and spiritual quality of her clergy both high and low. One of the most effective weapons in the humanists' armory was satire, which not only held up churchmen to ridicule, but also undermined the church's spiritual authority. The most prolific and the most effective of Scottish satirists, who unlike Erasmus wrote in the vernacular was Sir David Lindsay of the Mount. T.G. Law described him as 'perhaps the chief instrument in the downfall of the Church from which he never seceded'. He continued, 'It was the play, the ballad and the popular song which were doing the real mischief to the established system, and were preparing the ground for the coming revolution' (Law, 1884, xii). W.L. Mathieson made a similar comment paraphrasing a well known sentence from Genesis, 'The voice was the voice of Knox, but the hand was the hand of Sir David Lindsay' (Mathieson, 1902, 1.61).

Lindsay's place in the history of Scottish Renaissance literature has been discussed in Chapter II, here an attempt will be made to assess the impact of his writings on the religious scene. At one time it was suggested (Lindsay, 1849, 1. 209f) but without satisfactory evidence, that Lindsay had served as a soldier in Italy in 1510 and that like Erasmus, he had seen Pope Julius III,

> Pass to the field triumphantly
> With ane richt awful ordinance . . .

Be that as it may, Lindsay had visited the continent and was undoubtedly acquainted with the writings of fellow humanists. He was every bit as critical of abuse in the church as Erasmus. Indeed 'All his writings have for their object an unmistakable attempt to expose and reform abuses whether in Church or State' (Laing, 1889, xlvi). In 1529 in 'The Testament and Complaint of our Sovereign Lord's Papingo' he singled out for particular attention the avaricious practices of monks, friars, and canons regular, continuing the attack on the licentious lives of the clergy he had previously launched in the earliest of his writing, 'The Dreme', where 'the material is strictly medieval' (Hamer, 1931–6, 4.xv). He is not afraid to discover in hell popes, cardinals, prelates, priors, abbots and friars among whose many sins was their failure to instruct the ignorant, to preach, and to take care of the poor. He equally castigates the evil doings of secular rulers but especially in 'The Complaint of Schir David Lindesay' (Hamer, 1931, 1. 48 lines 321–7) of these priests who follow secular pursuits and do not preach.

> For Esayas, in his wark,
> Callis thame lyke Doggis that can nocht bark,
> That callit ar preistis, and can nocht preche,
> Nor Christis law to the peple teche,
> Geue for to preche bene thare professioun,
> Quchy sulde thay mell with court, or Cessioun
> Except it war in spirtuall thyngis.

And of course he complains of those being made priests who had 'neuer sene the scule' (Hamer, 1931, 1.49 line 334). There is also the Erasmian complaint against the emphasis upon ceremonies. He appeals to the prince (Hamer, 1931, 1.51 lines 413–23):

> Cause thame the spiritualitie mak ministratioun
> Conforme to thare vocatioun,
> To Preche with vnfenzeit intentis,
> And trewly use the Sacramentis,
> Efter Christis Institutionis
> Leyyng thare vaine traditiounis,
> Quhilkis dois the syllie scheip Illude,
> Quhame for Christ Iesus sched his blude,
> As superstitious pylgramagis,
> Prayand to grawin Ymagis,
> Expres agains the Lordis command.

Hamer, the editor of Lindsay's works, sees here this advocacy of a moral reformation of the spiritual estate in accordance with the scripture as the first appearance of Lindsay as a reformer (Hamer, 1936, 4. xvii), but the inspiration is probably more Erasmian than Lutheran.

The condemnation of ecclesiastical practices, especially the Church's treatment of those about to die is the aim of the brilliant satire 'The Testament and Complaynt of our Souverane Lordis Papyngo', written in truly humanist fashion. Here again the poet's criticism of the Church's practices expressed in a 'scene of grim humour' (Hamer, 1936, 4. xviii) is essentially a moral one. It is however in 'Ane Satyre of the Thrie Estaitis' which was first produced before the king, queen and court in 1540 that Lindsay by directing his main attack against the Church, in particular its oppressive financial exactions of the poor and its heaping up of enormous wealth, became 'the literary leader of the Reformers in Scotland' (Hamer, 1936, 4. xxviii).

There is, however, in his writings little of the theological or dogmatic reformer. Lindsay attacks abuses; he attacks the clergy for failing to fulfil the responsibilities of their office, especially those of preaching and caring for the poor. There are bitter satirical attacks upon pardoners and confessors and their promise of an easy way to obtain salvation which echoes much that is Lutheran but throughout the emphasis is a moral one. He advocates the preaching of the truth as it is found in the Bible, especially in the New Testament. Dame Verity in 'Ane Satyre' has in her hand the New Testament 'in Englisch toung, and printit in England' (Hamer, 1931, 2.125, line 1092; 129, line 1146). Later the Pardoner denouces this practice.

> Sen layik men knew the veritie
> Pardoners gets no charitie. (203 lines 2053–4)

Those passages which are most frequently quoted from the Scriptures are about justice and keeping the commandments: Matthew 5.6 (165, line 1572); Psalm cx (Vulgate: cxi, AV. 187, line 1875); Matthew 19. 17 (319, line 3444; 323, line 3504). The sermon delivered by the Doctor towards the end of 'Ane Satyre' is thoroughly evangelical and in accordance with Erasmian humanism (2. 319–23) extolling the love of God in sending his Son as a ransom to the Devil for man's salvation *Et copiosa apud eum redemptio* (321, line 3478). He asks from mankind only that they love God and love one another, and perform the corporal acts of mercy. (323 lines 3491–4)

> Luife bene the ledder quihilk hes bot steppis twa,
> Be quhilk we may clim vp to lyfe again,
> Out of this vaill of miserie and wa.

This theme is repeated in 'Ane Dialogue betuix Experience and Ane Courteaur', (1931, 2.197–386) completed by 1553. In Erasmian style Lindsay advocates the reading of the Scripture in the vernacular by the common man (1.215 lines 545–65). He wants all books necessary for faith in the vulgar tongue and although he is opposed to idolatry, he regards images as the books of the unlearned to remind them of the Gospel (1.268, lines 2325ff) but they are not to be worshipped. His approach here is thoroughly humanist, as is his attitude to pilgrimages, ceremonies and traditions contrary to Christ's institution (1.275, lines 2574). In his description of the last judgement, as is to be expected, judgement is according to the fulfilment of Christ's moral commands – the corporal acts of mercy (i. 374ff lines 5930ff).

In the introduction to his edition of Lindsay's works, Hamer (1936, 4. xli) considered that he did not qualify for the title 'humanist' as he knew no Greek or Hebrew. This, however, is to circumscribe the term too narrowly. Like all humanists of his day there is in his work a blending of the biblical, the classical and the medieval, but above all there is the humanist desire for a revived religion based on the understanding of the simple meaning of the scriptures, an emphasis upon a purified church, and on a return to the fundamentals of the Christian ethic – love to God and love to man. To help achieve these ends he employs the poetic medium in the vernacular and the sharpest of Erasmian reformatory tools, satire, his use of which is 'without parallel in Scotland' (Hamer, 1936, 4. xli).

It is impossible to gauge with any degree of accuracy the impact of Lindsay on the church of his day and on the progress of the Reformation in Scotland. Reference has already been made to the opinions of T.G. Law and W.L. Mathieson. No contemporary evaluation appears to have survived. In 1639 Archbishop John Spottiswoode, in his *History of the Church of Scotland* (Spottiswoode, 1865, 1.192) had this to say about his role: 'he was most religiously inclined, but much hated by the clergy for the liberty he used in condemning the superstition of the time, and rebuking their loose and dissolute lives. Nottheless, he went unchallenged, and was not brought in question, which shewed the good account in which he was held'.

There are in places clear indications that he was aware of Lutheran doctrines, but he cannot, except in the vaguest of ways be termed a Lutheran. Hamer refers to him as 'the lay apostle of the people of Scotland' and with this judgement there can be no quarrel. David Laing was in no doubt that 'his satirical writings had a powerful effect in preparing the minds of his countrymen' for the coming Reformation (Laing, 1889, xlix).

The relationship of the Renaissance to the Reformation has been and indeed continues to be the subject of lively discussion. In a recent incisive article Steven Ozment maintained that 'in terms of intellectual history Protestantism can be identified exclusively with neither humanism nor scholasticism, but was rather from the start a peculiar blending of both these medieval traditions' (Ozment, 1979, 134). In the reformed Church of Scotland something of these two strands can be identified in the Calvinism that came to dominate it. John Knox never wholly rid himself of his scholastic heritage both in the style of his argumentation and in his insistence upon the maintenance of right doctrine clearly defined, yet he was one of the foremost advocates of educational reform within the universities, of a school in every parish, of academies in every sizeable town, of the Bible in the language of the people and in everyone's hands, and of a ministry that was open only to those of approved and tested moral and educational standards. Just as there was a strong relationship between humanism and catholic reform as exemplified by such figures as Sadoleto, Contarini, and Gilberti, and also by certain elements within the Society of Jesus so too there was 'a fundamental and lasting kinship between humanism and Protestantism'. (Ozment, 1979, 134. See further L.W. Spitz, 'The Course of German Humanism' in Oberman and Brady, 1975, 414–36; and Spitz, 'The Impact of the Reformation on the Universities' in Grane, 1981, 22f.) This kinship was particularly marked in Reformed Protestantism; whose leaders all came to their protestantism by the way of their earliest humanist studies. Zwingli was influenced by Eastern European humanists such as Conrad Celtes and Joachim Vadian and later 'became an enthusiastic reader of the works of Erasmus, whose grateful and devoted student he felt himself for the rest of his life' (Locher, 1981, 233). Calvin's passion in his student days in Paris, Orleans, and Bourges for the languages, literatures, and cultures of antiquity are fully documented and formed much of the basis for his subsequent biblical study and exposition. Much the same must also be said for Martin Bucer and Theodore Beza. For all of these leaders, who in differing measures influenced Scotland, their protestantism was in large measure the theological fulfilment of their humanism. Thus the humanities became for Protestant theologians what Aristotelian philosophy had been to late Medieval Catholic theologians, the favoured handmaiden of theology (Ozment, 1979, 147). It is not therefore surprising that in Scotland fresh impetus should be given to the study of the liberal arts as the essential basis for making good the fundamental defect of the late medieval Church which in large measure had brought its popular downfall, viz. the lack of an adequately educated and morally acceptable parochial ministry.

The years that John Knox had spent on the continent, and particularly in Geneva, had coincided with the bringing to fulfilment of Calvin's plans for his Academy which he had largely based on the achievements of Sturm in Strasbourg and Baduel in Nîmes, plans in which the humanist curriculum, with its stress on the biblical languages was fundamental. In the century that followed this humanist curriculum became the enduring model for the arts curriculum in all the academies of reformed protestantism on the continent and in Scotland (R. Stauffer, 'Calvin and the Universities' in Grane, 1981, 76–98).

The plans of the Scottish reformers set out in *The First Book of Discipline* for the reform of the universities in which John Douglas of St Mary's College, whose humanist background has already been indicated, must have had a crucial role, had no immediate effect on the three existing universities (Cameron, 1972, 58–64, 137–55). Nevertheless in the longer term their importance and influence are undeniable. In the programme of reform, education was to play a major role, education in accordance with the highest aims of Christian humanism, ordered according to a graded progression of studies, especially in the languages, rhetoric and moral philosophy and available to all able to benefit from it for the service of the church and the nation. In seeking to reform the universities and thereby place the education for the ministry on a strong humanist and biblical foundation the church had the support of the celebrated George Buchanan whose own programme embodying the study of those classical authors beloved by humanists, as well as Hebrew and Greek was not taken up. It was not until the return of Andrew Melville from Geneva in 1574 that a marked interest in education for the ministry was seen in the activities of the General Assemblies. This was probably not unconnected with the more favourable educational provisions embodied in the settlement reached between the government and the church two years earlier (Acts, 1839, 214f.). Melville, whose introduction to classical studies dated from his own education as a boy in Montrose, which were reported by his devoted nephew to have amazed his regents in St Mary's College, and which were subsequently pursued in France and Geneva, was now to take a leading role in the reorganisation of university education, particularly in Glasgow and St Andrews and to have a share in that of King's College, Aberdeen (Durkan and Kirk, 1977, 262ff). Further, the desire 'to create a reservoir of learned and godly men . . .' who could make the educational blueprints of the Book of Discipline a reality (Horn, 1965–6, 297) led to combined efforts of the church and the city in the foundation of what we now know as the University of Edinburgh. Within the same decade plans were laid for the establishment of Marischal College in Aberdeen, both colleges being designed as centres of humanist influence. Primarily through the efforts of the Reformed Church, itself the product of an alliance of sacred and humanist studies, native educational institutions were being established as channels of humanism, and they in turn were to have a profound and enduring impact upon the Scottish Church.[2]

Fundamental in the education of future ministers was the study of Greek and Hebrew and allied Semitic languages. Not only the theology but all preaching was to be rooted in the study of the original texts of the biblical books which were to be expounded and commented upon in the pulpit. This approach to Scripture resulted in making sermons in Scotland essentially exegetical and expository. It also enabled subsequent scholars reared in this tradition to become international leaders in both biblical study and research. More immediately in the late 16th and 17th centuries the impact of humanism can be amply illustrated in contemporary theological and sermonic writings, and also in the participation of ministers in the encouragement of classical and vernacular literature. We may instance the sermons of Robert Rollock (1559–99), first Principal of Edinburgh University, and a pupil of Andrew Melville, which clearly illustrate that for him scripture understood philologically was the doorway to biblical truth – a phrase that enshrines a fundamental element of humanism dating back to Valla. Rollock won for himself through his theological writings an international reputation including the high commendation of Theodore Beza (Gunn, 1849, 1.lix–lxxxvii; Cameron, 1963, 331f.). Perhaps the most widely known as well as the most prolific of Scottish theological writers of this period was John Forbes of Corse (1593–1648), an outstanding member of that group of northern theologians, the Aberdeen doctors (MacMillan, 1909, 227ff.). Forbes, who had been brought up in the humanist environment of King's College and had pursued his education in Germany, France and the Low Countries, on returning home sought to pursue in the Scottish ecclesiastical scene the irenic policy that was favoured on the continent by men such as Franciscus Junius and Hugo Grotius whose humanist approach is well attested. His writings – *Instructiones Historico-Theologicae* and *Theologica Moralis* – illustrate his profound classical and patristic erudition which he employs in the discussion of theology often dominated by a keen historical perspective. For example in examining the nature of worship he inquires with the aid of writers such as Cicero, Varro, Vergil, Lactantius and of course Valla and Vives into the meaning of *religio, similacrum,* and *imago.* Nor does he restrict himself to classical learning. He knows the value of rabbinical commentaries in elucidating the sacred text. In the *Theologica Moralis* there is the humanist stress upon the innate morality in all men; he sees parallels in the Christian emphasis on worshipping God, upholding justice and cultivating a good conscience with the best classical authors. In his work on pastoral care (Forbes, 1703, 1.531–619) he revives and applies to his own day the humanist's abhorrence of clerical abuses such as pluralism, non-residence and engagement in civil affairs.

The impact of humanism on theological study could be illustrated in the works of Scottish churchmen who although initially educated in Scotland chose to serve the Church abroad (particularly in France) as well as in Scotland. One who made a distinctive contribution to French Protestantism was John Cameron (1579–1625) (Swinne, 1968; Armstrong, 1969, 42–70). He became involved in controversy on the nature of the freedom of the will. Another, a contemporary of Cameron, who served the Church both in France and in Scotland was Robert Reid of Trochrig (1579–1627). He returned to Scotland to become Principal of Glasgow University in 1615. His extensive commentary on the Epistle to the Ephesians, based on the Greek text, is his main contribution to biblical scholarship. In its use of classical and patristic scholarship it is outstanding and secured for its author a lasting international reputation (Cameron, 1977, 14.262f.).

Humanism had a profound and positive influence upon the Reformed Church in Scotland, an influence that has all too often been ignored. The Scottish post-Reformation Church has been depicted as lacking in humanity, harsh and dictatorial, indeed inquisitorial in its exercise of ecclesiastical discipline and in its attempt to bring about moral reformation. For such criticism there may be some justification. Yet it is frequently forgotten that Protestantism had imbibed the individualism of humanism, demanded an intellectual approach to religion, and required that one should both think for oneself responsively and act responsibly. Calvinism played a decisive role in Scotland's educational programme, ensuring that that educational programme was fundamentally humanist. The humanism encouraged by those whom we have named is reflected in their works which we have briefly cited and in the writings of others of lesser stature. This humanism did not, however, save the intellectual life of the Church from being eclipsed during a comparatively brief period of new protestant scholasticism, yet it was to re-emerge in the Scottish Enlightenment. That the Enlightenment flourished in Scotland at the hands of so many of its church leaders is probably in large measure due to its intellectual humanist heritage. The Scottish church historian aware of the difficulties in assessing the changes brought about in the Church's long history by the impact upon it of classical civilisation throughout the centuries of its existence will not readily come to a conclusion about the legacy of the humanism of the Renaissance period. Here an attempt has been made to show that humanists played a decisive role in seeking firstly to reform the Medieval Church, in ways which were both positive and negative; secondly to secure for the Reformed Church a firm basis in a revitalised educational programme for which the Church felt itself traditionally and morally responsible; and thirdly to provide the Church with biblical and theological scholars who sought to build upon the Church's heritage of learning from the past and provide for the continuing spiritual and intellectual needs of the people. It has been said of Erasmus that he envisaged 'reform in the sense of a union of the Scriptures, the church fathers, *humanitas* and *bonae literae* within the Church' (Spitz, 1863, 204). This vision may be said to have inspired all who sought renewal within the Church in Scotland in the sixteenth century.

NOTES
1. Douglas when a regent in Montaigu College received a small sum of money from Archbishop James Beaton in 1537. Hannay, 1913, xxxvi, xxxviii, 72, 96.
2. See further, Durkan, *IR* 4 (1953) 14ff.; Durkan, *IR* 10 (1959) 67–90, 382–439, and Cameron 1977, 251ff.

## REFERENCES

ACTS
1839
*Acts and Proceedings of the General Assemblies of the Kirk of Scotland*, Edinburgh.

ARMSTRONG, B.G.
1969
*Calvinism and the Amyraut Heresy*, Wisconsin 42–70.

CAMERON, E.
1980
'Archibald Hay's "Elegantiae": Writings of a Scots Humanist at the Collège de Montaigu in the Time of Bude and Beda', in *Acta conventus Neo-Latini Turonensis*, edited by J.-C. Margolin, Paris, 277–301.

CAMERON, J.K.
1979
'"Catholic Reform" in Germany and in the Pre-1560 Church in Scotland', *Records of Scottish Church History Society*, 20, 105–17.

CAMERON, J.K.
1972
*The First Book of Discipline*, Edinburgh.

CAMERON, J.K.
1977
'The Renaissance Tradition in the Reformed Church of Scotland' in *Studies in Church History*, ed. D. Baker, 14, 251–69.

CAMERON, J.K.
1963
*Letters of John Johnston 1565–1611 and Robert Howie 1565–1645*, Edinburgh.

DUNLOP, A.
1964
*Acta Facultatis Artium*, Edinburgh.

DURKAN, J.
1953
'The Beginnings of Humanism in Scotland', *Innes Review*, 4, 5–24.

DURKAN, J.
1959
'Education in the Century of the Reformation', *Innes Review*, 10, 67–90.

DURKAN, J.
1979–80
'Early Humanism and Kings College', *Aberdeen University Review*, 48, 259–79.

DURKAN, J.
1959
'The Cultural Background in the Sixteenth Century', *Innes Review*, 70, 382–439.

DURKAN, J. and KIRK, J.
1977
*The University of Glasgow 1451–1577*, Glasgow.

DURKAN, J.
1979
'John Rutherford and Montaigne: An Early Influence', *Bibliothèque d'Humanisme et Renaissance, Travaux et Documents*, Geneva 1, 415–122.

FORBES, J.
1703
*Opera omnia*, Amsterdam, vol. 1.

GRANE, Leif
1981
*University and Reformation*, Leiden.

HAMER, D.
1931–36
*The Works of Sir David Lindsay of the Mount*, STS Edinburgh vols. 1–4.

HANNAY, R.K.
1913
*Rentale Sancti Andree*, SHS, Edinburgh.

HORN, D.B.
1965–66
'The Origins of the University of Edinburgh', in *University of Edinburgh Journal*, 22.213–25, 297–312.

LAING, D., ed.,
1846
*The Works of John Knox*, Edinburgh, vol.1.

LAING, D.
1889
*The Poetical Works of Sir David Lyndsay*, Edinburgh.

LAW, T.G.
1884
*The Catechism of John Hamilton . . . 1552*, Oxford.

| | |
|---|---|
| LINDSAY, Lord<br>1849 | *Lives of the Lindsays*, London, vol.1. 207–62. |
| LOCHER, G.<br>1981 | *Zwingli's Thought: New Perspectives*, Leiden. |
| MATHIESON, W.L.<br>1902 | *Politics and Religion*, Glasgow, 2 vols. vol.1.<br>p.61. |
| MACFARLANE, L.J.<br>1985 | *William Elphinstone and the Kingdom of Scotland*,<br>Aberdeen. |
| MACMILLAN, D.<br>1909 | *The Aberdeen Doctors*, London |
| MCCRIE, T.<br>1856 | *Life of Andrew Melville*, Edinburgh. |
| OBERMAN, H.A. and<br>BRADY, T.A.<br>1975 | *Itinerarium Italicum; The Profile of the Italian<br>Renaissance in the Mirror of its European Trans-<br>formatons*, Leiden. |
| OZMENT, Steven<br>1979 | 'Humanism, Scholasticism and the Intellectual<br>Origins of the Reformation' in F.F. Church<br>and T. George, *Continuity and Discontinuity in<br>Church History*, Leiden, 133–49. |
| PATRICK, David<br>1907 | *Statutes of the Scottish Church 1225–1559*, Edin-<br>burgh. |
| RUPP, E.G. and<br>DREWERY, B.<br>1970 | *Martin Luther, Documents of Modern History*,<br>London. |
| SANDERSON, M.H.B.<br>1986 | *Cardinal of Scotland, David Beaton c.1494–1546*,<br>Edinburgh. |
| SPITZ, L.W.<br>1963 | *The Religious Reformation of the German Human-<br>ists*, Cambridge, Mass. |
| SPOTTISWOODE, J.<br>1865 | *History of the Church of Scotland*, London. |
| SWINNE, A.H.<br>1968 | *John Cameron, Philosoph und Theologue 1579–<br>1625*, Marburg. |
| WATT, D.E.R.<br>1969 | *Fasti Ecclesiae Scoticanae Medii Aevi ad annum<br>1638*, Edinburgh. |
| WEINSTEIN, Donald<br>1972 | 'In Whose Image and Likeness? Interpret-<br>ations of Renaissance Humanism' *Journal of<br>the History of Ideas*, 33, 165–77. |
| WINNING, T.<br>1959 | 'Church Councils in Sixteenth Century Scot-<br>land', *Innes Review*, 10, 311–37. |

## Conclusion
## JOHN MACQUEEN

I have heard it suggested that, although many Scots of the period before the Enlightenment were men of learning and genius, they existed in a kind of intellectual vacuum, at least so far as their native land was concerned. To give a relatively late example, the Royal Society of London had no immediate Scottish equivalent. The previous chapters of this book have gone some way to discredit such a hypothesis. Many Renaissance humanists still retain a considerable reputation. Even if Robert Henryson and Archibald Whitelaw are excluded as too early (something which need not be conceded), there still remain John Mair, Hector Boece, Gavin Douglas, David Lindsay, Florence Wilson, George Buchanan, Andrew Melville, John Napier and William Drummond. Despite the image left in the popular imagination, the claim for inclusion of John Knox is also strong. But it is not so much these celebrated names as the cluster of lesser ones surrounding them which make my point. With Douglas, for instance, must be linked not only Bellenden and such others as John Vaus in Aberdeen and his pupils, including Florence Wilson, but also John Mair and his circle. Douglas discussed Mair's *History* with Polydore Virgil. Mair wrote a dialogue between Douglas and his own pupil David Cranston concerning humanistic criticisms of scholastic Latin, a dialogue which throughout remains as temperate in tone as any humanist could wish, but which also makes it clear why neither Mair nor Cranston was prepared to abandon the terminology which Douglas found merely barbarous (MacQueen, 1967, 212). As bishop of Dunkeld, Douglas also became associated with the chapter appointed by his predecessor, George Brown, members of which had collaborated with him to reform administration and worship in his substantially Gaelic-speaking diocese, and whose concerns extended to architecture, libraries, manuscript hands and the history of the diocese. One of the chapter, Alexander Myln, afterwards first Lord President of the College of Justice, recorded (Myln, 1831, 72–75) Douglas's tumultuous arrival in his new see, and expressed admiration for the distinction in scholarship which made his incumbency appropriate. Douglas, it is clear, was no isolated figure. The same might be demonstrated for others.

Against this in a way is the fact noted by Dr Keller, that a high proportion of Scots pursued academic careers on the continent. He has primarily in mind physicians, astronomers and mathematicians, but Mair and Buchanan, neither of whom belonged in these categories, spent much of their working lives in Europe. So did many lesser figures. The great universities of sixteenth- and seventeenth-century Europe maintained an apparently insatiable demand for Scots as teachers and administrators.

This did not necessarily mean however that contacts with Scotland and Scottish universities were broken. Humanists were compulsive letter-writers and the trade in printed books was enormous. Travel too was rather easier than is sometimes supposed. Eventually many, like Mair and Buchanan, returned home to positions of importance in the intellectual life of their country. A late example is the Latin poet and physician Arthur Johnston, much of whose verse commemorates personal and political events in Europe, where most of his adult life was spent, but who returned to Scotland to become royal physician and rector of King's College, Aberdeen, to compose his best poetry on distinctly Scottish subjects, and to play a part in the preparation of the celebrated *Delitiae Poetarum Scotorum* for publication (1637) in Amsterdam (Geddes, 1895, xvii–xxv). Florence Wilson worked on the continent, but it was primarily (MacQueen and MacQueen, 1988, 240) a concern for Scotland which led him to write *De Animi Tranquillitate*.

The pattern of absence is not absolutely uniform. Some lawyers – Henry Scrymgeour, Edward Henryson, and William Barclay, for instance – spent most of their working lives abroad, whereas John Skene and Thomas Craig returned home after training in Germany and France respectively, one primarily to the profession of the law in public office, the other more in private practice. In the fifteenth century much the same appears to be true of Robert Henryson, who almost certainly gained his degree in decreits on the continent before returning to Glasgow University and eventually to the grammar school of Dunfermline. Some of the most distinguished humanists – Gavin Douglas, Bellenden, Lindsay and Napier – were almost entirely the product of local schools and universities.

The existence and activities of the older universities and the foundation of the 'tounis college' of Edinburgh in 1583 were themselves factors leading to cooperation and constructive debate among scholars and thus to the spread of humanistic ideas. In practice however the universities were limited to Arts and Theology; for Medicine and Law the services of a continental university remained essential almost to the beginning of the eighteenth century. The College of Justice, founded in 1532, had a judicial rather than a teaching function.

Nor should the influence exerted by the monarch and the royal court be forgotten. James IV was a man of multifarious interest in the arts and sciences. James V founded the College of Justice and patronised architecture and literature, most notably in the persons of Bellenden and Lindsay. During his reign the Chapel Royal of Stirling became an important musical centre. James's widow, the queen-mother Mary of Guise, who was present at the Edinburgh production of *Ane Satyre of the Thrie Estaitis*, rather remarkably continued the patronage of Lindsay, and seems to have taken another poet, Alexander Scott, under her wing. He travelled to France as part of the entourage for the young Queen Mary, and afterwards composed a New Year poem for her return which combines metrical virtuosity with satirical comment and much wise counsel. Professor Kemp and Dr Farrow have specially emphasised the reign of Mary in their treatment of the visual arts; it is also the intellectual and political heart of the Scottish Reformation. James VI's literary interests are well-known, his scientific ones rather less so, despite his contacts with Tycho Brahe and Kepler. In addition, he played a part in many of the legal and educational developments of his day. Charles I is a more remote figure, important nevertheless as an influence on William Drummond and Arthur Johnston and as the catalyst of a long sequence of events in cultural as in political history.

The Scottish Renaissance was based primarily on Latin. That is not to say that the influence either of Greek or of Hebrew was negligible. Buchanan produced Latin versions of Greek poetry and had a good knowledge of ancient scientific and philosophical writings, mainly in Greek. For others, Aristotle, the Hippocratic canon and Galen have often been cited. Plato affected Florence Wilson, Buchanan and Drummond. The pseudo-Platonic *Axiochus* was popular in a way which is now difficult to understand. Scots too played a significant part in the production of the King James version of the Bible; an untoward consequence of its use in churches and for private reading was the decline during the seventeenth century in the status of Scots as a literary language.

The Christian humanism of the Renaissance was first and foremost an involvement with the language, form and content of ancient Latin, Greek and Hebrew literature – a concept including not merely the poets, philosophers, orators and historians, but also the Hippo-cratic canon, the writings of Galen and the ancient astronomers, Vitruvius and the classical jurists up to and including Justinian. Hebrew was the ultimate source of law and the essential prelude to the Greek New Testament. Some familiarity with ancient art was gained through travel and from tapestries, paintings and the illus-trations in printed books. Under these circumstances and given the related stimulus of the Reformation, it is perhaps not surprising that the reflex of humanism was often a greater involvement with distinctively Scottish affairs, past or present, aspects of which might be seen to correspond with classical precedent. Something of this has come out in each of the previous chapters.

It is most obvious in the closely related areas of religion and education. Professor Cameron establishes the humanist basis for attempts at religious reformation before as well as after 1560, in the Provincial Councils of the 1540s and 50s, the *Catechism* of 1552 and the subsequent work of the Protestant reformers. A number of pre-Reformation bishops were themselves humanists and patrons of humanism – Bishop Elphinstone of Aberdeen and Bishop Brown of Dunkeld are particular shining examples, but even those like Cardinal Beaton whose later reputation is more tarnished, made some contribution. Andrew Melville, Robert Rollock and John Forbes of Corse were Protestant theologians whose writings were influential well beyond the immediate Protestant community. Professor Cameron notes (p.175) that Protestantism 'had imbibed the individualism of humanism, demanded an intellectual approach to religion, and required that one should both think for oneself responsively and act responsibly . . . That the Enlightenment flourished in Scotland at the hands of so many of its church leaders is probably in large measure due to its intellectual humanist heritage.'

The aim of the humanist teacher resembled that of Quintilian – to produce a classical scholar, capable in oratory and poetry, but also a virtuous citizen. The nation and the national church made the same demand, as a consequence of which we have what Dr Durkan calls (p.130) 'the development if not of a national, at least of a nation-wide, system of popular education . . . schools existed everywhere in Scotland by 1633 . . . and, in some favoured areas, were even fairly thick on the ground'. Attempts to produce a Latin grammar better suited to Scotland than the English Linacre or the French Despauterius conform to this pattern, as do the curricular changes instituted by Melville in the older universities and the establishment of the University of Edinburgh. The educational system which resulted persisted well into the nineteenth century.

National characteristics are least evident in philosophy. Although Mair and his circle have many points of contact with the humanists, their work is the last elaboration of the old rather than a fresh beginning. Dr Broadie does not commit himself but it seems to me that the humanists who followed were generally men of lesser attainments who contributed relatively little, nationally or internationally. Contrast the way in which the concept of 'notions' in Crab and Lockert anticipates the 'ideas' which formed a principal weapon in the armoury of the Enlightenment philosopher Thomas Reid, founder of the Scottish common-sense school, dominant for many years in Britain and America. Other logical concepts and problems elucidated by these late scholastics waited until the twentieth century before once more attracting attention. These are real accomplishments. The humanists have very little to set against them. Their greatest achievement perhaps was the Ciceronian clarity and elegance of the Latin style which they adopted. It is above all charm of language which draws the non-philosophical reader to Florence Wilson – something which cannot be said of Mair or his friends – a charm the example of which perhaps helped to produce the easy precision of style equally adopted two centuries later by Hume and Reid, although for opposed philosophical purposes. Matter of interest can be found in Rutherford and the others, but only Wilson retains any popular reputation at the present day.

In law one might have expected a recurrence of the emphasis on Roman law found in such scholars as Scrymgeour and Barclay whose professional life was passed on the continent. The result in fact is almost the reverse; the fountains of Scots law receive more attention than anything else in such works as the *Practicks* of Sir James Balfour of Pittendreigh, Sir John Skene of Curriehill's edition of *Regiam Maiestatem*, his *De Verborum Significatione*, and the *Jus Feudale* of Thomas Craig of Riccarton. To a considerable degree this results from the humanist *mos docendi Gallicus* particularly associated with the University of Bourges and such figures as François Hotman, Jacques Cujas and Skene's preceptor, Matthew Wissenbeck who introduced the new outlook to the German University of Wittenberg by way of the Netherlands. The immediate relevance of Balfour's work to court practice made his *Practicks*, which circulated in MS for more than a century, perhaps the most important among these pre-Institutional writings which paved the way for the philosophical and practical achievement of Stair in the late seventeenth century.

Law was not simply the perquisite of lawyers. Buchanan's *De Jure Regni apud Scottos* is a document with revolutionary implications which constitutionalists in Scotland as in England and elsewhere in Europe had to take into account. Notable too is the importance which Lindsay attaches to the series of acts passed in the assembly which gives its name to *Ane Satyre of the Thrie Estaitis*.

The discovery of logarithms may well be the most profound of all the contributions of Scots Renaissance humanism to the world. It is important not only for itself but for the mathematical method used by Napier to establish his system. Dr Keller has commented on similarities with the kinematics of Galileo and with the fluxions used by Newton in his *Principia*, but more immediately important perhaps is the way in which the method was used by the Scot, James Gregorie, as well as by Newton, in the development of the infinitesimal calculus which in turn made the *Principia* possible. Napier's achievement is also associated with that of Kepler and Descartes. A geometrical procedure based on fluxions was to be characteristic of

Scots mathematics until it was replaced in the late eighteenth century by the algebraic.

The intellectual repercussions of Napier's work were thus at once national and transcending national boundaries. On a somewhat lesser scale much the same was true of the medical innovations described by Dr Keller, innovations which eventually led to the foundation of the Edinburgh Physic Garden (later the Royal Botanic Gardens) and the influential Edinburgh medical school. As in England and elsewhere, the discovery and promotion of medicinal springs eventually came to play a considerable part in the social, as well as the medical, history of Scotland, later evidence for which will be found, for instance, in Scott's novel, *St Ronan's Well* (1824). A humanistic, or at least human, aspect different from anything envisaged by Gilbert Skene is set out in Scott's 'Introduction' to the Magnum edition of the novel:

> 'The scene chosen for the author's little drama of modern life was a mineral spring, such as are to be found in both divisions of Britain, and which are supplied with the usual materials for redeeming health, or driving away care. The invalid often finds relief from his complaints, less from the healing virtues of the Spaw itself, than because his system of ordinary life undergoes an entire change, in his being removed from his ledger and account-books – from his legal folios and progresses of title-deeds – from his counters and shelves – from whatever else forms the main source of his constant anxiety at home, destroys his appetite, mars the custom of his exercise, deranges the digestive powers, and clogs up the springs of life. Thither, too, comes the saunterer, anxious to get rid of that wearisome attendant *himself*; and thither come both males and females, who, upon a different principle, desire to make themselves double.'

The development reached its consummation in the hydropathics of late Victorian and Edwardian times, many of which continue in flourishing existence to the present day.

The supposed link between medicine and astronomy introduced a number of Scots physicians to the New Astronomy of Copernicus, Tycho Brahe, Galileo and Kepler. This in turn had direct side-effects, not only in Gregorie's observatory and reflecting telescopes at St Andrews, but in the cast of much Scottish literature of a later period, notably *The Seasons* of James Thomson. George Buchanan's Lucretian *De Sphaera* is an early example of the same phenomenon; it is strongly anti-Copernican, but shows some grasp of the theory as advanced by Copernicus himself and by his predecessors in the classical world, notably the Pythagoreans of southern Italy and the Greek astronomer Aristarchus of Samos (MacQueen, 1982, 9–17).

The confusing yet fascinating variety of accents in which the visual arts of the Scottish Renaissance speak to Professor Kemp is best summarised in the nationally individual baronial style 'in which any overtly Renaissance motifs were most commonly limited to a series of quotations within overall compositions which remained obstinately vernacular' (p.32).

Almost my entire chapter on the literature of the period is devoted to ways in which humanist writers adapted classical material to vernacular purposes or standards. It is not difficult to find further instances. The language of Gavin Douglas's *Aeneid* shares some characteristics with Bellenden's *Livy*; these were discussed many years ago by C.S. Lewis (Lewis, 1954, 81–7). Douglas also used the Prologues which he composed for individual books as a means of relating the poem to his own and Scottish life and circumstance. His methods sometimes are unexpected. Virgil's twelve books, for instance, he associated with the twelve months of the year and with the period taken to produce his translation. This is most clearly indicated by the prologue to the seventh and that to the supernumerary thirteenth book added to Virgil by the earlier Renaissance humanist Maffeo Vegio (1407–58). These mark the middle and end of the action, the first coming at the halfway point, with the emergence of Aeneas from the visit to the underworld described in book VI; the second following the struggle, concluded in book XII, to establish the Trojans in Italy, a struggle which entails the death of Turnus and the foundation of Alba Longa, which in turn will eventually lead to the emergence of imperial Rome. The significantly placed prologues centre on Douglas himself and on the opposed seasons of a year seen in a landscape which is predominantly Scottish. The first deals in grim, not entirely conventional, detail with December, midwinter with the sun in Capricorn, first as the season affects the countryside (Coldwell, 1959, 61–5):

> Bewte was lost, and barrand schew the landis,
> With frostis hair ourfret the feldis standis.
> Seir bittir bubbis and the schowris snell
> Semyt on the sward a symylitude of hell,
> Reducyng to our mynd, in every sted,
> Gousty schaddois of eild and grisly ded.    (41–6)

The imagery here belongs to the underworld which formed the climax of the first half of the poem. When the scene shifts to the translator's lodging as Provost of the collegiate church of St Giles in Edinburgh, the imagery begins to include overtones of warfare as it is described in the final six books (Palamedes, it should be noted, besides inventing the alphabet, was the victim of the treachery of his fellow-countryman Ulysses during the siege of Troy):

> Approching neir the greking of the day,
> Within my bed I walkynnit quhar I lay;
> So fast declynis Synthea the moyn,
> And kays keklis on the ruyf aboyn;
> Palamedes byrdis crowping in the sky,
> Fleand on randon, schapyn like ane Y,
> And as a trumpat rang thar vocis soun.   (115–21)

It is in this chamber and under these circumstances that he begins the translation of book VII.

As opposed to this, the setting of the final prologue is a garden in midsummer, when Apollo, the sun, occupies the zodiacal sign of Cancer (Coldwell, 1960, 141–6):

> Towart the evyn, amyd the symmyris heit,
> Quhen in the Crab Appollo held hys sete,
> Duryng the joyus moneth tyme of June –   (1–3)

The picture of prosperity and fertility is wholly appropriate to the completion of the action:

> I walkyt furth abowt the feildis tyte,
> Quhilkis tho replenyst stud full of delyte.
> With herbys, cornys, catal, and frute treis,
> Plente of stoir, byrdis and byssy beys,
> In amerant medis fleand est and west,
> Eftir laubour to tak the nychtis rest.   (5–10)

The planets whose astrological influence is strongest are the divinities who govern the action of the *Aeneid*, in particular, Venus and Jupiter:

> Goldyn Venus, the maistres of the yeir
> And gentill Jove, with hir participate,
> Thar bewtuus bemys sched in blyth estait.   (70–2)

This passage introduces a question which was very real for many humanists, especially those who like Douglas were churchmen. In what way was it appropriate for them to devote their lives to the study of pagan authors, however eminent? This is the primary reason for the apparition in a dream-vision of Maffeo Vegio, complaining about his omission from the completed translation. The excuses made by Douglas show that he was perfectly well aware that by any literary standards the thirteenth book was superfluous, but also indicate his reservations of conscience concerning the actual translation. In its way, the speech is an important humanist statement:

> "Mastir," I said, "I heir weill quhat yhe say,
> And in this cace of perdon I you pray,

Not that I have you ony thing offendit,
Bot rathir that I have my tyme mysspendit,
So lang on Virgillis volume forto stair,
And laid on syde full mony grave mater,
That, wald I now write in that trety mor,
Quhat suld folk demyn bot all my tyme forlor?
Als, sindry haldis, fader, trastis me,
Your buke ekit but ony necessite,
As to the text accordyng never a deill,
Mair than langis to the cart the fift quheill.
Thus, sen yhe beyn a Cristyn man, at large
Lay na sik thing, I pray you, to my charge;
It may suffys Virgill is at ane end.
I wait the story of Jherom is to you kend,
Quhou he was dung and beft intill hys sleip,
For he to gentilis bukis gaif sik keip.
Full scharp repreif to sum is write, ye wist,
In this sentens of the haly Psalmyst:
'Thai ar corruppit and maid abhominabill
In thar studeyng thyngis onprofitabill':
Thus sair me dredis I sall thoill a heit,
For the grave study I have so long forleit."   (107–30)

Maffeo replies that his book is at least short and Christian; a few
blows from his cudgel suffice to persuade Douglas to continue, with
the strongly implied suggestion that this will Christianise the whole
undertaking by changing the twelve pagan books into thirteen,
corresponding to the number of Christ and his apostles. This slightly
comic resolution of the problem by a combination of Renaissance
literary ideals with a more medieval form of Christian numerology
is typical not only of Douglas, but of the entire Northern Renaissance.

One cannot but speculate on the failure of the later sixteenth
century in Scotland to follow the example of Douglas and Bellenden
in translating classical and humanist authors. The contrast with
England is sharp. The later date of the Scottish Reformation may
have deflected most intellectual energies into other channels. Translation certainly mattered to James VI and his Castalian Band, but in
general they found their inspiration more in the literatures of France
and Italy.

The development of historical writing follows much the same
pattern as has been noted in other disciplines. The defence of
national interests in the course of the Wars of Independence had
already made Scotland the historical nation. The Renaissance gave
the concept new meaning. Despite its title, the pre-humanistic
*Scotichronicon*, composed in the middle fifteenth century, is both
national and international, making a deliberate attempt to set the

development of an independent Scotland within the context of world-history established by the *World-Chronicle* of Eusebius, Jerome and Prosper. Boece covers only a part of the same ground; as an associate of Erasmus whose book was published in Paris it was natural for him to be concerned that his audience should not be limited to his fellow-countrymen, but that continental humanists should realise the significance of his work. Thus he sets Scottish history against a background of classical cultural developments. In other respects however he tends to stress the uniqueness of Scotland and consequently devotes much less space than his predecessor to overseas political and social institutions and developments. The Reformation directed the attention of historians even more exclusively to Scotland and partly as a consequence assisted the movement from Latin to the vernacular seen in the histories of Knox and Pitscottie, both Reformers. Rather earlier than this a greater concern for local history and individual biography became evident in Myln's *Lives of the Bishops of Dunkeld*, Boece's *Lives of the Bishops of Mortlach and Aberdeen* and Ferrerius' *Lives of the Abbots of Kinloss* – all the work of men who in their different ways were humanists. Each tends to concentrate on a single figure – Myln on Bishop Brown, Boece on Bishop Elphinstone, and Ferrerius on Abbot Chrystal. Unusually detailed portraits of these three men, each of whom had extensive humanist interests, have thus been preserved. The emergence later in the century of the extended personal diary as a literary form is another manifestation of the same psychological trend.

The most striking feature of later sixteenth- and much seventeenth-century historical writing is the emphasis placed on the personal reign of Queen Mary. More was involved than her Catholicism, the question of whether or not the Casket Letters were genuine, her possible adultery and her eventual execution or martyrdom at the hands of her cousin, the English Queen Elizabeth. These certainly were issues much discussed from different points of view, for instance, by Knox, Buchanan, Bishop Lesley of Ross and a varied assortment of pamphleteers and versifiers. The deepest point at issue however was not so much Catholicism or Protestantism, as whether the monarchy under which Scotland and England were to be united would be Catholic or Protestant – indeed whether the illegitimacy of Elizabeth did not mean that union had already been established by the death of the Catholic English Queen Mary and the *de jure* succession of the Catholic queen of Scots, her nearest legitimate relation. The situation had been produced by the marriage in 1503 of Mary's grandfather, James IV, to Margaret Tudor, daughter of Henry VII of England, celebrated by William Dunbar and many others. The marital misadventures of Henry VIII and the consequent establishment of the Protestant church in England were at least partly the result of that king's fears of a Scottish succession. John

Mair, it will be recollected, had urged the benefits to be gained from union; the possibility is urgently present in Alexander Scott's New Year greeting already mentioned. Thomas Craig of Riccarton was a lawyer-commissioner in the negotiations which led to James VI's succession in 1603; he wrote *De Unione Regnorum Britanniae Tractatus*; the better-known *Jus Feudale* and all his other works 'were concerned, at least in part, with the legal, political and historical relations between Scotland and England' (p.51). Indeed this concern came increasingly to dominate all historical and political writing after the middle of the sixteenth century.

Traces of the old universalism are still to be found in Lindsay's *Monarche*, which deals with the progressively more miserable state of the world during its passage from creation to judgement. Scottish problems, lay and ecclesiastic, however, occupy an unusually prominent position during the sixth age, that immediately preceding the Second Coming.

Different aspects of humanism in Scotland developed according to different timetables. The literary and artistic is the earliest, coming clearly into view during the third quarter of the fifteenth century, and reaching a climax in the reigns of James IV and V. Thereafter it faltered, never quite recovering its earlier impetus, but equally never disappearing. The reign of James VI saw something of a revival, and Drummond of Hawthornden reached his peak as late as the reign of Charles I.

Science was later, but in compensation, as it were, there is greater continuity between its Renaissance beginnings and its maturity during the Enlightenment, a continuity particularly exemplified by the dynasty of the academic Gregorys, who span the period from the middle-seventeenth to the nineteenth centuries. This development of scientific method is to a degree linked with the rise of technology, illustrated in different ways by Napier's hydraulic screw, by the weapons which both he and Drummond of Hawthornden claim to have designed, and by James Gregorie's reflecting telescope. The comparison with Leonardo da Vinci is obvious, but the immediate adaptation to local conditions and requirements is perhaps rather closer. Coal mining at some depth, for instance, had long been a feature of the Scottish economy; for David Lindsay in the middle sixteenth century the coal pots (= pits) of Tranent in East Lothian were matter for casual reference. Under these circumstances a hydraulic screw for pumping water from mine shafts has an obvious utility. The device may never have been used, but Napier was at least thinking of possible practical applications. The rods known as Napier's Bones and his Promptuary of Multiplication are equally practical and more general in their possible application, forecasting as they do the later calculating machines of Pascal and Leibniz, the Analytic Engine of Charles Babbage and ultimately the

modern computer. Napier's work as a whole runs in close tandem
with that of his younger contemporary, the Frenchman René
Descartes (1596–1650), whose *Discourse de la Méthode* (1637) had
developed from a series of dreams which he had on 10 November,
1619. If, as has been claimed (Davis and Hersh 1986, 3–8), the
modern world begins on that date, Napier (and thus indirectly
Renaissance Scottish humanism) were agents, both in the production
of the dreams and in bringing them to fulfilment.

REFERENCES
COLDWELL 1939: D.F.C. Coldwell (ed.), *Virgil's Aeneid Translated into
Scottish Verse by Gavin Douglas, Bishop of Dunkeld*, iii (STS).
COLDWELL 1960: D.F.C. Coldwell (ed.), *Virgil's Aeneid Translated into
Scottish Verse by Gavin Douglas, Bishop of Dunkeld*, iv (STS).
DAVIS AND HERSH 1986: P.J. Davis and R. Hersh, *Descartes' Dream*
(London).
GEDDES 1895: W.D. Geddes (ed.), *Musa Latina Aberdonensis Arthur
Johnston*, ii (New Spalding Club).
LEWIS 1954: C.S. Lewis, *English Literature in the Sixteenth Century
Excluding Drama* (Oxford).
MACQUEEN 1967: J. MacQueen, 'Some Aspects of the Early Renais-
sance in Scotland', *FMLS* 3, 201–22.
MACQUEEN 1982: J. MacQueen, *Progress and Poetry* (Edinburgh and
London).
MACQUEEN AND MACQUEEN 1988: J. and W. MacQueen, 'Latin
Prose Literature', in R.D.S. Jack and C. Craig (eds), *The History of
Scottish Literature*, vol. 1 (Aberdeen), 227–43.
MYLN 1831: A. Myln, *Vitae Dunkeldensis Ecclesiae Episcoporum* (Banna-
tyne Club).

# Index